Daniel Libeskind

Daniel Libeskind
THE SPACE OF ENCOUNTER

UNIVERSE

Universe Editor: Richard Olsen
Studio Libeskind Editor: Carla Swickerath
Copy Editors: Iris Becker, Liana Fredley

First published in the United States of America in 2000
By UNIVERSE PUBLISHING
A Division of Rizzoli International Publications, Inc.
300 Park Avenue South
New York, NY 10010

Library of Congress Cataloging-in-Publication Data

Libeskind, Daniel, 1946–
    Daniel Libeskind: the space of encounter / by Daniel Libeskind.
        p. cm.
Includes bibliographical references.
ISBN 0-7893-0492-9 (pbk. : hardcover)—ISBN 0-7893-0435-X
1. Libeskind, Daniel, 1946—Themes, motives. 2. Architecture,
    Postmodern. I. Title.

NA737.L46 A4 2000
720.92—dc21   00-043419

00 01 02 03 / 10 9 8 7 6 5 4 3 2 1

Design by Juliette Cezzar, New York

The designer would like to thank Igor Siddiqui, Heather Roberge,
Robert Jamieson, and Ryan Ellsworth.

Printed in Italy

Photo credits:

All photographs © Daniel Libeskind except the following:

Cover: *Line of Fire* exhibition © Hélène Binet

pp. 14, 15, 124 copyright Christopher Duisberg

pp. 33, 97 copyright Uwe Rau

pp. 34, 35, 38, 39, 40, 41, 42, 43, 44, 46, 47, 108, 109,
114, 125, 126, 127, 128, 176, 219, 220, 222
copyright Bitter + Bredt Fotographie

pp. 36, 37 copyright Lars Gräbner

pp. 45 copyright Leo Torri

pp. 98, 99 copyright Dina Scrimali

pg. 104 copyright Sebastian Pfütze

pp. 110 copyright Studio 13

pp. 100, 101, 105, 106, 107, 111, 121, 161, 162, 163, 170,
171 copyright Torsten Seidel

pp. 112, 166, 167, 168, 209, 215, 216, 217 copyright Udo
Hesse

pp. 113 scene photograph copyright Jan Persson

pp. 113 model photograph copyright Sang Lee

pp. 115, 116, 117 copyright Foen X Photo Studio

pp. 118, 174 copyright Miller Hare

pp. 119, 211, 212, 213, copyright Hélène Binet

pp. 164, 165 copyright T. Waki for Shokokusha Pub. Co., Ltd.

pp. 172, 173 copyright Andrew Putler

pp. 176 rendering copyright Q-bus

The work in this book would not have ever materialized without the vision, inspiration, and passionate dedication of Nina Libeskind, who is both my wife and my accomplice. She dedicated herself completely to this adventure, not only managing the complex and ever-challenging tasks of running our office, but in bringing a totally fresh and critical discourse to the development of the work. Her penetrating intellect, keen insight, and extraordinary love make it all happen. But most of all, it is her spirit, integrity, and magic that turn every obstacle into fun and every challenge into a celebration. To me, she is inspiration. ■

Contents

Contents

Project Credits:

Markus Aerni, Louise Ashcroft, Donald Bates, Stefan Blach, Gerhard Brun, Damon Caldwell, Bob Choeff, Robert Claiborne, Thomas Deuble, Jan Dinnebier, Fergal Doyle, Christopher Duisberg, Christine Eichelmann, Lars Fischer, Hannes P.Freudenreich, Kimmo Friman, Thore Gärbers, Jean-Lucien Gay, Teresa Go, Wolfgang Gollwitzer, James Goodspeed, Elizabeth Govan, Lärs Grabner, Gerrit Grigoleit, Bernhard von Hammerstein, Boel Hellman, Manuel Herz, Jens Hoffmann, Barbara Holzer, Ariel Huber, Johannes Hucke, David Hunter, Wendy James, Yama Karim, Jason King, Jan Kleihues, Ulla Klot, Florian Köhl, Nina Lambea, Joachim Landwehr, Sang Lee, Dietmar Leyk, Santeri Lipasti, Karl-Heinz Maschmeier, Tarla MacGabhann, Noel McCauley, Susanne Milne, Anne Marie O'Connor, Martin Ostermann, Paula Palombo, Jason Payne, Matthias Reese, Claudia Reisenberger, Daniel Richmond, Guido Rörick, Todd Rouhe, Dagmar Quentin, Fernando Sanz, Robert Slinger, Eric Schall, Solveig Scheper, Marina Stankovic, Carla Swickerath, Attilio Terragni, Alexis Trumpf, Andreas Voigt, David Walker, Thomas Willemeit,

and

Stacey Ackermann, Jacob Atherton, Pnina Avidar, Gary Bates, Boris Bähre, Ruth Baumeister, Gregor Bäumle, Gisela Baurmann, Matthew Berry, Anja Böwer, Geoff Brown, Michael Brown, Lisa Cameron, Guadalupe Canta, Amiee Chan, John Cho, Gordon H. Chong, Ian Collins, Sid Conn, Rebecca Cotera, Lonn Combs, Sonja Dinnebier, Petr Dostál, Bruce Dunning, Britta Eichinger, Wim Eckert, Peter Fergin, Amy Finkel, Ted Finn, Simo Freese, Mari Fujita, Julien Gadrat, Matthew Geiser, Steven Gerrard, Daniel Grandy, Alessanrdo Gubitosi, Thomas Han, Helmuth Hanle, Christina Hansen, Pernille Birk Hansen, Jennifer Hauger, Sarah Heller, Francis Henderson, Juan Hidalgo, Matthais Hintze, Dean Hoffman, Catrin Homberger, Tom Houston, Sandra Hutchins, Gavin Hutchison, Juha Ilonen, Peter Ippolito, Christine Johnson, Matthew Johnson, Derek Jones, Berit Esbjöm Johnson, Jeannette Kuo, Claire Karsenty, Greg Katz, Katrin Klar, Patrick Keller, Ewald Kentgens, Ewoud Kok, Jerry Kopare, Simon Krohn-Hansen, Astrid Kurotschka, Peter Kutek, Maria Laurent, Michelle Lavigne, Bernd Lederle, Ruari Leeves, Pierre Lemaine, Katrina Logan, Karen Lohrmann, Diogo Seixas Lopes, James Lowder, Michael Maggio, Ajmal Maiwandi, Sascha Manteufel, Damir Masek, Nuno Mateus, Colleen McGrath, Marck McCarthy, Daniel McFarland, Michael McKay, Volker Mencke, Napoleon Merana, Mark Michaeli, Elke Motzkus, Pascal Müller, Jasmine Musharbash, Jost Muxfeldt, Uli Neumann, Brian Nicholson, Sam Nunes, Michelle O'Dea, Seth Orgain, Todd Osborne, Nicholas Ott, Nina Otto, Frank Petitpierre, Chris Perry, Nadine Petersdorff, Bernd Pflum, Kirill Pivovarov, Thomas von Pufendorf, Martin Puppel, Hani Rashid, Kelly Rattigan, Christine Regus, Stephanie Reich, Berit Restad-Jonsson, Tilmann Richter, Patrick Salomon, Blake Schauman, David Schatzle, Mortiz Schneider, Jessie Schook, Marc Schoonderbeek, Thomas Schröpfer, Tino Schädler, Werner Schultz, Jason Scroggin, Juliette Searight, Mark Shenton, Raphael Sidelski, Wilf Sinclair, Gregory Skogland, Kari Smith, Scott Specht, Lars Herik Stahl, Lucas Steiner, Miller Stevens, David Stockwell, Stephanie Strathmann, Peter Strzebniok, Mika Suominen, Ilkka Tarkkanen, Delia Teschendorff, Claudia Thomson, Yushi Uehara, Jeremy Wales, Karl Wallick, Michael Wilson, Daniel Wolkenberg, Eiffel Wong, Joseph Wong, Jens Wodzak, Christina Zahn, Walter Zausch.

With a very heartfelt thanks to Carla Swickerath who, against all odds, persisted in not only the technical and editorial, but in the conceptual vision of this book.

Preface
Jeffrey Kipnis

I first encountered the work of Daniel Libeskind as I sat in my art gallery in Atlanta, Georgia, in 1982. Having not sold a single work for six months, I had decided to mount a show of contemporary architectural drawings, hoping to lure young, successful architects into the gallery and convert them into clients for my artists—kind of a bait-and-switch strategy. Little did I know that young architects were, every one of them, flat broke—or that with the exhibition I would set into motion a small turbulence that would change my whole life, like the infamous flap of a butterfly's wing that expands into a hurricane. ■ To get started on the exhibition, I bought a coffee-table book entitled *Architectural Drawings*, my introduction to the field and—with the title—my first exposure to the wry, arid wit of architects that is so often misunderstood as solemn self-seriousness. As I thumbed through the watercolors, sketches, collages, and hard-line drawings, I withered at the lack of ambition and palled at the graphic naïveté of the work. I began to think that perhaps the show was not such a good idea—that is, until I turned the page to one of Daniel's *Micromegas* drawings. ■ To this day, I can still recall the visceral shock I felt, that sense that in an instant I had not only stumbled upon a singular talent, but had discovered the extraordinary powers of architecture itself, powers I had never before imagined, even if these were still latent, still unrealized visions trapped in a graphic world. Libeskind's drawing inhaled in a single breath the history of modern drawing, from Piranesi through Kandinsky to Held, and breathed out a typhoon of originality. It brimmed with intelligence, from the virtuosic command of pictorial organization to the eddying vertigo wrought from the interplay of line and sign, from the history of philosophy to the history of History, with a smiling nod to Literature—Voltaire and Kafka—in passing. Indifferent to the primitive and untutored work that held the art world in its nervous thrall, it adored knowledge, relished technique, and revered without apology the achievements of sophisticated self-consciousness. ■ I fell in love with the entire *Micromegas* set, and were it not for my subsequent encounter with another set of Libeskind drawings, I might have spent the whole of these short remarks reflecting in grateful detail on its riches. As it is, however, I look back at the *Micromegas* with the deep affection one reserves for adolescence's first true love. If they initiated me to the living possibility of architecture's profound passion, the other set of drawings would, eventually, transport me, mind, body, and soul, through infatuation and idea, through love and ideology, through ecstasy and insight, transport me to somewhere new, somewhere else. And that is, is it not, the very least of what we should ask of architecture? ■ About a year after the gallery failed, I moved to New York to pursue a career as an art critic. Scraping by as a freelancer, I got a small job ghosting an architect's essay for a folio of drawings called *Chamberworks*. With xeroxes of the twenty-eight drawings and several pages of notes in hand, my assignment was to cobble together a coherent essay, filling in background, segues, and other passages as necessary. After a day spent mulling over the xeroxes—every reference book I owned open and on the floor—I gave up on the drawings frustrated, befuddled, and irritated—actually, damned irritated. ■ Other than seeing the obvious—that the set of twenty-eight drawings divided into two sets of fourteen, each series progressing picture by picture from an oriented field to a horizontal and vertical line respectively—I could make no deeper sense of them whatsoever. Whenever I detected what I thought might be a key to unlock their mystery—chamber music, the tracks of a cloud chamber, the philosophy of Heraclitus, arcane numerology, cabala, Duchamp, chess, Rorschach, formal analysis—I was quickly thwarted. The gratings and grids, notational elements, zigs, zags, and curlicues all wandered adrift; they made no sense, followed no logic of seriality or process, obeyed no law, honored no esoteric structure, constructed no space, added up to nothing, depicted nothing, meant nothing. Neither individually nor collectively were they even beautiful or interesting, at least as I grasped those two guarantors-of-last-resort at that time. And, it should go without saying, I had no clue, no inkling that the chicken of these scratches was even remotely related to the Artist of my *Micromegas*. ■ But it did not matter; regardless of my scorn for the drawings, I understood where my architect-client wanted his notes to go, the point he wanted to make, understood it and admired it—enough to apprentice myself to his teaching for the next three years. Finishing the assignment was a snap. ■ More time passed, I began to find my way in architecture, and I finally met Daniel face to face for the first time. We sat next to each other in the audience of a blue-chip panel at Harvard discussing the recent Wexner Center competition—hard to miss each other, as we were the only two in the audience to interrupt the panel with questions. First impression? Mutually intrigued, but mutually suspicious is my best guess. But we talked, met again as panelists in Minneapolis at a conference called *The Irrelevance of Beauty*—thank God those times are past—where a friendship between us sprouted. ■ I launched this brief chronicle of our relationship to see if I could reconstruct just when and why *Chamberworks* erupted into my consciousness with such force. I realize, now, however, that I will never identify that moment. The drawings must have insinuated themselves into me that first madding day and started reorganizing my thought, my very being, without my ever sensing their covert operation. ■

So I will curtail the indulgence, set aside the anecdotes: Daniel's laughing attack in Como; the night we saw *Rambo*; our endless hours of talk; my shameless urging of his sons Lev and Noam to mischief; Stephen Wright jokes; teaching him to drive a straight shift only to have him total his automatic the next day; the birth of Rachel; the vicissitudes of Nina—itself a story of such intricacy as to paralyze even Proust; his phone call to me just after submitting the entry to the Jewish Museum competition in which he confided that, though he had abandoned any hope of winning, his entry would surely make an impact on the jury. I will set these stories aside, because, though the works documented in this book are saturated with them, like the elements of *Chamberworks*, they do not really add up to anything—other than a life. ■ Forgive me if I am not prepared to confront the smallness of my spirit just yet. Rather, allow me to retreat to a safe haven for me in a world that not only contains but sustains Daniel Libeskind, a daring world that on this evidence alone should admire itself much more than it does. Allow me to retreat to a reflection on *Chamberworks*. ■

If, while looking at a drawing, listening to music, or reading a book, you find your mind wandering, flitting over irrelevant details of your life, does that count as interpretation? Do the rambling feelings and thoughts that arise within a work's ambience belong in any sense to it, though they are in every sense disjointed from it as a matter of its history, form, and content? If not, why are we so often grateful to the work for them? I am, at least—so much so that I am increasingly of the mind that these collateral effects are the greater good of art, always adding up, one person at a time but inexorably, to more than the grandeur, the tragedy, the intellection, the spectacle, the virtuosity, or any other forms of impact that lend a work renown. ■ Those side effects are, like fumes and bubbles and sparks, evidence that certain qualities of the work are beginning to percolate with that preposterous goo of matter, mind, and memory that constitutes each one of us, stirring each of us yet again into a new brew. Because not one single ingredient in that concoction is unique, we organize always and automatically into vast and shifting organic collectives—species, nationalities, friendships, audiences, religions, tastes, even into our perversions and aberrations. But because the unlikely mixture of shared ingredients in any one of us is irreproducible, we are each singular, each a fountainhead. "Every individual is a potential sub-species," says Darwin, less histrionically. ■ Perhaps, then, this is why we sanction self-expression. Because, in the end, it is impossible, at least in terms of the utter solipsism it imagines of itself, hopes for, and fears. All expression, no matter how outlandish, is communal in its composure and organizing in its effect. And therefore it is political, spawning new organic collectives, bifurcating once unified ensembles into multiple new constellations. I remember listening again and again to Yoko Ono and John Coltrane (or was it Ornette Coleman?) in a wailing tone-duet that I felt to be the most incredible music I had ever heard. My grandmother burst into the room, yelling, "Turn that crap off, it's not music!" She was right, but so was I. ■

Chamberworks: Architectural Meditations on Themes from Heraclitus is a major work that will surely earn meticulous study. Already students of Libeskind's work are aware of the extent to which the drawings constitute a sketchbook of sorts, containing early graphic notes of many of the themes that develop into the architect's designs for buildings, though that's the least of its import. It is not hard, for example, to detect in the drawings an early version of the lightning-bolt figure that later joins with the hundred-letter thunder words from Joyce's *Finnegan's Wake* to become the red *Line of Fire* installation for Nervi's UN Headquarters in Geneva, a work that in turn evolves into the Berlin Jewish Museum addition. ■ Yet, to my knowledge, the only serious critical consideration *Chamberworks* has received thus far, other than the six invited prefaces included in the AA folio publication and Daniel's own account, is Robin Evans's entrancing miniature "In Front of Lines that Leave Nothing Behind" (1984). Ostensibly a review of the original exhibition of the drawings at the Architectural Association in 1983, Evans's brief essay is considered by many to be among his finest writings. ■ Evans begins by detailing how inadequately equipped criticism, obsessed at that moment with signification, was to cope with the work. "What is so remarkable [in *Chamberworks*] is the near total disengagement from signification of any kind. Such a condition is immensely difficult to achieve; mere abstraction does not begin to approach it." Evans laments that prevailing criticism often, if not always, treats a wholly original work, the emergence of a new species as it were, as a defective instance of a previously existing form—not as something new for better or worse, but as something familiar become monstrous. He senses in *Chamberworks* just such an emergence—and just such a response. And the ingenuity of Evans's astonishing critical leap is on par with *Chamberworks* itself. ■ Unity and fragmentation are the two major contrasted modes of twentieth-century composition in architecture as well as painting. A classic dialectic pair, married and bickering, they are unable to carry on without each other. The *Chamberworks* do not move towards unity, nor are they subject to fragmentation. It took me a while to realize that there was nothing to be broken, no virtual space, no subject matter, no substructure, no geometry. Lines that do not make bodies cannot be broken. The discovery of this area outside of unity and fragmentation may be the greatest achievement of the series. ■ The area outside of unity and fragmentation, a logic beyond same and different, an organizational diagram beyond congruence and collage. Does any topic more command our attention today? In science, political thought, and art, we explore complex ecologies that link vast diversities into fluid, coherent structures. Evans, in 1984, did not yet have in hand the conceptual apparatus to grasp the full consequences of his own intuition. That he took such a leap testifies to his courage and talents. That *Chamberworks* pushed him off the precipice... ■

To me, *Chamberworks* performs an eccentric history of the architect's sine qua non, the straight line. Actually, not a history in the customary sense, nor an unfolding, nor a genealogy, nor a myth. It is more akin to an ontogeny, a record of the genetic evolution of the straight line as a species, and an embryogeny, the development of that genetic diagram into the material specificity of an individual, the line in and as Daniel. ■ Already a miracle in absolute, ideality par excellence, transcendent or transcendental, the straight line lands on Earth as unparalleled world-maker, the possibility of geometry, proportion, and measurement, of order as such. The straight line inscribes the horizon, the very limit of the world, as well as the vector of verticality, orientation of rectitude, of solid footing, of the upright and normal, but also of ambition, setting the sky as the limit. The irruptive force of *Chamberworks*, however, resides not so much in its intensely personal admiration for the straight line, the horizontal and vertical, but in its meditation on the operations of history. ■ For centuries now, we are slowly, reluctantly becoming aware of the extent to which absolutely everything emerges from historical processes, every thought and feeling, every mode of existence, material and ideal, from the Earth to life to the universe itself. Working out the radical consequences of this underlies the achievements of Freud, Darwin, Hegel, Marx, all of contemporary science, and much of contemporary philosophy. ■ The great philosopher Edmund Husserl struggled with this problem as he grappled with the historicity of ideas. How, he asked, can ideas transcend the terms and conditions of their parochial historical emergence to become universals, timeless and placeless? The straight line and the geometry that follows from it were key examples for him; though a history of the emergence of geometry could be imagined, for Husserl, geometry transcended that history. There is, after all, no eighteenth-century triangle nor a California triangle: the Pythagorean theorem is true anywhere and everywhere, anytime and all the time, available as knowledge to anyone. Husserl tells his version of the story of this emergence of the straight line as an ideality in his *Origins of Geometry*, a story echoing throughout *Chamberworks*. ■ While at first thought it might seem that, as Plato would have it, the straight line is aboriginal, a form/concept anterior to all of history, on second thought it becomes clear that, after all, the straight line not only has a history, but one with red-letter dates! Even if we are reluctant to accept Egypt as the scene of the origin of geometry, we must admit that at the very least, geometry is tied to human history and is evident in abundance and with unprecedented rigor in Egyptian land governance. The Pythagoreans discovered the first inklings of mathematical magic latent in the line, Euclid generalized the finitude of the inscribed line to the concept of infinite extent, and Brunelleschi discovered pictorial perspective, the ability of the graphic line in relation to the horizon to invoke infinite extent and imitate spatial vision. ■ With Descartes the concept of the infinite straight line receives algebraic expression. Now, a straight line is no longer best represented by a graphic mark or a description, but by an equation of the form $y = ax + b$, a momentous synthesis of algebra and geometry. Not long after, an even more astonishing development made possible by Descartes occurs when Newton joins the straight line—and thus algebra/geometry—to the laws of the universe with his first law: every object in motion tends to stay in motion in a straight line unless acted upon by an outside force. Newton's law is all the more astonishing as a conceptual achievement when one realizes that another of his achievements, the law of gravity, argues that, because gravity is in principle infinite in its reach, nothing in the universe is ever completely free of outside forces! Newton's straight line of motion, therefore, is a transcending abstraction. Though it never finds material moment, it nevertheless rules all material movements. And, if one reflects on cosmogenic developments after the big bang, one realizes that a very long time passed, hundreds of millions of years, from the big bang to the decoupling and beyond, for there to be enough open space for that abstraction to have purchase at all. ■ There is much more to the history, of course, Picasso and Braque's discovery of the line's pictorial ability to embody time as well as space and Einstein's discovery that Newton's infinitely long straight line of motion is curved, though still and always straight, because the universe itself is curved—a discovery that grows out of a simple application of the Pythagorean theorem. The more we think about it, the more we realize that the straight line of our world today, though 14 billion years old, is far from being an ancient. It is, rather, a youngster, still experiencing growing pains.

And Daniel's *Chamberworks* adds one more step in its evolution, one that, for me, at least, ranks among the most profound. ■ At the radical limit of historicity, each of us, indeed everything existing today, is the culmination of billions of years of material processes. The miracle of matter is that it can, by using its organization as diagram and algorithm, compress each developmental step in that vast time into a breath. So, for example, the process of human embryological development—nothing other than a complex set of instructions for organizing matter—recapitulates the billions of years of cosmogenesis and the hundreds of millions of years of life's evolution in a mere nine months. ■ And though the straight line is a culmination of a vast history, each of us must recapitulate that history anew not only for the straight line to reside within us and shape us, but for it to continue its own life, to take on personality, for example, as a Horizon or a Vertical. *Chamberworks* is no depiction, not even a record of that process, but a step in it, as the haphazard mixture of matter and events that constitute Daniel's single life, from birth through adolescence to adulthood, reorganizes its available materials to resonate with the history and historicity of the straight line again, and in so doing allow it to evolve one step further. In this case, a very big step. ■ It is obvious that these remarks are far from a studied commentary on Daniel's drawings, far even from sober interpretation; they are the fumes, bubbles, and sparks the drawings evoke in me. ■

Jeffrey Kipnis is the Curator of Architecture and Design at the Wexner Center for the Arts, and a professor of architecture at the Knowlton School of Architecture at the Ohio State University.

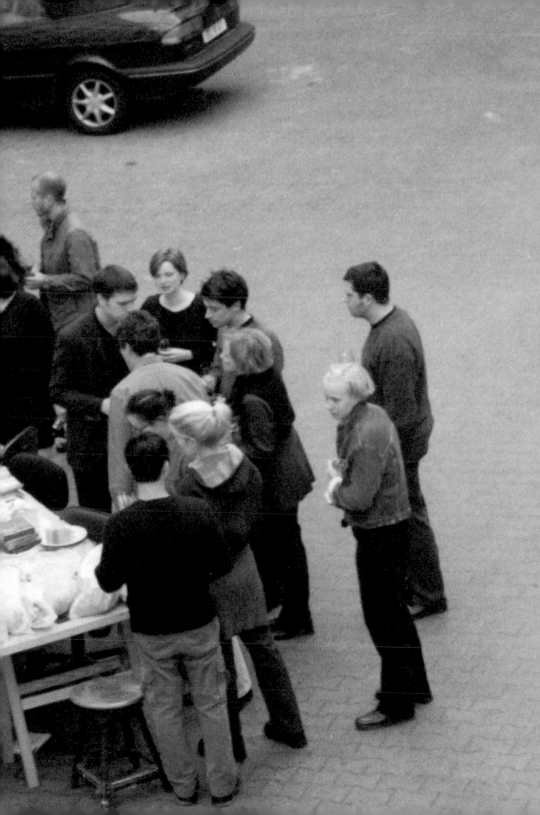

Daniel Libeskind is an international figure in architecture and urban design, well known for introducing, through a multidisciplinary approach, a new critical discourse into architecture. His practice extends from building major cultural institutions such as museums and concert halls, to urban projects, stage design, art installations, and exhibitions. ◉ Born in postwar Poland in 1946, Libeskind became an American citizen in 1965. After studying music in Israel and in New York on the America-Israel Cultural Foundation Scholarship, he became a virtuoso performer, then left music to study architecture. He received his professional architectural degree from the Cooper Union for the Advancement of Science and Art in 1970, and a postgraduate degree in the history and theory of architecture from the School of Comparative Studies at Essex University in 1972. ◉ In 1989, he won the competition for the Jewish Museum Berlin, which opened to the public in January 1999. His museum for the city of Osnabrück, Germany, the Felix Nussbaum Haus, opened in July 1998. His current projects include the Spiral Extension to the Victoria and Albert Museum, London; the Imperial War Museum of the North, Manchester; and the Jewish Museum San Francisco. ◉ Having taught and lectured at many universities worldwide, Libeskind is currently a professor at the Hochschule für Gestaltung in Karlsruhe, Germany, and the Cret Chair at the University of Pennsylvania. He has received numerous awards, most recently the Goethe Medallion in 2000; the Deutsche Architekturpreis (German Architecture Prize) in 1999 for the Jewish Museum Berlin; the American Academy of Arts and Letters Award for Architecture in 1996; and the Berlin Cultural Prize, also in 1996. He has received honorary doctorates from Humboldt Universität Berlin and from the College of Arts and Humanities at Essex University. His work and his ideas have been exhibited extensively in museums and galleries around the world and have been the subject of numerous international publications, influencing a new generation of architects and those interested in the future development of cities and culture. ●

Introduction
Daniel Libeskind

Ever since I began architecture, I've had an abhorrence of conventional architecture offices. There was something about the atmosphere of redundancy, routine, and production that made me allergic to all forms of specialization and so-called professionalism. Ten years ago we founded our office in Berlin as a result of a decision, an accident, a rumor on the street, and began an unimaginable journey down a path on which we are still traveling. ■ The work has developed in unexpected directions through a practice that does not mimic existing procedures, but instead attempts to break through into the excitement, adventure, and mystery of architecture. By dropping the designations "form," "function," and "program," and engaging in the public and political realm, which is synonymous with architecture, the dynamics of building take on a new dimension. The celebrations of taking drawing into building, the pathos of production, the dreamlike routines, configure into a substance that is not identifiable on any drawing board. This "substance" that sometimes appears totally opaque and inscrutable often glimmers with belief and offers a reality of the deepest hope. ■ The magic of architecture cannot be appropriated by any singular operation because it is always already floating, progressing, rising, flying, breathing. Whatever the problems—political, tectonic, linguistic—that architecture exposes, one thing I know is that engaging in architecture is exciting only because of the intensity and passion of its call. The work in this book addresses a multidimensional problematic that—at least in retrospect—seems to have the logic of a certain path. It is this path that is the most engaging construction, rather than any particular project found along its way. The exhilarating aspect of such a trajectory, at least for those engaged in it, is that its goals are unknown and its ends indeterminable and uncertain. The path itself substantiates that which is only imagined, and forms the evidence of that which is not yet built. ■ In one of my favorite books, *Two Sources of Morality and Religion*, Henri Louis Bergson comes to the conclusion that the universe, to paraphrase loosely, is a machine for producing gods. It seems to me that architecture is, in fact, the machine that produces the universe that produces the gods. It does so not fully through theories or reflections, but in the nonrepeatable and optimistic act of construction. Unlike language, music, or art, which are based on a trace that cannot be traced, architecture, through its transcendence and materialism, forever discloses its own opening but never sees its own end. Since it cannot be interpreted away, since it cannot disappear in its own disappearing act, architecture remains at a distance from the purely philosophical, communicable, and assimilable. The qualities of its resistance, which are as pragmatic as the materials from which it is built, form an irascible and volatile field whose smile is not that of Buddha. ■ The documents in this book demonstrate the fact that every impossible problem is worthy of pursuit. The means of building, which are always traditional, reveal the resistance of architecture to manipulation, whether technical or economic, which is the very index of its possibility. This does not mean that architecture is more expensive or more difficult to make; on the contrary, it becomes more fascinating, enigmatic, and certainly more rewarding. ■ I have found on this very particular path that people, whether here or there or now and then, always expect more of the spaces that they have been given. Tomorrow's citizens will no longer be amenable to receiving in reality what they can simulate in their dreams. We live in an age when economic globalization, the market economy, and technological advances make it possible for architecture to consume the immemorial. This book is a document of the unpredictable and an acknowledgment of the uncertain. In this, it reflects the nature of architecture itself. The spirit of architecture wanders where it will. ■

The Indecipherable Collective, 1988

30°, 45°, 60°, 90° *Villa, Lutzowplatz, Berlin, 1990* The "urban villa" seeks to demonstrate the complex, modern possibilities of building and living in Berlin. As such, the architectural order is one that displaces the traditional 18th- and 19th-century symmetrical type of "villa" and replaces it with another organization. The cube form is rearticulated into a set of distorted fragments, which, if reassembled in imagination and daily ritual, return the inhabitant to the yet-to-be order of the already been "out-of-place." ■

33

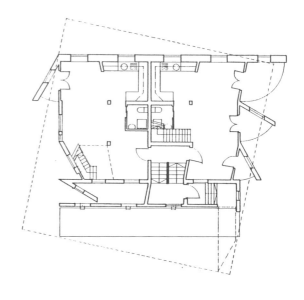

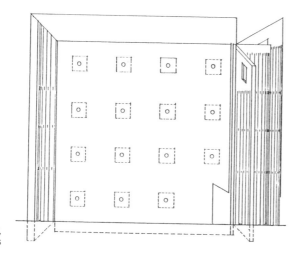

30°/45°/60°/90°,
elevation and plans

30°, 45°, 60°, 90°

Text (Novantique Berlin), 1990 House sheltering an absent yet significant fragment of the memory of the city. The memories embodied in old walls, peeling fragments, lost edifices. The rubble of decay are houses, preserved and revealed for a decision about what is forgotten and remembered, what is no longer and not yet; in other words, not only the history of the city, but the city of history. Through a precise designation of the potential place that each absence commemorates, a new order emerges, one that no longer imposes upon the city what is foreign to it, but rather one that reveals that what is already there is also what is still to come. By appropriating this ambiguous and suspended urban inscape, a landscape is disclosed. The urban villa as landscape reasserts the very "disorder" that has been ordered in the process of reconstituting the city. Thus the architecture seeks to guard an abandoned intersection, which testifies to the mutual infidelity between gods and mortals, between the visible and the invisible, between the house and the city. ■

The Urban-Villa Project is made visible as an activity of making an architecture that does not imitate, represent, or symbolize beyond itself, but simply shows—makes a site—and in so doing establishes a place where what is said is all that lasts. ■

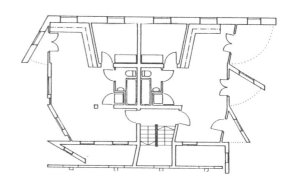

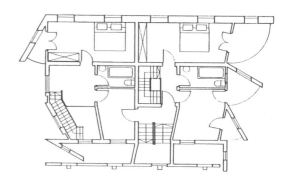

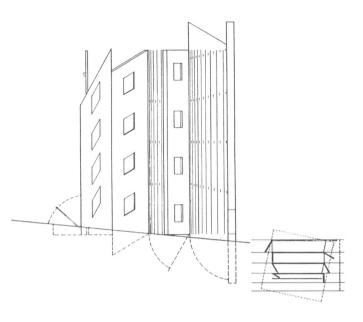

tinue the Jewish tradition across the desert of assimilation and annihilation is to return to the living sources of Jewish space and symbolism so that a community can be renewed. The new synagogue today should reflect an optimism and independence of Jewish culture amid its neighbors. In this way, the project continues the short-lived tradition in Germany of synagogue-building that began with Erich Mendelsohn—a tradition that does not model the synagogue after the typology of a Christian church. ■ Urbanistically, the project is sited and aligned to the historically prominent features in the city of Duisberg. The building stands with the vertical hinge of the book facing the river and the main entrance to the complex facing the promenade, which is the focal point of the new city development. The book opens in two directions: a solid-colored, tiled page and the Star of David looking toward the city; a vertical, scaffolded page interwoven with greenery looking toward the East, toward the light of Jerusalem. The extended wall of the book shields the school and echoes the old city wall. On the eastern side is a proposal for a large landscaped park with a children's playground. There is also a special festival entrance for large groups and large functions, accessible from the inner court at Springwall. The main body of the synagogue and community center is located centrally between the foot (school and administration), the book, and the head (foyer and apartments). ■ The synagogue is conceived as a central gathering place for service, worship, and study.

The Aleph before the Beit
Competition for a Jewish Community Center and Synagogue, Duisberg, Germany, 1996

The aleph before the House. The aleph represents the unity of Israel—the unity of G-d. The aleph stands for more than a letter, more than an emblem, more than the fiery beginning from which the בראשית stems. The aleph gives substance and connection to the four letters of the tetragrammation: yud (י), heh (ה), and vav (ו)—the ineffable and unpronounceable Name. These letters have their seat and are given form in the One. The structure of the aleph is related to the book in which it appears. Therefore the book and the aleph together represent the spiritual and cultural identity of the Jewish people. The aleph and the book are the twin elements used to organize and structure the urban, architectural, and functional dimensions of the project. ■ The letter aleph is the beginning. Like all Hebrew letters, it has the structure of the body. It is structured in three dimensions of unity: the head, signifying the teacher; the body, standing for the community; the supporting leg, representing children's education. ■ To con-

Rabbi Elazar bar Abina said in Rabbi Aha's name: For 26 generations the Aleph complained before G-d: I am the first of the letters yet you didn't create Your world with me! Don't worry, said G-d, the world and all its fullness were created for the Torah alone. Tomorrow when I come to give my Torah at Sinai the first word I say will begin with you.

The Torah is contained in a tablet wall, the movable structure of which allows for a diversity of services and their varying relationships to the community center. The movable wall is a functioning symbol that worship is not frozen in space or in objects and that "since the Exodus, freedom has spoken with a Hebrew accent" (Heine). ■ The configuration of seating allows for flexible arrangements, and unites the community in service while respecting orthodox rules. The wooden ceiling refers to the now-gone Polish synagogues and articulates their forms. The two heh skylights represent two poles of light, the secular and the religious, the intensities of which differ though their sizes remain the same. The synagogue is part of a bigger social space, which includes community activities such as eating, studying, and gatherings. This space contains a kosher kitchen with its own direct-delivery access. In this way, worship and community are integrated into a fluid relationship reflecting life. The facades of the synagogue are structured around windows that bring the text of light through the intricate patterns of the Talmudic page. The synagogue building is constructed of wood. ■ The school is an articulated part of the complex and is connected to the synagogue and community space by the courtyard. This inner courtyard, filled with the laughter of playing children, is part of the everyday atmosphere of the synagogue. The school is embraced by an outer wall, which responds to the city wall across the street. It is constructed of concrete with colored tiles, which in their polychromatic quality clad the building and extend its surface toward the standing page of the book. The inner wall of the school is light and opens toward the court. This building also contains the administrative offices. ■ The "head" of the letter contains the main entrance and the foyer. From this point, the community members kinetically trace the aleph in circulating through the building. On the uppers levels of this building are the apartments of the rabbi and the circumciser. This building is constructed of concrete, with windows and patterned reliefs relating to the tiling system. ■ The entire aleph configuration is expressed in the verticality of the "Open Book";

the lineaments of the buildings held together organically by the functional relations of schooling, meeting, and worship. Learning and interpretation of the book constitute the visible structure of reality. They are the external and internal form of this architecture, which positions, unites, and articulates the building in the historical and urban space of the city of Duisburg. ■ The scheme celebrates a true rebirth of the Jewish community in a building that accommodates a complex program and is itself part of the open and eternal tradition of intellect and faith. ■

Architecture Intermundium:
An Open Letter to Architectural Educators and Students of Architecture
1987 Why spend time tediously applying gold leaf onto a pinnacle of a tower (impressive!) when the foundations are rotten? Before that delicate task will have been completed, the entire edifice will collapse, destroying both the work and the worker. Invisible disasters precede those that can be seen. . . . ◉ No amount of research, discussions on "relevance," or compiled information can disguise one obvious fact: Architecture as taught and practiced today is but a grammatical fiction. Enough to see the gulf that separates what is taught (and how!) and what is built (and why!) to understand that somewhere a lie is being perpetrated. Only a sophistic method could mask a situation where so many spend so much to do so little—with such damaging results. ◉ Here will resound a chorus of

The Aleph before the Beit, competition panels

protests. Have we not introduced new teaching methods and up-to-date theories? Have we not retrieved lost precedents? Are we not producing a great new generation of educators and the educated? A success story, in short. Precisely. It is this "success" that has transformed a realm where "angels once feared to tread" into a supermarket of commodities, or worse, a whorehouse of opinions about them. Students are corrupted early into believing that only that which succeeds is a paradigm. They are prepared within simulated frameworks where future success can be insured. This constitutes a precondition for the school's ability to rob systematically each student of his or her problem. By the time they have become "professionals," the process had indeed succeeded in brainwashing them so they are no longer even able

to remember that there is a problem: the problem of architecture's existence in a corrupt society, and how to resist this corruption. ◉ But the problem of architecture just won't go away by manipulating history, scavenging through other fields, contemplating techniques of action. For architecture can solve no problems—it itself is inherently problematical and questionable. ◉ Having relinquished love of the divine *epistème* in favor of opinion, the architect has become a purveyor of opinions, has lost participation in *sophia*—that wondrous dimension of architecture that Alberti called angelic. Architecture

The Architect

`36` `37`

Scenography and costumes, National Theater, Oslo, 1997 The set is constructed from a precise number of universal architectural elements. The configuring and reconfiguring of these abstractions allow certain figures to emerge and others to recede. The universality of architecture is caught in the web of illusions while alienating itself in the process. To what extent architecture is an alien phenomenon or a cozy sign of homecoming depends on the participant's belief in its stability. Home and homelessness are not conditions of material, but refer to the ever-groundless belief that here/there, now/then have been given once and for all. And in this sense we all live in an Eden Court that will soon be implicated in a crisis of foundations. Whether this crisis is referred to the architect or to the society that constructed the architect, one thing is certain: **You can go home again, but your home has nowhere to go.** ■ The play is a parable of the contemporary situation, using architecture as its basic symbol. Architecture, however, is a symbol that can actually be inhabited and domesticated, thus erasing the boundaries that divide reality and its representation. Architecture opens onto a horizon in which the absurd, the farcical, and the socially pressing become confused. I have used this capacity of architecture to both represent and de-present reality in the making of the set. Its mobility and dynamic quality, its elementary nature, and its nonfigurative dependence on language are counterparts of the drama. The "scandal of architecture" is precisely that its figures are mute and that architecture's silence speaks resonantly to the soul. ■

Bauhaus

Lecture, Weimar, 1998 The thread that runs through my work is best expressed, perhaps, by the phrase "The Trace of the Unborn!" This phrase refers to a sign that is itself not traceable, because it is generated by an act that remains forever absent. Absence, the fact that the trace points to the Holocaust and to those who can never again be, simultaneously refer-

ring to a future still unborn, still waiting for a present that is at once entangled in history and yet has no part in it. To do justice to this absence, to give body to the unfathomable sacrifice requires the realization, once again, of a spirit that animated each and every dying breath; each Jew's extinguished resistance to the eternal tide of inhumanity. And is it not at this very moment of solitary resignation that the very condition of happiness, law, and ethic is established? For those of the future and of the past—the unborn—depend on us today to embody the dimension of an eternal ethic and an undying culture in the city and in its architecture. ◉ This, then, is the place where the ideal of the Bauhaus intersects with my own belief that the ethic is indeed an optic since it makes visible our own relation to and responsibility for history. History is not a story with a happy or unhappy ending, but rather a process that in its very anonymity produces no meaning at all. Rather, this process calls for a human response to its own injustice. The call of the process asks one to preserve the trace of the unborn—not to obliterate its absence or evade its groundlessness—to do justice to it through the work of memory. A work that, like a light we forgot to turn off at night, reminds us the next day by its very own faintness of the forgotten events of the night. Staggering testimony speaks, making us witnesses no longer called to martyrdom but to action. Is that not what the very word survivor embodies today? It is incredible that some people have forgotten the connection between memory, action, and construction; forgotten that, they too, removed from the trace, have become part of it and are thus destined to undergo the obligation to cry out in opposition to every falsification and obliteration of the truth by politics or by the deception of homecoming and place. ◉ The Bauhaus ideal of modernity was a call for an exodus—an exodus from the mythology of space, from slavery to idols; that is, from all forms of aesthetics, of hollow rituals and banal responses. This ideal calls one to sever the root, to leave one's soil, tribe, and place in order to create an architecture that is universally naked in its freedom toward others, an architecture permanently displaced. ◉ The beauty of the works of that irretrievable time lies for me in the explicit nonfittingness of these buildings, with not only their immediate surroundings, but the Earth itself. These buildings, whether in Tel Aviv or

becomes everybody's (the managers', renovators', interior designers', space planners'—a "good profession") and no one's. School becomes a pluralistic cover, under which attention toward the nonexistent basis of architecture is converted into each person's opinion as to how to supply it, and thus diffused in its potentially explosive content. Problem solving is simply another term for transforming the nowhere-to-be-found ground of architecture into a piece of "real estate" in order to sell it. ("Start with the site....") ◉ Neither teachers nor students today

are encouraged to undertake an adventure. Dangerous, risky—perhaps hopeful?—that understands itself as a search for the whence, the whereto, and the why of architecture's condition. A quest for the miracle, or at least the abyss that illuminates it. And if someone is still bothered by a problem to which no curriculum answer can be given, then he or she should refrain from raising it, because that to which technicized thinking can give no answer is irrelevant—a "pseudoproblem." (A few history courses, some humanities, and—hocus-pocus-architecture's

meaningful once again!) ◉ I believe that the atmosphere of unease that is felt today in architecture cannot be eliminated, though the climate in which it is taught and practiced can be regulated by sophisticated control systems. ◉ The experiential core of architecture has sunk below the horizon of visibility so that even when it appears it is unrecognized. The process of de-culturation called education and practice has eclipsed architecture so far and so thoroughly by the fictions of "common sense" and the "real world" that one hesitates even to speak

Berlin, in Prague or Amsterdam, refuse to become the "world incarnate in matter," but express in their artificial structure an intellectual construction and a human departure from that communion that takes place whenever home is the fulfillment of the divine and prior dwelling. The visibility of modernity in architecture and planning is its explicit manifestation that "meaning" is not rested in worldly sources but belongs to the internal authority immanent in the object's relationship to a free and disillusioned humanity. A revolutionary attitude that dispels the illusory contact with the "sacred object." An idol is not dissected by the mediation of reason! ◎ Ravaged by transformation, this culture distances itself from the persistence of modernity to illuminate real needs by the unreality of presence. The "white city" offers the citizen at once an infinite task to build a wholly new and just world, a world that does not age, and a critique of any present in whose name the future is sacrificed. It puts the world between two impossibilities: the impossibility of the present and of the nonpresent. For these buildings make vivid that the whole spectrum of biological life—sleeping, eating, working, etc.—is on the way to becoming part of the mechanics of the spiritual. These rooms and their public visage offer the dweller an environment that, in its desolateness, reveals that the adult needs no figure to hide the just dessert of the human condition and the body ready to experience the eternal. ◎ Their eyes remain open to see through. The "strip window," the transparency of space, the openness of plan, the homogeneity that makes each point interchangeable—as if in outer space—with any other, are not conceived for any future topic. Rather, they are impressions, each time the future is conceived, of a state of lucidity. The superfluity of reality over architecture becomes the permanent tour de force of this architecture, which allows one to scrutinize diversity and yet allow the heresy of the singular that refers only to that which is not a thing. For these objects fling a truth at one's face: building cannot be inhabited; the only space one can inhabit is the space of the world, the country whose boundaries are those of the unsaid, the unnamed. Ultimately, the pitiless nature of architecture is revealed in the fact that its material reality is a revelation of a fiction, and as fictitious nature it is an embodiment of a reality that has no place—so long as existence is conceived as a deviation of the sacred into the profane. That is,

so long as architecture is seen to be a refuge for the divine rather than exposing its placelessness. ◎ Moreover, the lack of institutional or political reference in this project of architectural form makes visible that these buildings and spaces show themselves as they are, with nothing remaining for later. Their heroism lies in that immediacy where justice and matter join together without bowing to one another. Their heroism, prefigured in the Bauhaus, is that of insomnia, of these buildings against places—lest any one of them appear as a stand-in for memory, thus confining the word with stone. ◎ This is very different from the contemporary obsession with style and ideology; products of a twentieth-century legacy of nihilism, which today culminates in the works announced by Nietzsche, Heidegger, and all those for whom the human is about to disappear. This "tradition" of nihilism—a tradition of dealing with the world as object—has sought to reduce reality itself to that of an object. Whether one calls this object the tool, the heart, artwork, nature of temple, one thing is clear: Nihilism seeks to found the world on the basis of objects and places rather than on that of the human encounter and its light. ◎ The Bauhaus demanded a radical destruction of the superstition of form and habit. Instead it advocated existence in the transparency of constructed and geometric space, which would free one of the magic and constraint of place. It sought a placeless world in the plenitude of universally available space, space whose very homogeneity was a metaphysical guarantee of a democratic emptiness that could only be filled by the weight of the just and the free. ◎ Mystery and opacity have become virtually synonymous with building and its foundation. An immemorial tradition observes the sources of human intelligence and seeks to speak in the name of the unremembered. This aura of mystery and shadows is the very materiality art for which building matter works. At the same time, this mystery—in its essential originality and inaccessibility—is the ever-present source of violence, servitude, and cruelty. For in the name of the mystery of things there continue ignorance and injustice; in the name of the origin there speaks the unoriginal repetition of the same. ◎ The dispelling of this "mystery" is a task that the Bauhaus embraced with determination and an almost messianic zeal. It was precisely here, in the domain of the sacred, that the Bauhaus declared war and wrought havoc. For there is no more to the

of indifference toward it. By simply being silent the educational establishment has eliminated questions; "practice" has developed a blind spot for that which threatens its success. ◎ But the decentering of being toward nonexistent grounds is actually felt as reality. Indeed it is this very groundlessness that moves the participant in architecture toward the void. This void has become the mover, the seeker, the moved. Reflection upon this process of participation constitutes the true literacy of the architect. ◎

Education as the art of turning around toward reality—the truly revolutionary art—has become a technique of adjusting students so completely to the times that they no longer feel a desire to know anything else. The school has become a device that prevents students of architecture from acquiring the knowledge that would enable them to articulate the fundamental question of architecture: being or not. Pressed into a state of quiet despair or aggressive alienation, students abandon the mystery

of architecture. But this kind of attitude and reason is not reasonable. There are other ways to think and do Architecture: noninstrumental reason, nonmanipulated architecture. ◎ Architecture—that divine luxury of faith, highest crystallization of the material liberty of humanity, its imagination and spirit—must never succumb to being the degraded product of necessity provided by the technicians of educational and monetary utopias. ◎ This is why I started *Architecture Intermundium*. ●

sacred than the empty ritual, a formalism, the desire for salvation through grace, the evil of senseless habits, the purpose of which is to deprecate reality in the name of convention so it may become fulfilled through an image. Gods were toppled, orders broken, walls smashed, the center removed. These buildings pass the death sentence on the magic of pagan protectors, on the idols who protect the threshold and the health. With the breaking of the boundary of the threshold every stranger may enter; with the removal of the hearth, the family transforms its genetics into an ethics and ethics into a look—whichever, if not considered divine—looks and in looking testifies to an ongoing construction-destruction defining responsibility. "Only God can save us now." Let the German philosopher ponder the acute irresponsibility in that statement. One can not reproach reality for one's own faithlessness. Is it not an evil to resign oneself to futility; the stuff redemptions are made of? Precisely to have confidence in the fundamental void of God as well as in one's own incapacity to hide this absence is to give credence to a human being who is free from all forms of infantile advocation and weakness. Such a human being, when he or she is an architect, dispenses between substances and void at the very moment of constructing this absence called space out of tangible materials. Such constructions do not lull one to the emptiness of conventions, but demand rather the mastery of political situations through thought and memory. Unlike those who constructed cathedrals and sacred graves, this kind of architecture seeks not to approach the other by hiding the normal face in front of the supernatural. Rather, he or she demands that human beings— in the absence of the supernatural—speak to the other without contempt (the so-called user) and without putting the other in servitude or to treat him as an object of functions. ◎ After all, only a personal and genuine response to reality can come to grips with the perverse manifestation of a city reduced to a violence and expressive of a justice that does not triumph. ◎ This temerity or chutzpah is also an acknowledgment of a deep patience opening the Bauhaus ideal, which is at once an engagement and disengagement with history [Kafka quote]. But this is not an ambivalence. It is, rather, a process of demystifying the universe, particularly of the illusion that one traverses history only by taking up its course and results. The permanent or "eternal," Bauhaus (a Bauhaus one can discover even two thousand years ago on the notion of the Art, the Book, and the tabernacle) "lives on" by judging history while refusing to accept the verdict of history that proclaims the Bauhaus as a "style" and "moment." In thus proclaiming the momentum of anonymous events as the judge of spiritual ones, the ideologization of the Bauhaus deforms and distorts its essential core: Light never shines collectively; it shines permanently, even in the darkness and as long as eternity itself. This is perhaps the real relevance of that whiteness, eternity, and purity, which refuses to compromise with history and any form of realism; a refusal that gives all these works the light of ever-present dawn (for are they not always young?). The relevance of this light might be even greater tomorrow than it was yesterday. ●

Between the Lines *Jewish Museum, Berlin, 1988—99* The dis-

38
39
40
41
42
43
44
45

cussion about a Jewish Museum in Berlin was in process for almost a quarter of a century. Many eminent experts and Holocaust survivors discussed this issue and its implications. The conclusions reached were formulated in a brief for the competition held in 1988–1989. ■ When I was invited by the Berlin Senate in 1988 to participate in this competition, I felt that this was not a program I had to invent or a building I had to research; rather, it was one in which I was implicated from the beginning, having lost most of my family in the Holocaust and myself having been born only a few hundred kilometers east of Berlin in Lodz, Poland. ■ There are three basic ideas that formed the foundation for the Jewish Museum design. First, the impossibility of understanding the history of Berlin without understanding the enormous intellectual, economic, and cultural contribution made by its Jewish citizens. Second, the necessity to integrate physically and spiritually the meaning of the Holocaust into the consciousness and memory of the city of Berlin. Third, that only through the acknowledgment and incorporation of this erasure and void of Jewish life

Between the Lines, Jewish Museum Berlin, Star Matrix

in Berlin, can the history of Berlin and Europe have a human future. ■ The official name of the project is the "Jewish Museum," but I have called it "Between the Lines." I call it this because it is a project about two lines of thinking, organization, and relationship. One is a straight line, but broken into many fragments; the other is a tortuous line, but continuing indefinitely. ■ The site is the new-old center of Berlin on Lindenstrasse, next to the distinguished Kollegienhaus, the baroque former Prussian courthouse. At the same

Between the Lines *Opening Speech, Berlin, 1999* I am thrilled and honored to be here on the occasion of this wonderful opening and to welcome Chancellor Schroeder, Bundestag President Thierse, along with the many other distinguished guests who are here tonight. ◎ I would also like to recognize my father, a survivor of the Holocaust, whose ninetieth birthday we've just celebrated in Israel; Nina, my wife and collaborator, who was so integral to the spirit of this project; Noam and Lev, my sons, who endured the stresses of this project and who flourished and grew through it; and Rachel, who was born exactly on the day when I started working on this project and gave it its luck. ◎ So, where to begin—perhaps with the visa which I received in my passport to live and work in Germany, with a letter from the Senate, upon winning this competition. The visa was inscribed in patient handwriting by a border official, and it stated that Herr Libeskind is allowed to enter Germany in order to plan and realize a single building, namely the Jewish

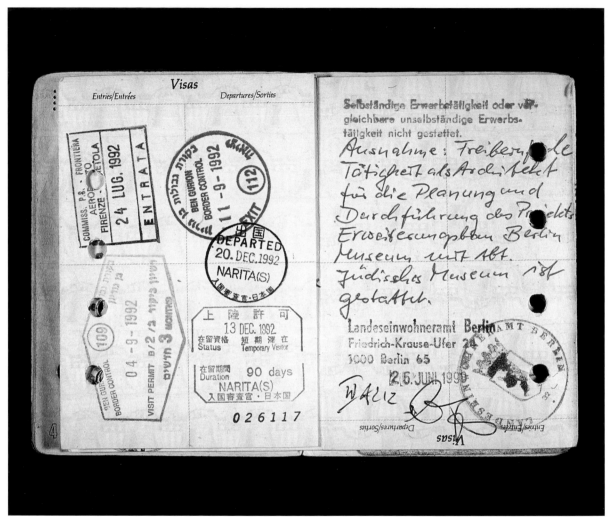

Between the Lines, Daniel Libeskind's passport. "Ausnahme: Freibeinfelde Tätigheit als Architekt für die Planung und Durchfuhrung das Projekte Erweitesungsbau Berlin Museum mit Abt. Judisches Museum ist Gestaltet." ("Condition: Free to work as an architect for the planning and realization of the project of the Berlin Museum with the Jewish Museum.")

Museum of Berlin. Having a permit to specifically realize a singular building, I saw it as an unconscious manifesto given to me at the border, which I had to honor through the reunification of Germany, five different governments of Berlin, different senators of Building and Culture, and different museum directors. ◎ Despite the many name changes of the museum, from the Extension of the Berlin Museum with the Jewish Department, to the Extension of the Berlin Museum with the Jewish Museum, to the Jewish Department in the Stadtmuseum, to the Jewish Museum in the Stadtmuseum, to the Jewish Museum Berlin, I was unwaveringly committed to building a museum that would portray in an uncompromising way the Jewish dimension of Berlin's history throughout the generations. ◎ From the competition proposal, which were lines on paper, to the building in which you are now sitting, I sought to incorporate the Jewish experience. This experience is not just a residue of a vanished culture, but a living and vital dimension of Jewish and German history. And this experience is no longer an abstract one, having been incorporated in the space of architecture; something that cannot be described in words or texts, but now belongs to the city and to the museum. ◎ The construction of the Jewish Museum has reached completion. Whatever an architect says about his work may only seem to be a redundant commentary on what is obviously built. Yet when it comes to this Jewish Museum, there are dimensions that are not purely in space, dimensions inscribed in time, which the lineaments of the building and its construction present. The conception with which I worked from the very beginning was that the physical space and form should give substance beyond the visible; a dimension that forms a permanent trace of the past in the future,

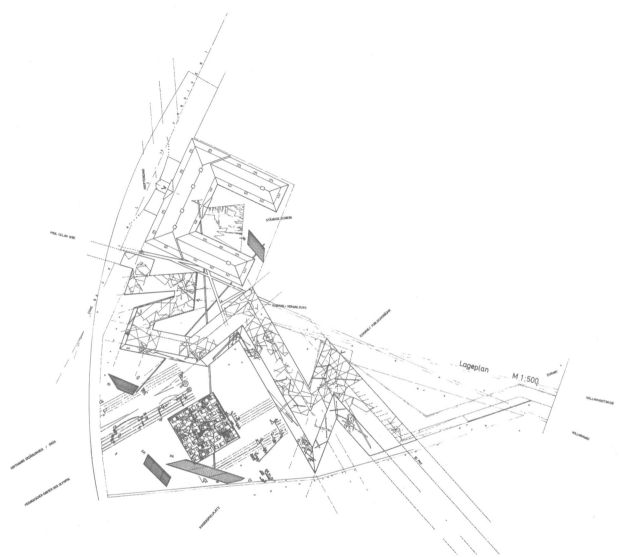

Lageplan M 1:500

Between the Lines,
Jewish Museum Berlin,
competition site plan

of exhilaration and tragedy, of the closed and the open, of fatality and hope. ◎ Tonight I would like to share with you the thoughts and the emotions that have formed the backdrop and underpinnings of this building. These concepts and feelings did not simply begin in 1988, when I first participated in the competition for the museum. The spirit with which I designed this museum is part of me as a person, and as a Jew, born to survivors of the Holocaust, someone who was born in Lodz, emigrated to Tel Aviv then to New York, and who moved to Berlin with his whole family in order to realize what, after all, was then only

an idea. I have always believed that this Museum should represent the future, not only the past; the beginning, not only the end. I wanted to design a museum that would communicate and engage the visitor on a mental, visceral, and emotional level with the Jewish dimension of Berlin and German history. The uniqueness of Jewish history here is not only something abstract and theoretical, but that which is also part of the emotions and of the heart. ◎ Audiences were fascinated with the possibility that despite the erasure of history, the people of Berlin and of Germany believed that there was a future to that history. For

the Holocaust was not just one more event in time; it was a reorientation of space—an event more drastic than what had occurred in the thousands of years of Berlin's previous history. This museum gives possibility to exhibit the past in the light of the future, and the future in the light of the past. For the Jewish Museum represents the tension and the struggle to appreciate not only the Einsteins, the Liebermanns, the Schoenbergs, the Benjamins, but all those nameless Jewish Berliners who are now inextricably bound with the identity of this city. ◎ When this building seemed simply a theory, people described it as a zigzag

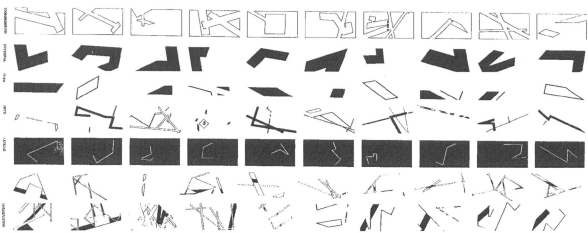

Between the Lines,
Architectural Alphabet

time that there was this actual visible site, I felt that there was an invisible matrix of connections, a connection of relationships between figures of Germans and Jews. Even though the competition was held before the Wall fell, I felt that the one binding feature that crossed East and West was the relationship of Germans to Jews. Certain people, workers, writers, composers, artists, scientists, and poets, formed the link between Jewish tradition and German culture. I found this connection and I plotted an irrational matrix that would yield reference to the emblematics of a compressed and distorted star: the yellow star that was so frequently worn on this very site. This is the first aspect of the project. ■ I was always interested in the music of Schoenberg and in particular his period in Berlin. His greatest work is the opera *Moses and Aaron*, which could not be completed. For an important structural reason, the logic of the libretto could not be completed by the musical score. At the end of the opera, Moses doesn't sing, he just speaks, **"Oh word, thou word,"** addressing the absence of the word, and one can understand it as a "text," because when there

is no more singing, the missing word that is uttered by Moses, the call for the word, the call for the deed, is understood clearly. I sought to complete that opera architecturally, and that is the second aspect of this project. ■ The third aspect was my interest in the names of those persons who were deported from Berlin during the fatal years of the Holocaust. I asked for and received from Bonn two very large volumes called the *Gedenkbuch*. They are incredibly impressive because all they contain are names, just lists and lists of names, dates of birth, dates of deportation, and presumed places where these people were murdered. I looked for the names of the Berliners and where they had died—in Riga, in the Lodz ghetto, in the concentration camps. ■ The fourth aspect of the project is formed by Walter Benjamin's *One-Way Street*. This aspect is incorporated into the continuous sequence of sixty sections along the zigzag, each of which represents one of the **"Stations of the Star"** described in the text of Walter Benjamin. ■ To summarize this fourfold structure: The first is the invisible and irrationally connected star that shines with absent light of

or a blitz, surely an image only seen by an angel. Today, as you walk through the building, the walls, exhibition spaces, and the building's organization generate an understanding of the scale of disrupted tradition—and the trace of the unborn. ◉ The main doorway to the museum is through the baroque Kollegienhaus, the former Prussian courthouse, which is near completion in its renovation. Programmatically, it is important to enter that baroque Berlin with all its rich history and then to descend through the entrance void to the underground connections. These connections link the visitors with the new Jewish Museum—an underground con-

nection which asserts the profound foundation between German and Jew. There are three streets, each having a singular destination: The Garden, the Holocaust Tower, and the Stair of Continuity. ◉ The garden is upside-down, containing forty-nine columns in a rigid grid and on a sloping surface. Forty-eight of these columns are filled with the earth of Berlin, signifying the birth of the State of Israel in 1948; one representing the city of Berlin is filled with the earth of Jerusalem. ◉ The garden is upside-down because the vegetation grows across only at the very top and is completely hidden in the 7-meter-high columns. Upside-down

because there is a distinct disorientation produced by perfect right-angle geometry rooted in a sloped floor vis-à-vis the buildings surrounding it. This instability is akin to the disorientation which awaited those who left Berlin and the disorientation of Berlin. ◉ Another road ends with the Holocaust Void, an abrupt deadend. This 27-meter-high, acutely angled space is built of raw concrete. The space is not heated in the winter and not cooled in the summer, and is connected from the underground, but disconnected outside. There is only a reflection-without-source of a narrow line of light, which ends high above. This chamber res-

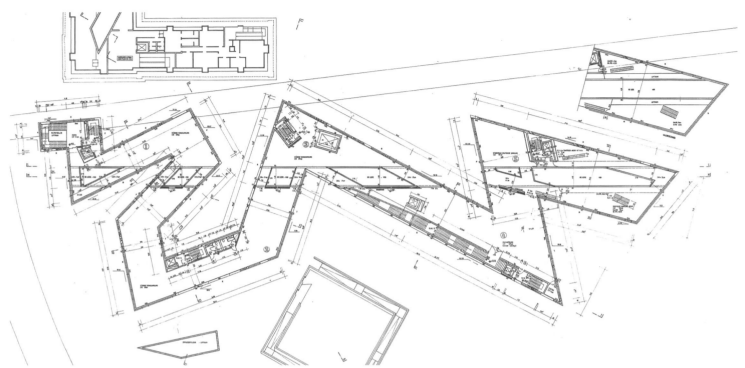

Between the Lines,
Jewish Museum Berlin,
ground floor plan

individual address. The second is the cutoff of Act 2 of *Moses and Aaron*, which culminates with the not-musical fulfillment of the word. The third is the ever-present dimension of the deported and missing Berliners; the fourth is Walter Benjamin's urban apocalypse along the *One-Way Street*. ■ In specific terms, the building measures more than 15,000 square meters. The entrance is through the baroque Collegienhaus and then into a dramatic entry void by a stair, which descends under the existing building foundations, crisscrosses underground, and materializes as an independent building on the outside.

The existing building is tied to the extension underground, preserving the contradictory autonomy of both the old building and the new building on the surface, while binding the two together in the depth of time and space. ■ There are three underground "roads," which programmatically have three separate stories. The first and longest "road" leads to the main stair, to the continuation of Berlin's history, to the exhibition spaces in the Jewish Museum. The second road leads outdoors to the E.T.A. Hoffmann Garden and represents the exile and emigration of Jews from Germany. The third axis leads to the

onates with the hum of the city. The Holocaust Void is a place that has to be experienced as an end, which will forever remain a dead end. For they will not return. ◎ The third and longest road leads to the main stairway and to the continuation of the museum, giving access to the different exhibition floors. ◎ The central structure in the building is the void, a disconnected straight line cutting through the building. This void—different acoustically, materially, architecturally from the white walls of the exhibition spaces and illuminated by skylights—refers to that which can never be exhibited in this museum, no matter how

many objects are brought to it and stories told in it. The bridges provide the physical connection from one side of the museum galleries to the other. Surrounding the void are the white spaces of the exhibition. ◎ Another dramatic feature which you might become aware of as you explore the building is formed by the window configurations, which radically penetrate through the walls. These configurations are a topographical record—the writing of the walls: a matrix of lines and addresses connecting Jewish Berliners to their fellow citizens. ◎ I believe that the space of the Jewish Museum is part of the cultural process that

provides and extends a different sensibility, a discountinued discourse, and sheds another light. The source of this light is the very ground of Berlin. But what is the ground of Berlin on which this building stands? Certainly it is the obvious piece of land here in Kreuzberg. Yet both beneath and above this ground there is another one to which the Jewish Museum refers: the ground of an incredible Jewish culture of Berlin which flourished here, became assimilated, annihilated, and reborn in hope. ◎ Whatever theories and written text have been published about this building, we are now in a concretized space of encounter. A space

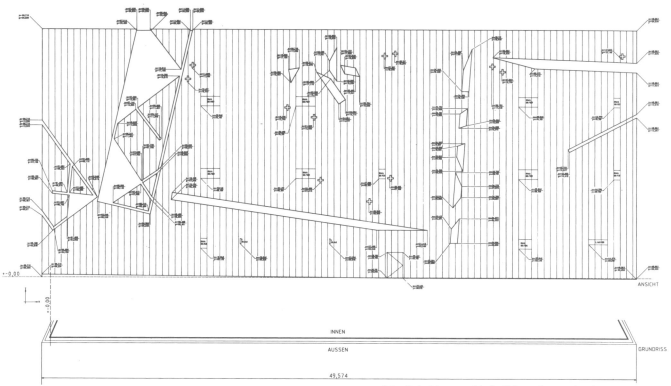

Between the Lines, Jewish Museum Berlin, elevation

dead end—the Holocaust void. ■ Cutting through the form of the Jewish Museum is a void, a straight line whose impenetrability forms the central focus around which the exhibitions are organized. In order to cross from one space of the museum to the other, the visitors traverse sixty bridges that open into the void space—the embodiment of absence. ■ The work is conceived as a museum for all Berliners, for all citizens. Not only those of the present, but those of the future who might find their heritage and hope in this particular place. With its special emphasis on the Jewish dimension of Berlin's history, this building gives voice to a common fate—to the contradictions of the ordered and disordered, the chosen and not chosen, the vocal and silent. ■ believe that this project joins architecture to questions that are now relevant to all humanity. To this end, I have sought to create a new architecture for a time that would reflect an understanding of history, a new understanding of museums, and a new realization of the relationship between program and architectural space. Therefore, this museum is not only a response to a particular program, but an emblem of hope. ■

whose figures are not neutral. But neither is this history. Neutral architecture is perhaps appropriate for non-events. The articulated spaces in the Jewish Museum make the incredible fluctuations of Jewish history, with all its highs and lows, move through the abyss created by the Holocaust into the future. ◎ Perhaps it is appropriate to point out that this Jewish Museum is not one that looks to the nostalgia of yesterday, but one that propels itself towards the future of existence in Germany. Whatever the reaction to this museum, the expectations and anticipations of the visitors will be connected to their own view of this history. Like a cloud passing in the sky that some see as a face, others as a fish or a monster, this building gives permanence to the figure of hope dressed in the guise of every visitor's response. ◎ The Museum is open to many interpretations and many routes, just like the pages of the Talmud, where the margins are often as important as what is being commented on. This experience is dependent on the engagement of the visitors with the implication of an ongoing history. For this history is not over. It is not, in my view, a story to be told with a happy or an unhappy ending, but a story that continues over irreversible events, in which every participant and visitor is implicated and made aware. History is not the statistics of the six million Jews, but of a unique Jewish individual multiplied six million times. This architecture provides the spaces for the involvement and participation of the public in an institution that communicates that Jewish culture, despite these tragic events, has a vital future in the capitol of Germany. ●

BETWEEN THE LINES

A Museum for the City of Berlin must be a place where all citizens, those of the past, of the present and of the future, must find their common heritage and individual hope. To this end the Museum form itself must be rethought in order to transcend the passive involvement of the [   ] actively confronting change.

The extension of the Berlin Museum with a special emphasis of housing the Jewish Museum Department is an attempt to give voice to a common fate: common both to what is being and what is other than being. The Museum must serve to inspire poetry, music and drama, (etc.) [   ] must give a home to the ordered/disordered, chosen/not chosen, vocal/mute [   ] [   ].

The particular urban condition becomes the spiritual site wherein the nexus of Berlin's precarious destiny is at once mirrored, fractured and transformed.

The [   ] [   ] of the German-Jewish cultural relation in Berlin is enacted now in the [   ] of the invisible. It is this invisibility which must be brought to visibility in order to give rise to a new hope and to a shared inner vision. Thus this project seeks to reconnect Berlin to its own history which must never be forgotten.

[   ] figures in the drama of Berlin who have acted as bearers of a great hope and anguish are traced into the lineaments of this museum: Heinrich Kleist, Rahel Varnhagen, Walter Benjamin, E.T.A. Hoffman, Friedrich Schleiermacher, Arnold Schoenberg, Paul Celan. They spiritually affirm the permanent human tension which is polarized between the impossibility of the System and the impossibility of giving-up the search for a higher order. Tragic premonition (Kleist), sublimated assimilation (Varnhagen), inadequate ideology (Benjamin), [   ] science (Hoffman), displaced understanding (Schleiermacher), inaudible music (Schoenberg), last words (Celan); these constitute the critical dimensions which this work as discourse seeks to transgress.

The new extension is conceived as an emblem wherein the invisible has made itself apparent as [   ] Void, as the Invisible. Void/Invisible: these structural features have been gathered in [   ] space of the City and laid bare in an Architecture where the unnamed remains in the name which keeps still.

The existing building is tied to the extension underground, preserving the contradictory [   ] of both on the surface, while binding the two together in depth. Under the [   ] [   ] like Berlin and its Jews, one common burden - this insuperable [   ] contradictable burden - is outlined in the exchanges between two architectures and forms which are not reciprocal: cannot be exchanged for each other.

The urban, architectural and functional paradox of closed/open, stable/added [   ] [   ] [   ] [   ] can no longer presuppose the fictitious stability of State, power and organization. In contrast, the paradox presupposes the Unchanging, i.e. change proceeding directly out of that which would exclude changing attitudes and unchanging opinions alike.

Urban Design Concept

The proposal gives new value to the existing historical context by transforming the urban field into an open, future-oriented urban matrix. The proposed extension is characterized by a series of real and implied transformations which go beyond the existing forms of the site. The compactness of the traditional street pattern is gradually dissolved from the [   ] origins and related diagonally to both the housing developments of the sixties and the I.B.A. projects.

The new structure reasserts the urban importance of the "Collegienhaus" and through a series of contrasts engages the existing housing and public structures in a new dialogue. Thus the proposal interacts as an intense field whose old boundaries withdraw, exposing the vitality and [   ] dimensionality of Berlin.

Organization of the Building and the Required Functions

The new extension provides the Berlin Museum with an exciting set of new and flexible spaces. These spaces act in series of "open narratives", which in their architecture seek to provide the museum-goer with new insights into the collection, and in particular, the relation and significance of the Jewish Department to the Museum as a whole.

The Jewish Department is closely interwoven with the rest of the collection, yet is entirely independent and can be experienced alone as an integrated whole: both outside and inside, and from the outside and from the inside.

Standard exhibition rooms and traditional public spaces have been dissolved and disseminated along a myriad of complex trajectories in, on, and above the ground. These trajectories [   ] tily and systematically transform themselves in their form, function and significance.

Linear structures interact to create an irregular and decisively accentuated set of displacements, providing an active path and distancing the viewer in the investigation of the exhibits. These may be arranged both horizontally (plan), vertically (section), or in combinations of the two.

[   ] contain functional and circulation elements (stairs, services, and funicular platforms), as well as "walled-in" meditation spaces for the presentation of audio-visual materials.

Library books are disposed along the walls to become part of the exhibits themselves [   ] [   ] necessary.

The lecture room is transformed into a dynamic "mechanical theatre" by the movement of a single platform. This offers the possibility of truly spatial-kinetic exhibits, and puts the audience into a new relation to performance.

[   ] [   ] set in relation to the underground Museum connection. It is independent, [   ] Die and works in juxtaposition to the Bierstube in the 'Collegienhaus'.

The Museum ensemble is thus always on the verge of Becoming - no longer suggestive of a final [   ].

Link to the Existing Building

The link between "Collegienhaus" and the new extension is made through the central spine of the old building re-establishing this stair in its original baroque position. The underground Jewish Berlin collection thus serves as the "interchange station" between the different levels of the Museum and the collection itself. In this way, the "Collegienhaus" is restored and preserved in its autonomy, while becoming all the more integrated with the new building.

Fragments of the Museum - in the form of indeterminate closed/open voids - lodge themselves in all parts of the territory to become dispersed traces suggestive of past and future public [   ].

In this way, the link itself becomes - as connection - the structural key to the full integration of the underground galleries, restaurant, external Museum fragments, the extension, and the disjunctive interior.

Structure, Materials, and Facade Design

Structure: Pre-cast and cast-in-place concrete elements, constituting a tube with variable [   ].

Cladding: Various cladding materials including metal, mosaics, and glass. Special emphasis (see elevations) on light quality and lumination control.

Facade Design: Richly textured, visually de-naturalized, luminous surface, creating tension between the hand and the eye.

Concept for Open Spaces, Parking

E.T.A. Hoffman plaza whose focus in the "Mechanical Garden of Olympia" this moving image of Berlin is unique to all of four planes, 196 surfaces and 98 hidden facets. The space [   ] is oriented for the benefit of the museum-goer, but is also accessible to the public [   ] at large outside of the Museum and in the Restaurant.

To be included in the rotation: 1) Atrani - The gently rising baroque staircase leading to the church 2) Navy - Children's playground in the form of tall sailing ships 3) Versailles [   ] - Orderly apple planting and topiary 4) Heidelberg Castle - Ruins jutting into [   ] sky 5) Seville, Alcazar - Wooden dance platform 6) Marseilles Cathedral - Stepping stair to eternity 7) Freiburg Munster. 8) Moscow, Saint Basil's. - Life-size wooden dolls 9) discotheque. - Stone-pine forest 10) Naples, Museo Nazionale. - A child holds out freshly picked flowers 11) Florence Baptistry. - Helplessly stretched arm reaching for a fruit that [   ] beyond the reach. - Sky. - Vine, a Maiden, a Scale is Polar Sea.

The "fresh-air corridor" includes the children's playground, pedestrian paths and the anticipated bicycle pathway. Above-ground parking on a reinforced grass field for 53 automobiles.

What all this amounts to is two lines: one straight but broken into fragments, the other tortuous but continuing into infinity. As the lines develop themselves through a limited-infinite "dialectic", they also fall apart - become disengaged - and show themselves as separated so that the void centrally running through what is continuous materializes itself outside as void, or rather as the solid residue of independent structure, i.e. as a voided-void.

Fragmentation and splinter do mark the coherence of the ensemble because it has come undone in order to become accessible (both functionally and intellectually). The open spaces both inside and out never pre-existed as a whole (neither in the ideal Berlin or in the real one) nor can they be put together again in some hypothetical future. The fragmentation is the spacing, the separation brought about by the history of Berlin which can only be experienced as the absence of time and as the time fulfillment of what is no longer there.

The absolute event of history - the Holocaust - with its concentration camps and annihilation - the burn-out of meaningful development of Berlin and of humanity shatters the place while becoming a site of that which cannot be given. The preservation of the sacrifice, the offering: guardian night-watch over absent and future meaning.

And out of the disorder of time and Late there raises what is Early: Out of what is too Far, the Near.

Beyond the Wall *Exhibition, Netherlands Architecture Institute* (NAi), Rotterdam, 1997

[46]

[47]

This project is composed of architectural models and drawings as well as their extension into the concrete space they open to the public. This particular exhibition represents the search for architecture and is a microcosm of ideas and thoughts. It is the intention of the exhibition design that the public co-participate in a scheme by following an imaginative and nonlinear path in order to experience "the other side": "the substance" of hope and the proof of what remains invisible in space. ■ The public is invited to reflect on a different relationship between drawings and thought, building and construction. The design of the exhibition itself transforms and alters the original hall of the NAi and proposes a new understanding of the materiality of ideas. ■

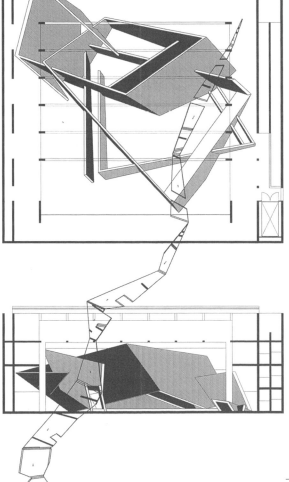

Beyond the Wall,
plan and section

The Books of Groningen *Drawings and texts, Groningen, 1990*

[48]

The Books of Groningen are the emblems whose marks outline the spiritual destiny of the city.

In turn, the city marks the trace of the historical text read and written by the citizens of the once and yet-to-be city, permanently remarking the boundaries of Groningen in time and space.

The differentiated intervals of time erased by each citizen's heartbeat and the articulated openings measured out in the space of the world are the dimension in which the written-read, imagined-realized, deserted-fulfilled is enacted.

The Beginning is: the letter—ancient initials that tie together traces and erasures.
The Book is: the letters—sent through the present to those awaiting the reply of the future to the deed of the past.
The Leaf is: the double-sided field suspended in the anticipated breath.
And Angle is: the position to which each letter turns the book—from closed/unread to unread/open.
The Measure is: the openness of the angle—stability that declines by thirty degrees around the axis of imagination.
The Ray is: the trajectory along which the city slides to the other side of the world and back again.
The Spiral is: the section cut through the structural spine, inclined toward the beyond.
The Muse is: the poetic guardian—the necessity of inspiration.
The Technique is: the manifestation of that which has been opened/veiled.
The Time is: the hidden measure—millennial.
The Heartbeat is: the unit of the future.
The Material is: the color.
The Inner Organ is: the known place that has not yet been. ■

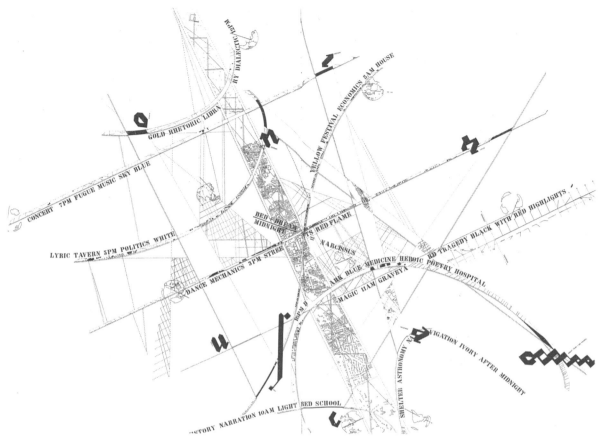

U
A Walk along the Boundary
Magic / 11 A.M. / Graveyard / Tragedy
Black with Red Highlights / Melpomene
Discipline: Architecture

Book U (A Book of Groningen, 1990)
Bouvard takes a rosy view of the future of mankind.

▨ Modern man is progressing. Europe will be regenerated by Asia. The law of history being that civilization goes from east to west—role of China—two branches of mankind will finally be merged. Future inventions: means of travel—balloon, submarine boat with windows, always in calm waters, as the sea is only disturbed on the surface. It will be possible to see fish go by and landscapes at the bottom of the ocean. Animals tamed. All kinds of cultivation.

▨ Future of literature (other side of industrial literature). Future sciences: Control magnetic pull.
▨ Paris a winter garden—fruit espaliers on the boulevards. The Seine filtered and warm—abundance of artificial precious stones—lavish gilding, house lighting—light will be stored because certain bodies have this property, like sugar, the flesh of certain molluscs and Bologna phosphorus. House facades will be compulsorily painted with the phosphorescent substance and their radiation will light up the streets.
▨ Evil will disappear as want disappears. Philosophy will be a religion. Communion of all peoples. Public holidays.
▨ There will be travels to the stars—and when the earth is used up, mankind will move over to the stars.
▨ Pecuchet takes a gloomy view of the future of mankind. Modern man has been diminished and has become a machine.
▨ Final anarchy of the human race (Buchner, I–II).
▨ Impossibility of peace (id).

Barbarity caused by excessive individualism and ravings of science.
▨ Three hypotheses: 1) pantheistic radicalism will break every link with the past, and inhuman despotism will result; 2) if theistic absolutism triumphs, the liberalism that has pervaded mankind since the Reformation will collapse, everything is overturned; 3) if the convulsions existing since the Revolution of 1789 continue endlessly between two outcomes, these oscillations will carry us away with their own strength.
▨ There will be no more ideal, religion, morality.
▨ America will have conquered the world.

Future of literature
▨ Pignouflisme universel. Tout ne sera plus qu'une vaste ribote d'ouvriers.
▨ Fin du monde par le cessation du calorique.
Gustave Flaubert, **Boulevard and Pecuchet**, 1872–1880.

The Book of Groningen,
master plan

Manual Piety

▮ Theatre-religious gambler wearing a mask made of shark fins. Each individual should resemble a building made of small forks; a score for faint sounds permitted by the chairman, who directs the sale of metaphors, packed sorrel in his rucksack. The maids mumble demurely.

▮ For example, there are plenty of men whose names stand for yearlings because they start each year with a revolution. An anointed epistemology is terribly linear yet not as empty as the space of the stomach that consists of a tropological volume large enough to contain a potpourri of neurasthenic possibilities, the remaining volume still positive when compared to the ocean. This garrulous, three-dimensional fold is selfishly developed into two-dimensional prodigy surpassing the perfect meter even when it falls straight from the sky toward the right point of the observatory. Iridescent paws, like projectiles, are purified by the night curve, touching the erudite.

▮ Without a net or a bag you cannot capture the just robbing a hermit near the brittle jetty, nor please the unjust distributing alms on the cliff. Your task will be to divide an assigned place by cutting it in half with color; each pile, mutating unpredictably in an elevator going down when the oxygen is used up, will be clearly distinguishable from the last. Light purple appears to be thinner than dark red, more pleasing when mixed—**mutatis mutandis**—with drizzling rain. Sojourn in the open nearness of presence. Say "bright green," and so on. It might be necessary to climb the Universal Fixture—longest existence—to reclaim what Africans call "dollars." The lyrical will reduce its own edifice for a time, but in lyricism it has always been true that design stood for simple end concepts that could be pictured by sowing graphic seeds instead of these residual hairlocks and hoping to grow a being that, inside itself, looked like this: Oh, what a charade!

▮ Footprints, basically religious, have no epic function. All decorum secretly vows to murder any object in emulsion (silicate compound with extra H_2O). Painting, bouncing up and down to determine its relation to gravity, is a map that can be refolded without dogmatically aligning each precreased lineament. It will be made of flexible puma skin. Art will possess an exact unit of measurement: mosquitoes trapped in an attic, aeroplanes inside a coal mine—the sand king's spoils. Jehuda ben Ezer should have been sued! He would have done better to study the laws of anatomy than fancy radioactive metaphors.

▮ Recruit all dithyrambic verse, prescientific fractions. The anguished triple was the last worthy goal for humanity. Don't bother selling Renaissance perspective to fossils whose reaction is Einsteinian, sacrificial, entirely fantastic—in short,

as rundown as confidence that avoids all external influences but follows its own terrific path.

▮ Are you soaking a menhir—irascible record—in a kidney-shaped pool? Playing embryonic soccer with attractive xenophobes? Rearing the little jet turbine? Miracles will happen! Outrageous nouns will bury the leaping clown—trembling enemy on the march—beneath acid-gray loam covering the skin in layers, especially when a nasty taxidermist has centralized all the flesh into a single bundle. Meat tastes like lead to beasts capable of intercepting the call with a snare made from edible earth. When the table is fully laden with beautiful gifts—all rocks—the living forgive animals and plants their resistance.

▮ They should cart away the debris of the city, but not trample the heart frame, which gives a semblance of reality to popular films. Many choke to death on the slide rule though they have soaked it in soup for months. Serviettes are elegant at a dinner, not at the requiem, when sneezes designate that toxic green mucus is already slithering like a putto in tervalent carbon rings. Man was only happy when he was depressed and lacked a few numbers needed to civilize the Turks. Now twenty-three is indistinguishable from five! Without these fumbles the mujik would not be oppressed nor remain caged like an animal who fell into a hole dug by each lucky communist who went to the grave before private property was completely vindicated. Name all the spiritual leaders who began life by inventing feeble adjectives rather than by imitating animal sounds howled by their parents. The Eve of the Chicken is a phrase that moves toward the distended axiom, in which motion stalls at its maximum, ridicules the movement of the cosmos. In simple terms, this means that the absence of pain creates an empty field clinical revue, onomatopoeic silence.

▮ Invent a staircase that gets you to the revolving involuntary summer day—a really tough project for drinkers. But the more clever have their bodies filled with round, affable geometric signs pointing to various internal spaces in which respect can be bought and events are representable in the language common to triplets who possess a built-in dictionary for gestures—relational interfold—allowing them brief spatial respites between the glutinous, nonsocial concerns they have for civilization. A muscular man thinks the Sputnik a monstrosity while bearing his own never-elated anti-silt devices. Savor a pound of lies. Hope to become an azalia at best.

▮ "**Blood is beautiful, in ounces**"—a very eloquent maxim when one is freed from the burden of claws, telegrams from Moses that arrive via Murmansk, messages that induce a recluse withering in the pulsating dawn to inhale through his own mouth. Substitute "tsum" for

"must." Use semantics as a coast on which an ellipse can park itself, defying convention. Ruffle your hair. Human happiness shows that it has no head, but only a long wooden stick, which a coiffeur can twist and turn around to imitate a permanent-in-verse.

▮ Exactly sixty tits: Diana of Ephesus was mixed up about reserve. But an orangutan from Borneo prefers opium to a spiritual burlesque. He can read Zetl, but only when written in italics without ethnic spots. The prescription of colorful lion semen mixed with holographically preserved algae is a remedy against being attacked by longevity whose only sinecure is the god's anthropomorphic, rent-controlled slum life. And once more we leap when serious fits of coughing wake the lion sleeping curved on the lower lip.

▮ One should act like Stalin lost in satisfaction that tapers into moral ice. He built his city directly atop a naked matron using mock missionaries as workers. Let's not underrate the embalmed body heating the Kremlin wall! Organs frequently titillate the learned, who wear glamorous clothes, knockout style, to protect themselves. The city with body power in plentiful supply will eventually replace lascivious visions with its own **hotspots**.

Still Life with Red Predictions

Letatlin will fly back without Ulalume.

▮ Sharp staccato sounds will bypass Cerberus barking, sui juris, at the stranger in us; will be transmitted by heredity to the abracadabra violincello playing a solo motet in slow neon without the bow, without the cello.

▮ Odors creating the illusion of rotating, difficult-to-taste conventions will ripple the water already agitated by a continual barrage of ancient texts thrown into it. Both odor and water will become things permanently verging on spinning, like the Ring. A similar example of metal: willful arcs of polished metal siding fused with astral fibers, will be used for making discus or the shield protecting local poverty from being beaten up by an alien ratio.

▮ One will acquire a funny hypnotic power over flattened minds, particularly those of stupid museum curators who reject ornithological art because it is influenced by Chopin's flighty spirit. One will censor the invisible writings by General Petain, which hide in the delicate art nouveau ornament of the Metropolitan—provided one is willing to reconnoiter a flat cladophyll with a feeling of remorse.

▮ Inside each piece of furniture—even tall ones—there will be a play performed. A delicate young lad in the dead of winter will be able to participate in a sensory-ritual quest for lost birch, pine, and linden trees now replaced by single-fit smells of ionization exclusively designed to furnish each living room with rapid, national bursts of sneezing. Tulips anyone?

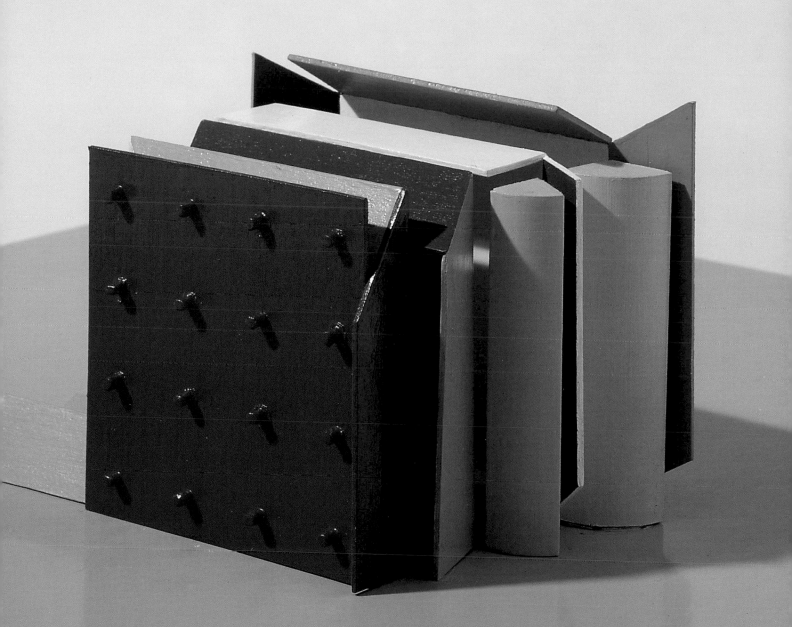

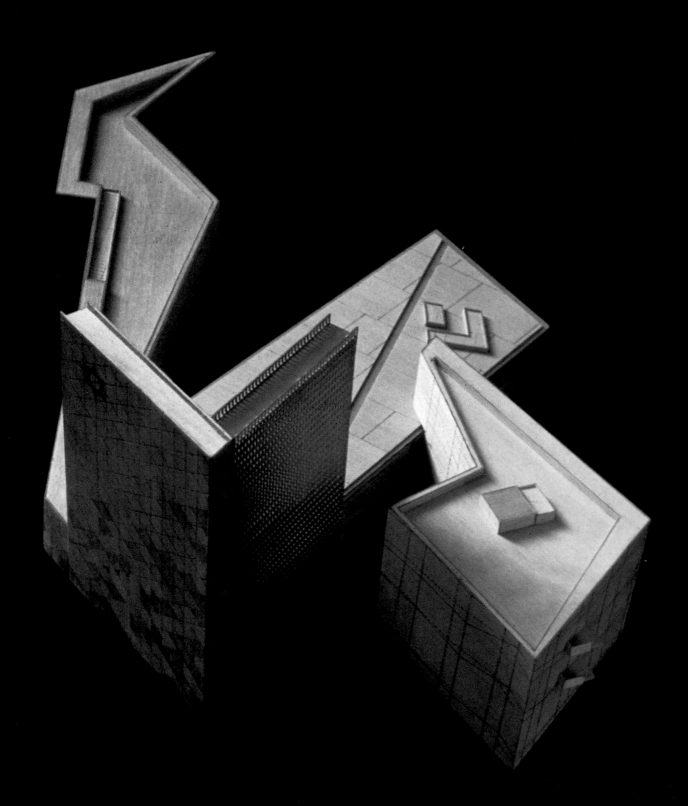

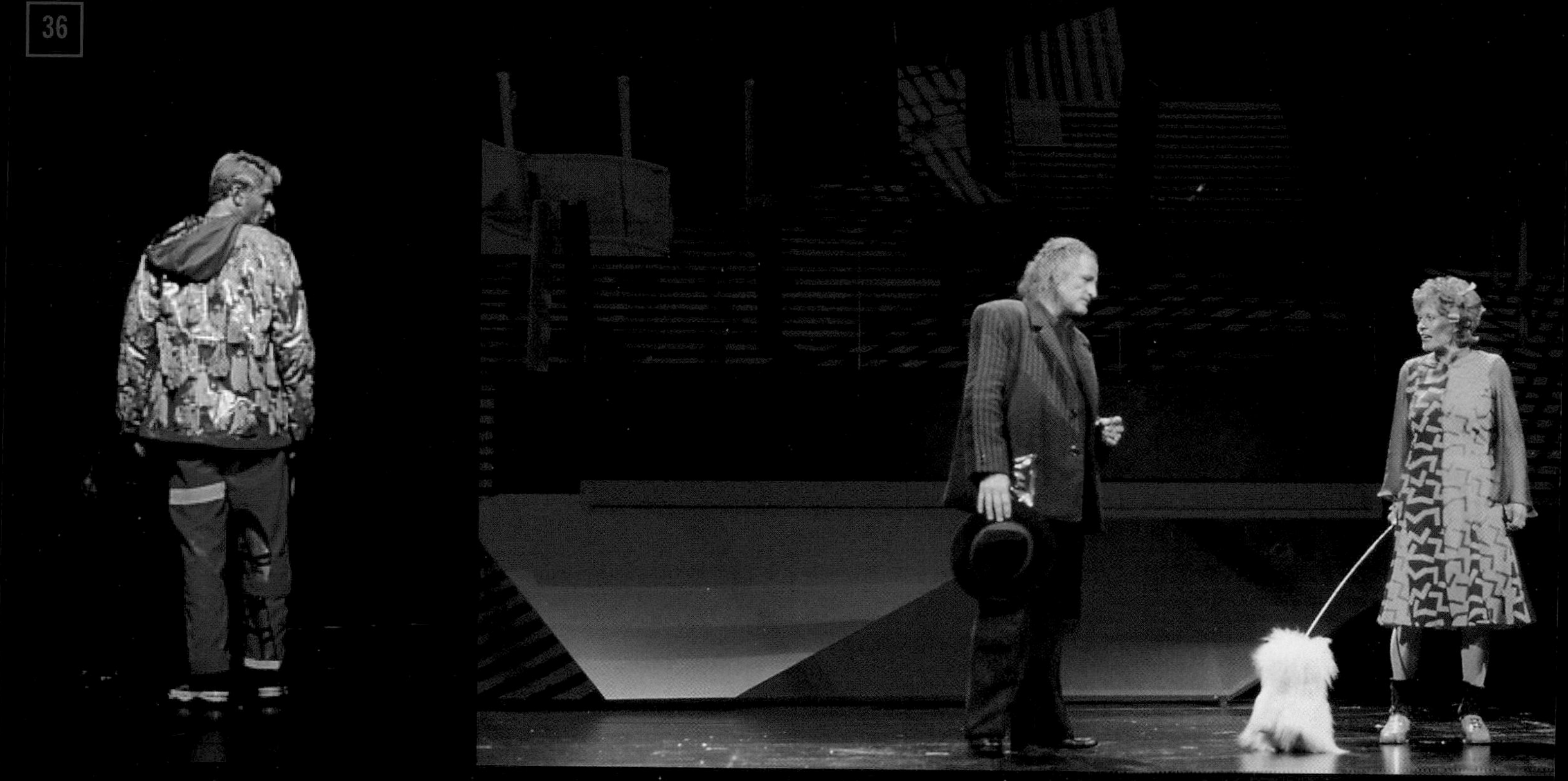

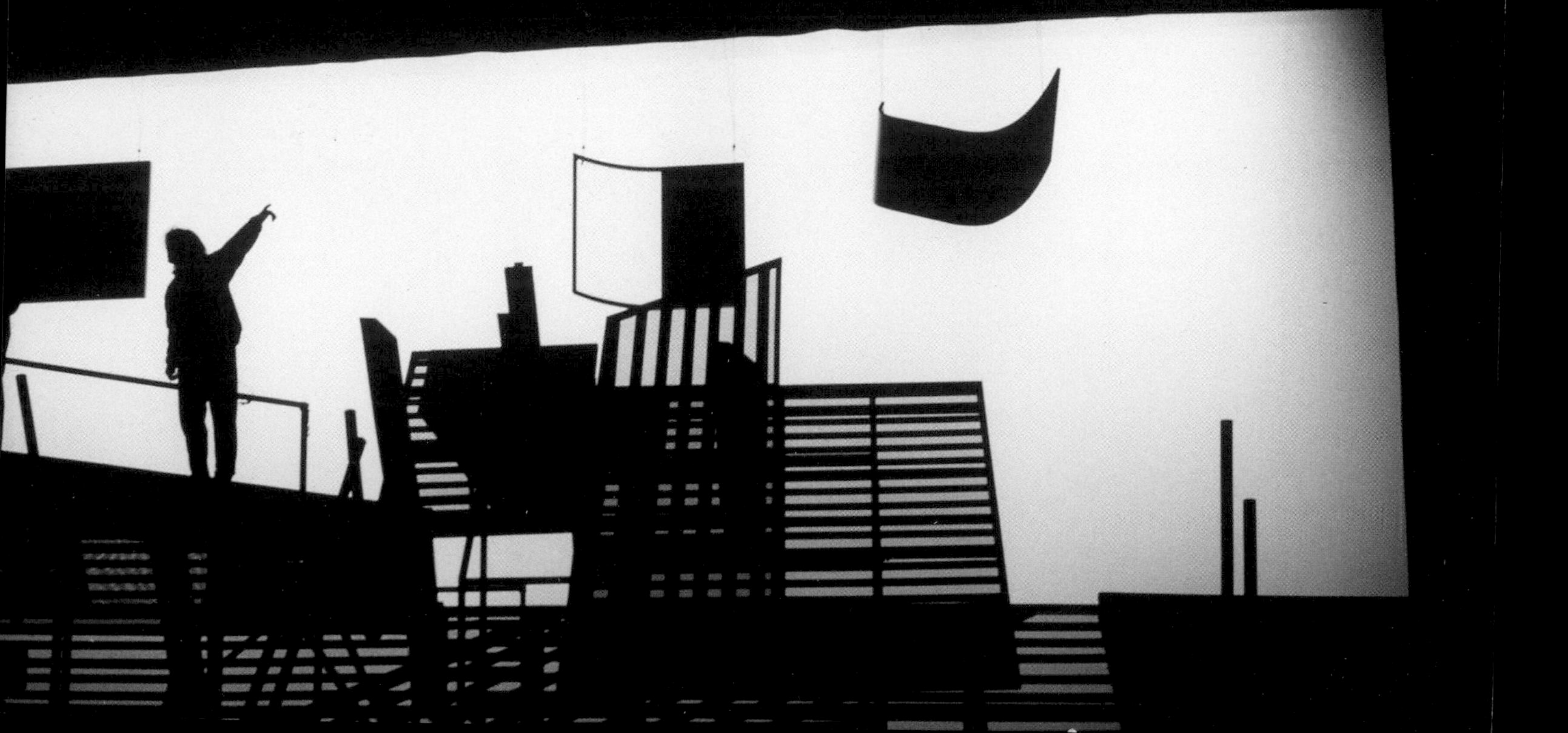

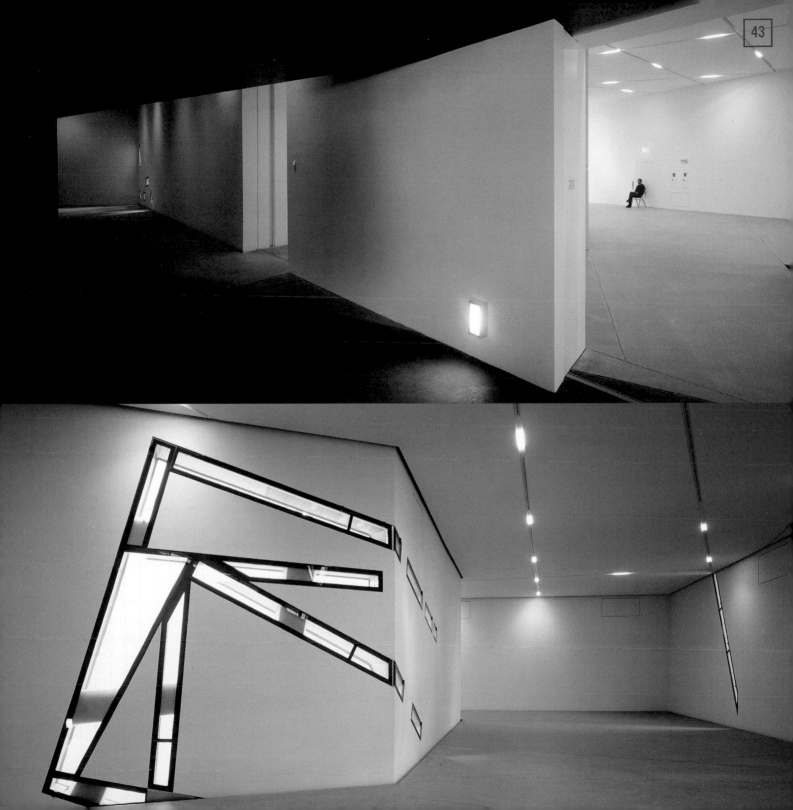

Behrend, Dora R. | Bendix, Albert | Berg, Simon | Berlin, Albin | Berliner, Edith
Behrend, Edith | Bendix, Alice | Berg, Sophie, geb | Berlin, Alfred | Berliner, Else
Behrend, Elisabeth | Bendix, Cilly | Berg, Walter | Berlin, Auguste | Berliner, Else
Behrend, Elsa | Bendix, Edith Pa | Berg, Werner R. | Berlin, Bernhard | Berliner, Emmi, g
Behrend, Else, geb | Bendix, Hugo | Berg, Willi | Berlin, Denny | Berliner, Erna, ge
Behrend, Emil | Bendix, Hugo | Berg, Willy | Berlin, Elli, geb. | Berliner, Ernst
Behrend, Emilie, | Bendix, Hugo | Bergas, Frieda | Berlin, Erna, geb | Berliner, Ester, ge
Behrend, Erna, g | Bendix, Ida | Bergas, Minna, g | Berlin, Erwin | Berliner, Eva
Behrend, Erna, g | Bendix, Jenny, ge | Bergas, Wilhelm | Berlin, Eva, geb.
Behrend, Flora, g | Bendix, Julie | Berge, Emanuel | Berlin, Fanny, geb
Behrend, Helman | Bendix, Julius | Berge, Ignatz | Berlin, Flora, geb
Behrend, Helene | Bendix, Julius O. | Bergel, Josef | Berlin, Frieda,
Behrend, Henny, | Bendix, Leopold | Bergel, Marianne | Berlin, Gertrud
Behrend, Henriet | Bendix, Levi Mei | Bergel, Rosa, geb | Berlin, Gertrud
Behrend, Henriet | Bendix, Mélanie | Bergen, Albert | Berlin, Gudula
Behrend, Hermin | Bendix, Meta, ge | Bergen, Anton | Berlin, Gustav
Behrend, Hertha | Bendix, Otto | Bergen, Charles | Berlin, Helene, g
Behrend, Hertha | Bendix, Paul | Bergen, Clara S. | Berlin, Hilde, geb
Behrend, Ida H. | Bendix, Recha | Bergen, Ella J., | Berlin, Hildegard
Behrend, Isaak | Bendix, Regina | Bergen, Erna | Berlin, Horst
Behrend, Israel | Bendix, Rosa, geb | Bergen, Hedwig, | Berlin, Ilse, geb.
Behrend, Jeanette | Bendix, Rosalie | Bergen, Max | Berlin, Irma
Behrend, Judith H | Bendix, Rosalie | Bergen, Sally | Berlin, Jeanette
Behrend, Julius | Bendix, Selma, ge | Bergen, Samuel | Berlin, Josef
Behrend, Kathari | Bendix, Sophie, g | Bergenstein, Klar | Berlin, Josef
Behrend, Marta, | Bendix, Taube | Bergenthal, Elsa | Berlin, Kurt
Behrend, Martha | Bendix, Thekla | Bergenthal, Ernst | Berlin, Leiser
Behrend, Max | Bendix, Wilhelmi | Bergenthal, Mina | Berlin, Lotte
Behrend, Max Ju | Bendkower, Regin | Bergenthal, Nane | Berlin, Malchen
Behrend, Minka | Bendorf, Dina, ge | Bergenthal, Regin | Berlin, Max
Behrend, anny | Bendorf, Edith, g | Berger, Adelheid | Berlin, Max
Behrend, ula | Bendorf, Emanuel | Berger, Adolf | Berlin, Paul
Bendorf, Joseph | Berger, Adolf | Berlin, Regina R.
Bendorf, Katharin | Berger, Adolf | Berlin, Ruth
Bendorf, Manfred | Berger, Adolf | Berlin, Ruth, geb
Bendorf, Max | Berger, Albert | Berlin, Sally
Bendorf, Moritz | Berger, Alexande | Berlin, Selma, geb
Bendorf, Moses | Berger, Alfons | Berlin, Sigismund
Bendorf, Paula, g | Berger, Alfred | Berlin, Simon
Berger, Alfred | Berlin, Wilhelm
Berger, Alfred | Berlin, Wilhelmi
Berger, Alfred
Berger, Amalie
Berger, Amanda,
Berger, Anna, geb

Chamberworks: Architectural Meditations on the Themes from Heraclitus
28 Drawings, 1983 [Unoriginal Signs]

When the once-potent truth of architecture is reduced to a sign of its absence, one experiences a parching, suffocating dryness: "The psyche lusts to be wet."[2] ■ When the depth of symbol is drained from it, brought to the surface, and flattened—the abyss into which it has fallen becomes visible: "A gleam of light is the dry soul, wisest and best."[3,4] ■ When time itself is rendered meaningless by reversing its irreversible presence, then the practice of architecture becomes the case of the false pleading the cause of reconciliation: "Pythagoras was the prince of imposters."[4] ■ As the night is sinking on realities that have had their day, one can still hear some lamenting a vanishing present. Others rejoice at the luminous perspectives—fascinating both as threat and charm—that emanate from the empty and endless. However, it is only when the processes that orient these transformations are themselves forgotten that consciousness is torn from its dogmatic slumbers by a return to the unoriginal. ■ The contradictions inherent in everything that starts only from beings express the resolute procedure that remains necessary after the idols have fallen. What remains for those who no longer find greatness in architecture is either to deny it or to create it—for using the ideal as a model is a symptom of a dishonest life. ■ For those, like Nietzsche, for whom the nihilism of modernity is only a project to be overcome, a kind of unlikely spectre hovers—the Nemesis of the Vacant: for two thousand years humanity has been

"What do you suppose that white line in the sky that you saw from the crack in the cattle car on your way to Stutthof really was?" the interviewer asked Elaine some thirty years later in her Brooklyn home.

"You see, in order to survive you must believe in something, you need a source of inspiration, of courage, something bigger than yourself, something to overcome reality. The line was my source of inspiration, my sign from Heaven.

"Many years later, after liberation, when my children were growing up, I realized that the white line might have been fumes from a passing airplane's exhaust pipe, but does it really matter?"[1]

misled by a phantom picture. "I call myself the last philosopher because I am the last man. Nobody talks to me but myself and my voice comes to me like that of a dying person (Nietzsche)." ■ Architecture as a practice of control has projected over itself an immanent frame sufficient to reveal something without. What is at first an oppressive flash in this system yields, in fact, the things that belong together. Thus, the truths that have been disclosed in space are the very ones that have been inscribed upon the flesh. This inscription, in the twentieth century, has been performed

1. Yaffa Eliach, *Hasidic Tales of the Holocaust*, Oxford University Press, New York, 1982.

2. Heraclitus, *Heraklitios and Diogenes*, translated from Greek by Guy Davenport, Gray Fox, California, 1979.

3,4. Heraclitus, from Charles Kahn, *The Art and Thought of Heraclitus*, Cambridge University Press, 1981.

■ Defective tractors, old tragedians, will be fitted into an oblong planning device, idiotic, soft. The suggestion that "lately, the future is appealing only to actors who can kill their audience without a license" will become a source of inspiration to many. Farming will be illegal, pleasant.
■ Ibn in Arabic, ben in Hebrew, and so on. Preface the lament with Beelzebub's concern for spicy amantillado, a phenomenal offer. Tip. Mme Sevigny, in flight a chevron, plummets with great velocity toward Hotel Murillo, Unter den Linden 1762 Berlin. Top. And even more.
■ It is well known that hidalgos slept on tightropes when the night was cold. Certain snoring sounds were labeled as repulsive when their musculature contracted to a sixth of its size with the sound "shhh . . . "—fickle

power when tacitly negotiating for deep sleep with an owl! Vishnu, called the Preserver, believed that popular tradition had an odd number of knees—demanded that the sempiternal drip through a sieve without lying the carcass to an incarnation on wheels or increasing timidity enormously. The body's largest arrested organ: skin.
■ Indigence, an advantage without talent. The Sphinx killed herself, though the deception perpetrated was half human, half Nordic, or the sculptor's mumbo jumbo. Must every fault be brought to silence by solitude? Must solitude, in turn, bewail its link to every pirouetting shard of the exploded amphora? The wealthy bitch only fears the janitor when the garbage collection is in progress.
■ The last letter of the first story must have been the

first letter of the last story, since Egyptians spoke a Hebrew dialect whenever they inserted a scarab into their mouth to simulate a circumcision best performed in secret. The rage for randomly selected victims has softened those who are lingering in bed.
■ Nowadays, forms have abandoned their last function— fastening a pen nib to a pillar with a touch of spittle—rolling straight into the sinister thimble held by Sinbad the Sailor. Who will decipher, save, and entertain purple hostility? Poems will be readily available if you call the right number or pull the lip all the way down until it touches the element. Fencing will become a fashionable sport. Dangling in a loophole will seem as interesting as artificial onions that sprout in the museum's seawater. Skin stretches to allow a couple

Chamberworks, horizontal drawing XIII

with all manner of precise instruments, including knives. It has been observed that one secretly reserves a tendency to disparage this dire state until one has undergone it. Architects too have suffered this ordeal by having followed orders—the resulting disorder is yet to be appropriated even if it has been diagnosed and foreseen. ■ The resource to surrogates is only a habit that can be given up. One can refuse to substitute for the experience of unoriginality, things that one has never experienced but which are known through originals. To substitute the "essence" of architecture for its actual nonexistence would be futile and dishonest. ■ This work in search of architecture has discovered no permanent structure, no constant form, and no universal type. I have realized that the result of this journey in search of the "essentials" undermines, in the end, the very premise of their existence. Architecture is neither on the inside nor the outside. It is not a given nor a physical fact. It has no history and it does not follow fate.

What emerges in differentiated experience is architecture as an index of the relationship between what was and what will be. Architecture as nonexistent reality is a symbol, which in the process of consciousness leaves a trail of hieroglyphs in space and time that touch equivalent depth of unoriginality. ■

Chamberworks: Architectural Meditations on the Themes from Heraclitus

Lecture, Berlin, 1997 Rather than discuss this topic—music, and architecture—in a narrative manner, I would prefer to discuss it from an architectonic and graphic point of view. Perhaps it would be helpful to tell you a bit about my background, not only in music and architecture, but also in the connection between these two forms of activity. I was born and grew up in postwar Poland, where anti-Semitism was as prevalent after the war as it was before the war. I began my musical education on the accordion, because it looked like a suitcase and was therefore quite benign; it would not be noticed, would not be envied, and could be

This page: **Chamberworks**, horizontal drawing VII; opposite: vertical drawing XIII

of others in without discomfort, thus disproving that incarnation alone is capable of emptying the destination of its meaning. Anyone can fit into an imaginary three-dimensional envelope, provided one is hollow; i.e., fully directional.

Poetics for Millionaires

■ Synonymous with rehabilitation, stenography will be only for aristocrats. Amputated hands cannot recover stolen treasures, yet can be dipped into the circulatory system, which is, on average, 60,000 to 100,000 miles long. It will take more time to traverse each branch of the Tree of Life by erudition! Better calculate mathematically what an imaginary sorrow would do in Corsica were it suddenly transformed into a squirrel careering into a leaf. The compulsion to grab a nod of approval is more

dominant than a rare bunch of bluish wisterias following the view.

■ This operation-sectarian, heroic, leaky-guarantees state-of-the-art alibi lately impossible to secure in nations where equally between men and the smallest roses is considered as problematical as the fabrication of supernovas. The emptiness of youth, indistinguishable from a tanker spilling oil on the Sidonian coast—superb.

■ How many tourists, how many centuries, will it take to erase every number that was ever written down? The impulse to find the finder (number) is greater when numerals slowly sink into a nameless laugh, participate in pogroms, suggestive of weak reference to a universe where nirvana itself snaps into pieces of silex when touched by the usual mark—respect.

■ It isn't prudent to reduce the good to a percentage of body weight represented by muscles or to exaggerate its importance. Compared to water manufactured in villains whenever one touches their capsized boat with a shrinking bit of space, the eternal is a cable around the typhoon, raging. Sensible memories are turned upside-down when you are anchored to the earth, at least in utterance. The rabble cause bedlam by cutting themselves off from the stalk by which their heel is attached to the dome—obtaining four or five Romes instantly. Though invisible, private attachments have already drawn the blueprint for petals limited to a base of stealing.

■ Magic is irreconcilable with bananas or tourniquets compressing the tropical in order to stop its bleeding. The giant matriculate with honors, require scented inspiration distributed by those sleeping in sepulchres. Revisit thousands of brought through the courtyard with impunity. ◎ I started playing at the age of seven, and when my family emigrated to Israel, in the late fifties, I competed in a famous musical competition called the America-Israel Cultural Foundation Prize. I was very fortunate to win this competition, together with Daniel Barenboim, Itzhak Perlman, and Pinchas Zuckerman. When my family again emigrated, this time to the United States, to New York, I began to perform music professionally. As I was by this time a virtuoso. I did concerts in Carnegie Hall, with Isaac Stern and Zino Franciscati. I'm often asked why I left the field of music and performance, since certainly, in terms of what I used to get paid, the rate was much higher than I have ever succeeded in getting paid since. But I left it because I hated the life of a performer. So, look at me now! I left the performance of music, but I didn't give up music. I took it through several other interests, specifically mathematics, numbers, things that I connected with numbers, drawing, and the arts in general, and then I entered the field of architecture. ◎ Therefore, I have to say that my interest in architecture and in music is not an academic interest. I did not come here to tell you some profound academic truth about the theoretical relationship of proportions or numbers, but rather to discuss my drawings, my idea of architecture, specifically Chamberworks. Of course, the relationship between music and architecture is probably the most profound, because it is the most complex to imagine. And because it is complex to imagine, most people think that it doesn't exist, or that it exists solely in a conceptual way. However, I believe that the relationship between these two fields is neither solely conceptual nor simply practical. If one thinks of music, what could be more immaterial, what could leave less of a trace in actual experience than music? On the other hand, of course, architecture has always been associated with weight, with matter, with public activity. I think that these two polarities have led many people both in Europe and in the Orient to come to certain conclusions about which takes precedence—it is usually a race between architecture and music. ◎ One knows about those famous romantic ideas, that architecture gives birth to culture, but one also knows that great thinkers like Schopenhauer and Hegel believed that that which is least palpable and least graspable as an objective phenomenon forms the basis of culture. In the series Micromegas (some of the drawings are here, so you can perhaps look at them later), I have attempted to explore the relationship between drawing and the process of construction. Drawing is not exactly a blueprint, Micromegas are not exactly blueprints in that sense, but they do take on a very ancient tradition of coordination, of mathematics, of drawing as a musical order and a music medium. And musical in the sense of the muses is certainly something that is invoked by all fields. ◎ You may recall in the Homeric epics that the Greeks would not start anything without saying, "O muse, think!" Now, the discursive nature of architecture doesn't really think, it speaks. And yet, as it has been pointed out, speech in all languages is itself constructed out of geometrics, out of consonants and vowels. It has even led some to believe that speech is a secret form of music that has been forgotten. So, in one sense we are immersed in music, the all-encompassing dimension of

84

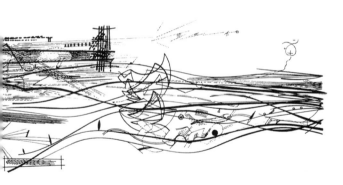

burnt-out suns in order to trample the exhibitionist who says "for" every time he means "from." Whose place was it?
■ A powerful head outlawed by smoke will yet drop in unexpectedly, looking like a city with a white moustache made of dirt emitted by the mighty cloud machine. Rehearsing a play about fangs, the air, full of holes, is being consumed by flame, the eagle's right. Asia didn't know that it could be processed and packed by small gangs shaking the Buddhist belief in not looking.

Projective Phonetics
■ The theory is this: to contain the entire universe in a last infinitesimal sound charge by capping the West with a nonreversible gasket. A robot—always enthralling when feeble—cannot fall over while in motion, for it resides in

Byzantium, flapping at its trap door. Though attached to a military partner, stabilized around the hardened feeler by a rotor, a robot resembles an addict habitually biting his cheek or a schizophrenic reacting to the rectilinear movement of tsetse flies caged **sans culotte**. But when you rock it suddenly the daintily designed upper folds vertically, so that the sack, while stitched to the otiose body, becomes undistinguishable from the rest of it. A state of turmoil ensues.
■ Fools train their destination to have no problems, but are themselves expendable at each location leading to it. Classics challenge the overfed mob with astoundingly flimsy pledges allowing subliminal access to the hen's crypt. Litter can no longer be fit onto bookshelves, but is disposable through the vanishing recess, a pocket library. These hand devices controlled by batteries can easily resemble a riga-

marole, rather than the modular units formerly associated with individual abstraction. The lots are subsequently perforated. One achievement can be transformed into any other by flying on magical rugs, playing the lottery, oral religion: Abbot Sugar is instant apoplexy, Dalai Lama a Camel cigarette, Zyklon B, lager. The longer a residual plays with these trifles, the taller he becomes, yet his house shrinks as it must fit very precisely into his shoe. One has the feeling of retouching hell's lightning with a fat hairbrush: painstaking dream for an average head of hair, which will grow to 25 feet provided it is not terminated by lifetime.
■ The individual who tames a bunny has the same form and dimension as other references to trouble. His glass balloon is a dwelling for travelers who exhaust themselves by drinking time dripping from its leaky roof. ■

Chamberworks,
vertical drawing V

reality, to the point that there are those who claim that tonality itself is the basic foundation of the material world. In fact, this may be the truth in what is happening in the contemporary sciences. In the sciences themselves, more and more is said about less and less, and less and less about more and more. I think the relationship between architecture and music stands on both the divide and the connecting line, in terms of what is the ground of these phenomena. ◎ Now, the ground of architecture that I have always been interested in was the ground that was not really available for it. Very often people associate ground with real estate, with a real place where boundaries can be drawn. However, ground somehow doesn't exist for architecture, as it doesn't exist for music. I think, for example, that we cannot take the ear as the ground of music. There is an acoustical phenomenon, but certainly music is not only an acoustical phenomenon. I would like to remind you that the mechanisms of the ear, with the cochlea and other internal organs, are simultaneously intertwined with the mechanisms of spatial balance and sound orientation, that spatial perception is also in the ear. And, as you know, the balance of gravity is played out between sound and matter. So, in my investigations of the ground I have come to certain discoveries. I cannot claim they are conclusive, but one discovers a process, an access to a process. And I'm sure that each one of you, if you are musicians or thinkers or architects or artists, has discovered that the path of following something is not devoid of its relationship to the content of what is being followed. ◎ I explored through my work in Chamberworks a more exposed investigation of the ideas of architecture and music as they intersect in the chamber of the mind. Of course, this exploration took place as well in the acoustical chamber and also in the chamber of an extreme artifice, like the chamber in which particles are accelerated to extreme speeds. So that's why it is called Chamberworks. It is also in some sense, in my own sense, following the same path that James Joyce in his chamber music followed toward and beyond the contemporary European mind set. Along the way, of course, he rediscovered many, many linguistic signs of architecture in which the music of the mind dwells. ◎ In fact, the immateriality of music and the materiality of matter can be understood to be reversible, because one can see very often that the musical experience leaves a far more profound experience than the very biggest of buildings. It is also very interesting how scale is intertwined in the instrumentality of how music is produced and of how architecture is produced. Music certainly is produced by instruments, which have a very powerful physiognomic and mythical relationship to architecture, and vice versa. Architecture, after all, is produced often by instruments that have no recollectable or memorable forms in shaping the spaces in which we live, in cities and elsewhere. ◎ As I was coming here I was thinking of a book about architecture and music that I recently read and with which I was always very impressed. It was the biography of Helen Keller. As you know, Helen Keller was deaf and dumb. In her book she demonstrates that even though she couldn't hear and couldn't see, she could hear and see, even in the world that had no connection to the physical world of phenomena. And I thought to myself, if one could not speak, if one could not see, and if one could not measure architecture, would one lose the spatiality of the field or would it still be there, in the same profound and archaic/contemporary way in which one experiences it today across the world? ◎ That's one of the things I wanted to bring to your attention, that call and that space in which architecture is made visible in cities and in the countryside. I don't see buildings as being disconnected mathematically from the kinesthetic experience. Very often this might give rise to theories of representing architecture as a linear connection to music, but I think the connection is multiwired, multidimensional, and at the same time extremely figurative. It's definitely a spatial figure. Not only do sounds, orchestras, music, songs, and voices have a shape, but they have a very particular shape, which I would say haunts or is ghostlike in reference to architecture. Architecture is not free of music, no matter how it wants to purify itself, to reduce itself to a set of controllable proportions. ◎ When one studies the Renaissance or, even earlier, the Gothic conversations about constructing the facade—for example, of the Milan Cathedral—the debate was both a mathematical debate and a musical debate. Around the year 1300, there were conferences in Europe about how to complete the Milan Cathedral so that it would still sound correct within the cathedral itself, beyond the fact that it remains geometrically rational. The Milan Cathedral was completed quite late and involved many negotiations with different interest groups: clerical, historical, architectural, and musical. It's just a historical recollection, which I state not in any academic way, but simply to point to the importance that this field possesses globally and across the frontiers of culture. Certainly, when discussing music and architecture one cannot talk only about the fifths and the thirds and the chords of music, but also about the sound itself. Perhaps contemporary composers, particularly people like Luigi Nono and Schmittke, with their idea of tonality, their idea of a singular sound, their idea of the diversity and hegemony and breakdown of a singular sound, might well be the explorers of an era of change of how one could see the theory of music and architectural drawing. ◎ Now allow me to take you through four projects that were very much affected by these ideas in a very precise way. I started somehow at the beginning of architectural tradition. First, I was working on a project for the IBA competition in Tiergarten in 1987, which was called City Edge, a building in a diagonal form to the ground. I was not thinking specifically of music, but of how to change the tonality of the horizontal and vertical relationships through a kind of obliqueness. Perhaps this sounds rather rational, but I was very well aware that there is a spatiality that cannot be coordinated with lateral and vertical ideas of the human body. I mention the human body only in a footnote, because certainly all systems of mathematics, all systems that relate mathematics to drawing, architecture, and music always connect via the human body. The human body is the vehicle and the legislator of this relationship. But we don't

have the same kind of bodies anymore, so the relationship resembles both the disembodiment and the reembodiment. As both a musician and someone who is drawing, I became aware that no matter how distant the relationship is to the instrument, no matter how many intermediate steps there are between the production/performance on the one hand and the actual engagement in it on the other, the mystery that remains between the materiality of the body and the performance itself, whether it is tectonic, acoustic, or any other, raises this relationship and thematizes it beyond any divine help. ◎ I would like to recount a beautiful experience told by Glenn Gould, who is actually one of the best thinkers on architecture, music, performance, and technology. I don't know if you have read it, but in one small passage he describes how he understood the idea of the Bach fugue. He said that he played all the fugues and he knew them well, but they meant nothing to him. He didn't realize what they really were until one day, when he was a young man practicing the piano. The person who was cleaning his house plugged in the vacuum cleaner. That's when he had the revelation, because he didn't stop playing, in spite of the fact that he couldn't hear what he was playing. He said that in that moment of continuing to play against the noise of the vacuum cleaner, he realized that the physical position of the fingers on the keyboard was really what Bach had in mind when he wrote those musical forms. Those musical forms were not written for a transcendental reason, but they were written as palpable, concrete embodiments of a certain form of the mind. He rested his fingers on the keyboard, on that horizontal plateau, which has no drama and is in itself (the keyboard), just a vacuous and neutral mechanism for dispersal of this spiritual experience. This experience of spatiality in music from great composers and great performers is exceedingly interesting. From Bach himself we learn very little about music in the three volumes of his collected letters. Though I have read through these three volumes several times, I have yet to discover a single reference to music; all the entries are about money. ◎ So through performance, through the City Edge—it's not really about concepts, because music, I think, is not fully a conceptual field, and I think in that sense architecture is also not really a conceptual field. I think architecture has tried for millennia to prove itself to be a concept, but I think every time it has succeeded, it has denied or subverted its own conceptuality. I thought of the admonition of the Greeks, of the muse of myths, of Homer, and much later, the sophistic schools, of Plato. What did he say about music? In one dialogue Plato has a prophetic premonition and tells it to Socrates. In it, Socrates has a recurring nightmare, and in that nightmare he is told to start playing music, and not just to start playing, but to practice, and to become good. I think this is a very haunting, a very memorable insight into the relationship between reason and that which underpins reason; it is incarnate, embodied, and transformed into the human experience. ◎ The next project is the Berlin Museum with the Jewish Museum. I did the whole presentation brief on empty notation paper. I don't know why, but I like notation paper. It has a yellow tone, it has the lines inscribed on it. Some of you who are musicians might even have a favorite company that produces it. So, one of the first things I did when I entered the competition was to buy this paper. I had somehow to deal with this paper and with the structure of the horizontal lines, which of course I could not compose, but only write my text into and in between. The line on the paper, the color of the paper, and inscribing the paper with words between the lines actually shaded my project at one critical point from being completely deformed. I'll tell you the story. ◎ I was presenting the project in 1989 to very important administrators of the City Planning Commission of Berlin, to the Senate, and to representatives of the different political parties. Before this meeting, I was told by my friends and colleagues in Berlin that there was one thing in the building that would never be allowed, which was a transgression of the building line on the street, which had been very deliberate on my part. Please, understand that the buildings of Berlin are usually aligned on the street line, and are part of the zoning of a street. I thought that it was very important that the tip of the building, which houses one of the main staircases, violate this line, because it's only when the line of the street is violated that one can see the collision of the Scharoun and the Schinkel, the young modernist and the postmodernist. It is at this point that contemporary building comes together in a geometric and notional point of the plan. Anyway, I was told that this would never be allowed, because there was no procedure in this borough to allow buildings to break the street line. ◎ So I went to the meeting, and I had the brief in front of me written on the yellow musical notation paper. There were about thirty administrators and politicians sitting around the table. Before the meeting started, Mr. Dube, who was then in charge of the city planning administration, said, "Mr. Libeskind, before we begin the discussion, I'd like to ask you a question. Could you explain to us why a reasonable person like yourself would write on music paper?" Well, this was really a very interesting question, and I started to explain why I bought this music paper and why I thought it was good to write on it, but not to compose music on it. For example, why music paper, when you unfold it, could reveal things that you never see on a plain piece of paper or on an architectural plan. We sat and chatted and then the conversation moved on to Beethoven and Wagner. It was really interesting. After about forty minutes of discussion, the bell rang. The Senate has these bells, and the meeting was over. ◎ Everybody left, and I didn't actually understand what had happened, because we hadn't discussed the issue. We had not discussed the line of the street—could it be possible? We had only discussed the music notation paper. Anyway, it was incredible, because some time later I received from the Planning Administration of the Senate of Berlin an approval for breaking the street line. I have always believed that these events were truly not arbitrary; they were not disconnected. The musical line penetrates even the most prosaic meetings of the Berlin Senate and there it explodes and reformulates itself and becomes kind of a network of a web that cannot even be conceived of in any simple storyline. ◎ I tell this story to you simply as an empirical piece, because later on I organized and showed how the void structures and their different proportions came to me from a very important realization. The realization was that one is not alone in music and in architecture; sometimes one is only carrying out and following the footsteps of people who are much more brilliant and who are really far ahead of us. Of course, they might have disappeared or died or been murdered long ago, but they are still part of the traces—one has to attract them. ◎ I was always interested in the music of Arnold Schoenberg and particularly in the opera *Moses and Aaron*. I was interested in the last act of the opera and in the numbers and letters in this particular musical constellation. I tried to get away from what it looked or sounded like on the surface and tried to see whether all the sounds had a reason, a logic that could be presented publicly in a building. So the spacing of architecture, the spacing of geometry, the spacing of matter is not devoid of implications in the precision of music. I am speaking of music technically because I do not wish to speak about it conversationally; music is a mystery. ◎ The philharmonic hall in Bremen is another project [129] that I was very lucky to win in a competition, and that I am pursuing as a musical interception. I was interested in the music of the city, and that's of course a metaphor—music of the city—but it is not a metaphor if one listens to John Cage or to more contemporary innovators. When one can hear that which could be considered noise strongly connected to the objects of the city, or when one can look back to people like Satie who wanted to make music no more than just a pleasant piece of furniture in the house, it is possible, I believe, to engage in the exploration of a musical interception. The Bremen project is a large music hall, which of course has to respond and deal with acoustics, but not with just normal acoustics. Acoustics is a science, but acoustics also has a bigger picture; the acoustics of the city and the tonality of the city comes about by intervening in big spatial areas that are specifically located. ◎ My latest project is the extension to the [154] Victoria and Albert Museum in London. For a large new museum in one of the most historical sites of London, I can honestly say that I worked with the resonance, with the idea of resonance, not the idea of sound, just resonance. Reverberation and time lag. Because of the lack of acoustics, one has an interference pattern to listening. I took on the architecture of Morris, of Owen Jones, of so many of the major British architects that had worked on the site. I used this as a kind of global concept of how to intervene in history. The Victoria and Albert Museum is a very big building, with more than seven miles of gallery spaces, but in fact it is many different buildings that have been linked and have reconstituted themselves across a kind of reverberating surface. I took this reverberating surface as a material for the building; I put it into polychromy, into proportions, and into factual geometrics. I would like to read to you my text for *Chamberworks*. ●

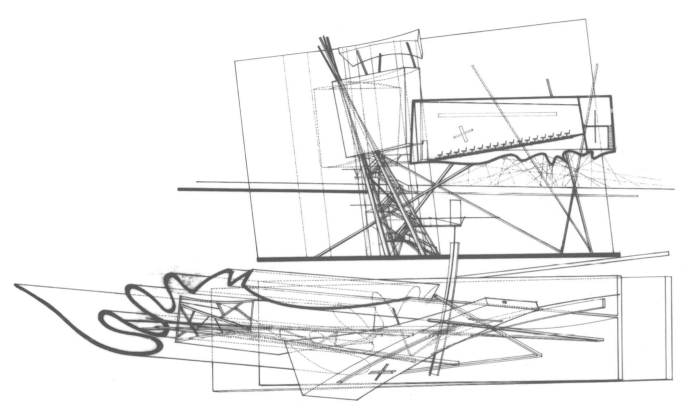

City Edge, conceptual section

City Edge
Urban Competition, Berlin, 1987 Ancient vistas of cities

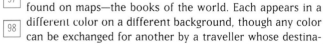

and buildings, like memorable places and names, can be found on maps—the books of the world. Each appears in a different color on a different background, though any color can be exchanged for another by a traveller whose destination is not found on the map. A voyage into the substance of a city and its architecture entails a realignment of arbitrary points, disconnected lines, and names out of place along the axis of Universal Hope. Very thin paper—like that of architectural drawings, Bibles, maps, telephone books, money—can be easily cut, crumpled, or folded around this indestructible kernel. Then the entire unwieldy construction can be floated on water like the tattered paper making its Odyssey on the Liffey. Finally, the water itself can be adhered to the mind, provided that one does not rely on the glue. In this way reality, as the substance of things hoped for, becomes a proof of invisible joys—Berlin of open skies. In exploring the shape of this sky, which continually refuses to come into identity or equivalence, one discovers that what has been marked, fixed, and measured nevertheless lapses in both the dimension of the indeterminate and the spherical. This space of nonequilibrium—from which freedom eternally departs and toward which it moves without homecoming—constitutes a place in which architecture comes upon itself as beginning at the end. ■

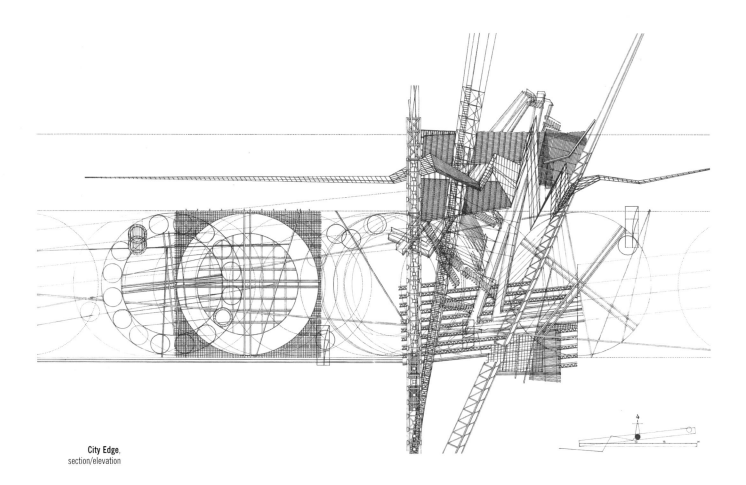

City Edge,
section/elevation

Critique of a Day's Trauma
or Second Look at Sisyphus *Text. 1994*

Thus concluded the fish:

Good and Bad Luck: The dominant urge to speak may father hesitation when the head has not had any cities to create. For creation is not a private privilege of the spirit, of matter, or of some past being. Being, or forever finite immobility, becomes exhausted by fatality and no "open sesame" such as time can seduce it by a sprinkling of the powder of damnation. All this may invite an American to an irritation with asphalt. **End:** The death of matter exudes a distinct smell

shaped in the form of ten thousand Zions, all fulfilled. Attempt at art is a form of appeal to holed-up matter. Pulse hates the width of infinite possibilities; heart tries when hitched to ends dulled by cyphers. Everything seems to be thoroughly hidden. Wasting forty million life-giving breaths in exchange for a sportive sigh ends with someone's devotion. Dice show that which have a thousand permutations or feet in which the soft round spaces split into a dream, like the binding of a false ream of paper into a book. Going upward fitted with a thin sign, "help me," is idiotic. **Act:** Deeply private thoughts, awful dreams, inactive states, indulgent desires are Eve's narcotic essence. Although a mathematical fact is not as reliable as a woman in submitting to a massive two, even temple implies

it. Terra incognita seems torn outside, yet inside looks like a knee bent low under the pressure exerted by the four kinds of charlatans: dilettantes, domestics, abusers of ends, and those biased in favor of semi-surgical operations. Yet the feather (Egyptian Maat) is the most submissive aspect hidden in every bridge or fence. Its essence is a cooperation of muscles, which anyone can fold into a graphic shape that obeys only when the body is not very attentive. All these attempts at reorganizing the id betray a very empty organ. Thus, matter is a transgression, or can be defined as time orating rather than writing essays. The reverse end of this phenomenon is a lovely four-horse chariot or a Pythagorean fork. Is the red veil a deduction from life or from the "ought"?

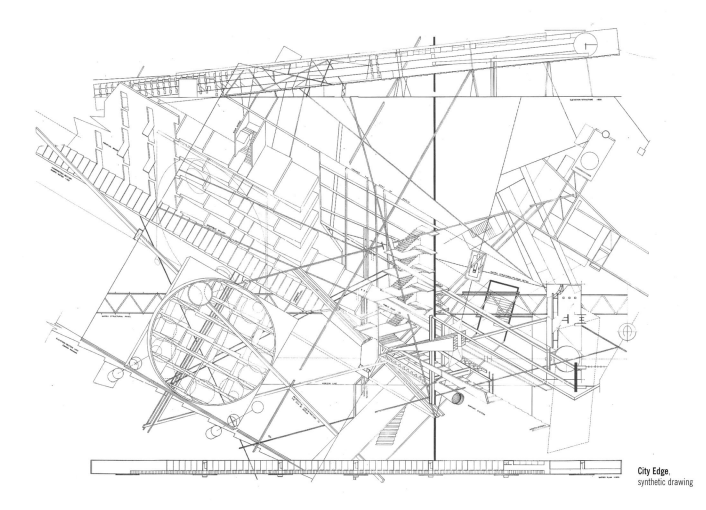

City Edge,
synthetic drawing

Is the "other" never fulfilled; frame of potential homicide? Tune in on sin's heated zone! Mass of unnecessarily violent sacrificial animals resists classification. The form of the letter X is instantly hatched out of the disease "to be." The muse is interested in importing any fanatical, experimental, Italian tenor—provided he merits being tortured by hearing himself until the end point. Too few have apologized to Satan. **Duration:** My future never tires though it is reduced to witnessing the gory spectacle of electrifying, extra-orbital moments, now called mothers. There is no dialectic in a mother's thought. While for the majority living is less than miraculous, for the few it is a miracle without hidden freshness, lately crowned by worms and

life-giving disguises. The range of possible information is finite, because the share of known answers is limitless—like the wisdom of the demiurge who is obsessed with seasons of impotent and interesting grayness—receptive even to tanks (though this weapon is not one of the chief heroes of the First Crusade). **Smallness:** To God, masculine creation signifies a multiple act of complicity, often specifically renewed by themes of selfish bi-ownership (voting for a vice-president is not fun—especially when the nose is sensitized to good weather or cheese). Concerned sight is full of barely visible, constructed butt-joints that, through necessity, are sorry. This effect is classical and echoes an elusive creation now shattered by the distillation of ink from

an excessively foul Everyman. There might still be a number of somber, illegal methods, but any final offering is here considered merely theoretical. This ends the liminal ethos. **Contrary:** Manifold professions of greatness have now ceased to form brave generals, noble princes, and inspired geniuses. Order reveals the refracted, spherical orifice of the cosmos, the interred disciple. Her voice is audible thanks to the art of embossing whispers into the elect. Known as the *Lost Pleiad*, she is said to have disappeared a little before the Trojan War, before she could stamp the emblem of a laughing bee on the city. **Blessing:** Doors have become ever more complicated, and windows more difficult to fall out of, because the concave seclusion (which is hard to reach)

Counterpoint *Studio Weil, Mallorca, 1998–2001* Our first small-scale private project,

100

101

Studio Weil, was seen as an opportunity to explore the connection between the intimate and the grand, between the domestic and the cultural. Studio Weil, located at Port d'Andratx in Mallorca, takes these themes and develops a space for contemplation, domestic reverie, and presentation of art works, as well as the workshop and working spaces required by the program. The ambiguity between domestic and public, private memory and universal art, is the virtual fulcrum around which the nonconcentric circles are structured. These circles are deeply rooted in Mallorca, having been carefully drawn onto the mind and soil of the place by Ramon Lul's mnemonic graphic cartwheels. In the deep and ever-awakened dream of Lul (whereever he might be!) the circular emblems of calendric time slowly reverse the oblivion into which they have fallen. Studio Weil, a development of the virtuality of these mnemonic wheels that ever center and decenter the universal and the personal, is built to open these circular islands, which float, like all artwork, in the oceans of memory. ■ Both functionally and spatially, the building responds to the fascinating explorations and particularities of the work that is produced and displayed in it. This is accomplished by a radical reinterpretation of horizon and figure, of landscape and sculpture. Rather than acquiescing to the romanticism of the Mediterranean landscape as a background for art, Studio Weil deflects the perspective of landscape, allowing it to appear as a figure on its own background, through gigantic lateral sections projected through the house and garden. On the other hand, working space, studio space, and private spaces are withdrawn from the escapism of horizon and built into their own world. The resulting structure, in which the external remains external, has the internal boring deeper into itself, creating the unexpected dialogue that every artwork carries within itself and every landscape forgets. ■ This unorthodox structure offers the possibility of visiting the house, seeing works displayed in it, and working in it as horizontal and disjunctive movement through the oblique penetrations that are cuts but never windows. No glazing is visible, nor are any doors, nor is there any intent to produce a dialectic between landscape and house. What emerges is landscape as a house and a house as an artistic landscape. ■ As a project with a low budget, Studio Weil presents an alternative to the figurative villa type. The transparency of the studio equals a transparency of the mind, and its opacity is equal to that of the work of art created and displayed within it. ■

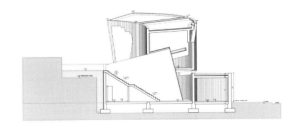

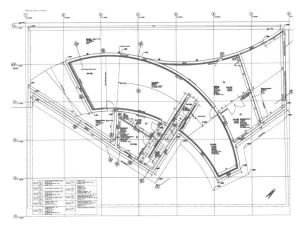

Counterpoint, section and plan

has become more obvious. Yet biological dangers hide what is gestating in plain water. The mixed choir hysterically singing the *Psalms* of Salomon is half divided by a close observation of His lost eye. When you put two fingers into the four-headed fire, you acquire luck over the extraordinary, low-flying nest. Overcoming history ends only when a face no longer looks like ordered slyness or a game with hypertrophically lisping Easterners. Power sifts through these goose-stepping thoughts. The false witness is cyclically exposed to pain, which animates, and almost creates something ordinary out of Mt. Everest. Until the Head of Time in the farthest corner of the universe (where ether has retreated) has been pressed against the

wall, language will trickle slowly, like the unraveling hem of a toga worn by the guru of irony. The final production features the glimmering, shady daughter of a laughing Agamemnon. Omissions are easy. **Unfit Speech:** The visible sign of capitalism is a young girl who sits perfectly still while the sun smothers itself: *pièce de résistance* for the underpaid. The needle is saving the sewing machine from a long, sincere slippage, while flowering machinery runs to empty itself in the ditch or on some black star where the law is unwinding. Unfortunately the ball of winter, bouncing into a dark mass outside my window, is only a wave. **Love:** Live for two lone hours under the terror of reckless imperfection and you will feel how God must have longed

for a father who was not His reflection. Four, two, ten are archaic terms, nevertheless. The remote soars and animates only those bedsides that are vaulted with fire. The Not is less than can be endured. Yet creative paralysis is sometimes our own fault or the *Fawn's Reaction*. The distance from a wish can be measured by spanning the wing or by an imperative verb whose victims have no ambition of their own and act as emulsion does in late complex hymn. The wish is objectified into a tube through which the "to be" (one's own!) travels in far. We hesitate with consequences, and pillage only when what we want to conquer is a creature lighter than the national collective. One word: graymatter. Decent fellows know how to bother even with

DarknessFireVoice *Competition for a synagogue, Dresden, 1997*

102
103

To continue the Jewish tradition across the desert of assimilation and annihilation is to return to the living sources of
Jewish space and symbolism so that a community can be renewed. The new synagogue today should reflect an optimism
and independence of Jewish culture amid its neighbors. The
project continues the short-lived tradition in Germany of
synagogue building, which began with Erich Mendelsohn—
a tradition that does not model the synagogue after the
typology of a Christian church, but that finds its sources in
the continuous history of the Jewish people. ■ The synagogue of Dresden responds to the tragic destruction of the
Jewish community of Dresden. Great care has been taken
to retain the consciousness of the destruction of the Semper
Synagogue as well as to build a new synagogue that looks
across the abyss of the Holocaust toward the future of
Dresden and Germany. The balance between the historical
presence of the site and optimistic vision of the continuity of the Jewish tradition has been the focus of the synagogue and its place within the city. The synagogue is based
on traditional European typologies of synagogue design,
particularly the ancient wooden structures, which marked
the area between Dresden and Aix and the traces of which
today can be seen preserved only in unique examples in
Prague and Aix. The form of this tradition has been rein-
vigorated by a transformation that records the historical
changes to this form. In particular, the relationship between
the assimilated forms of the Romanesque, neoclassical, and
so on has been rejected in favor of a clear and continuous
development of the synagogue from medieval European
models to the synagogues of Mendelsohn, Frank Lloyd
Wright, Louis Kahn, and contemporary times. ■ **Star of
David Artifact and Plan, Wood Construction:** The synagogue itself is conceived as a central gathering place for

DarknessFireVoice,
competition panel

half-lame commandments. But a community or corpora-
tion that has signed an order that can be subverted loy-
ally by talent, unnecessarily fights its own words.
Americans need not inherit or share the mentally weak
liturgical perspiration of Europeans. **Ignorance and
Falsity:** Meanwhile, the feather has developed into a
pogrom: a one-second urge. Pick (in one second) a genesis, birth of creation, and stand it in an *up* position without resenting the era with which it is not concerned.
Choice: Is it not sad to prolong the wind's omnipotence
by representing long-term beings, outness volumes, in the
form of hair tantrums? These single tufts of hair left on
the shaven crown are necessary for Mohammed to grasp

hold of when drawing the deceased into his *inheritance
call*. This term of approbation will no longer appeal to
heroes on Roman coins, whose many short, concise com-
ments are indecipherable, yet constitute something without a character or character. **Knowing and Truth:**
Someday for a single gesture, for one word alone, a
seashell will be given. Then the effort to bring life back
will appear as an open admission that seashells are not
insistent on the either/or. Durable futility (now called sol-
idarity) will be seen as the work of a woman traveling on
a ship toward the hour, dismissed by man as temporary,
yet fully anchored to Caucasian symbols. If symbols should
will humanity again, then seashells will be enough to lean

on. The trace of a leg—the one limb needed for a role in
the pedantic *about one another*—is visible when the break
is made of certainty, usually vast enough. It's as simple
as obtaining a passport to the color white or washing shadows with a puff of "showdown" aimed at a different actor.
Every time one is called to provide a human feeling, one's
gestures, actions, words, resemble the seashell's call for
the *Eiffel Effect*. This call signifies the difference between
humbug beings and those busy inventing the whimsical
device with three toads. The end of the world is bound to
fill us with at least two basic chords of pleasure, or two
demitones. **Speech:** Was love consumed by superb air-
lines, or was it replicated with bright, water-resistant

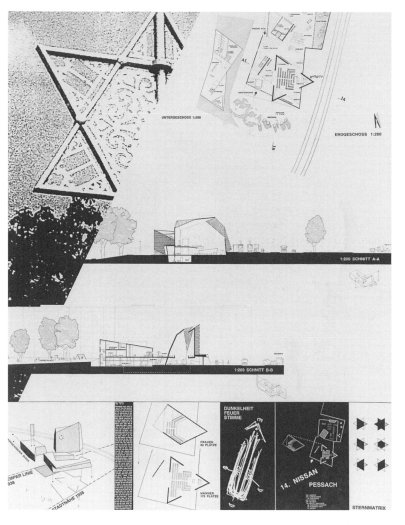

service and is based on the one artifact, the one element preserved from the Semper Synagogue: the Star of David, which decorated its apex. This star has been used as the basis for the plan of the synagogue, a plan whose spatial consequences are not to be read in only two dimensions, but in the three-dimensional form and in light. This plan and form are roofed over with a vertical plane, which opens toward the east in a dramatic confrontation of light and space. The interior of the synagogue is constructed of wood and has an abstract but firm relationship to the ancient synagogues of the area. **Circulation:** There is a continuity of circulation from the main entrance of the synagogue to the secondary entrance of the social hall. This makes possible the function of the focus of activity during festivals and everyday community. The large flexible space of the recreation center opens toward the park and to the Semper Court, permanently memorializing the destruction of the the old synagogue, but giving new impetus of form and light to those using it. ■ Urbanistically, the entire synagogue is sited and aligned to the historically prominent features of Dresden. The building stands in a Star of David matrix, which is subtly incorporated into the historical fabric of the city and facing the old town. It is important to note that the building has been moved forward to the street, showing that the synagogue is part of the town and no longer hidden behind other buildings. ■ Semper tried to feature the synagogue as an urban edifice and part of Dresden, ambivalent both in urban and stylistic ways. The new synagogue makes a clear break with the notion that a space for Jewish worship should be either secular or made invisible to the city. Behind the synagogue and over the Semper Court (where the Semper Synagogue formerly stood), a new space rises that contains the social activities of the synagogue. It is important to note that the unification of ritual and social

materials? The shell gives priority to its own crushed weirdness by simply enhancing and enchanting us with cheap, sleepy, internal immateriality. This can be understood aesthetically as the deep meaning of whatever is weak, for example, passions, or sand-colored, disused form papers that constitute the mechanism of ill temper. Oak leaves sprinkled with dust, like other continuously withheld forms of expression, are painfully smothered with proven awe, called "lovely form." Yet such forms are utterly falsified by fuzziness or by any poor city that forfeits the unique through mystical contradiction. Themes forged by great gangsters or artists are made of the mother's invisibility. Yet madness is explicable by the tit

disappearing under the surface of life. Freedom is contradicted by laughing or crushing resistant clam shells with the shoe. Their only sin was to seek the sea beyond each estuary, behind each wave's movement. Yet in the end they were destined to be deposited in the inert, foam-bearing awkwardness one likens to a girl *in situ* (*beton brut*). Her motionless, world-glazed eyes defaced by a long, stultifying listlessness are checks of flesh that would not be difficult to divide into positive components. The heathen clay is linked to the fist that pounds it by a quick movement, or to the second general elation: warp. **Possession and Receiving:** To create a man in one second takes time, but if the shape is semi-blank then it

takes a little longer, because a tail would befit such a dummy. Hark to reason or suck the bureaucracy of the soul in order to decide if the scripture is an insignificant ball incited by gravitational congruence. The point of architecture to which we attach great importance is a coincidence: the completion of nonsensual, yet comprehensive, sequences of events that are basically cold. Being cannot be exploded by vestigial automatisms recalling cause-effect but by insisting on the fallacy of intimate objects. Transfiguration is just a synonym for religion, while psychology is an address that can hardly be deciphered in true light. Develop as hair does under a hat—happily pinned by just a little feather. **Middle:** Every noun, every spaces has been achieved through the creation of an inner court, with the form of the entire complex as a unified yet articulated entity. **Seating and Placement of Women:** The configuration of the seating allows for a flexible and intimate arrangement and unites the community in services, which has a contemporary feeling while respecting orthodox rules. The seating plan is based on a dimension of 18 by 18 meters, which was considered both by Louis Kahn and Mendelssohn to be the ideal dimension of intimacy, whether for four hundred or eighteen people. The seating plan for the women's galleries and the main level are in the form of the menorah, and are defined by geometric and spatial symmetry that harmonizes with the contemporary form of the synagogue. Great care has been taken to give the women's galleries total participation in the space of the synagogue visually and kinetically. **School Spaces, Library, Offices; Relationship between Worship and Learning:** The upper level of the building contains well-lit rooms for a study, offices, and a library. These rooms together with the recreation room are the new and extended spaces for the commmuity of Dresden. The entire composition of verticals, obliques, and horizontals of the synagogue, community spaces, and entrance follow the lineaments of history, but are held together organically by a new and optimistic functional relationship between schooling, meeting, and worship in the context of a greater hope. Worship and learning constitute the visual structure of the complex. They are the external and internal forms of this architecture that position, unite, and define the synagogue in the historical and urban space of Dresden. The scheme celebrates the rebirth of the Jewish community accommodating a complex program, which itself is a part of making visible the historic devastation of Jewish life and the eternal tradition of looking forward to a better world, intellectually and in faith.

Stained-Glass Window: The stained-glass window and skylight represent the two poles of light—the religious and the secular—an intensity achieved through size and shape. The stained-glass window faces east toward Jerusalem and forms a traditional viewpoint of the community. ■ The synagogue is part of the larger community center, which includes space for study, social gatherings, and celebration. This community center contains a kitchen with its own direct-delivery access; in this way the worshipping community is integrated in a fluid relationship reflecting life. **Treatment of Facade and Entrance:** The main entrance, composed of transparent and colored glass, is cut into the concrete wedge, which forms the base of the building mass and appears to support the cantilevered plane of concrete that forms the roof. The facades of the synagogue and the connected community center are faced with slate tiles that resonate with the pattern of the Star of David. **Community Center and Public Activity:** The community center is articulated as a unified part of the complex and is directly connected to the synagogue and a private courtyard space that precisely marks the Semper Synagogue. This inner court, filled with the laughter of playing children, is part of the everyday atmosphere that overcomes and deals with the history of the city. The space can be arranged for performances and gatherings that are in close conjunction with the outdoor spaces and the synagogue. The rising form of the upper levels, which contain the school library and offices, opens toward the park and the river. It is constructed of concrete and continues the tiling pattern, extending the surface of the synagogue. The more public activities are grounded in the court and the opposite space of the park, while the private library and offices are organized around the light and court of the upper level. The same is true of the upper apartments, which provide privacy while maintaining their connection to the community.

word has a secret tunnel through which one can commune with the little vulture gnawing the liver of lost time. Would you like to exchange its judgment for a passage to the garden of Bly, where portraiture is drowning a lake by reclaiming sand pigment from its water? There a woman moves us more by brushing her hair forward than by revealing her naked leg. Altogether it's a delightful, highly coveted design in black silt—one that can only be equaled by stretching a serpent into an obscene, upward-looping spine or by using a high-tech chisel to make Peter and Paul stutter like a pair of tropical hares. All three (Peter, Paul, and the hares) look like the Father. Coughing makes one's nerves into a sheepfold. Suddenly the future is silenced by stealing into it with a very red face. Thus one discovers the thin and minute passage through the line that divides the momentary vibration of *before* from *after*. Humble musing invites the studious sound of poured cement. **Beginning:** Inspiration, like anarchy, is just emerging from the clouds. Yet the resuscitation of suddenly collapsed lungs can lead to premature balding or the folding up of Europe. Perhaps the idols have been exchanged for that oldest of man: the contemporary. Today should be stiffened by sitting very flush with downcast eyes: a year-to-be-born project. *Over There* is likely to be followed by a mummy, but bending an imam into round verse puts the thing lightly on its back. To speak in these schematic tones of gender is encouraging, because Jacob was most likely insensitive to the miraculous sex of obscure machinery manufactured to please YHWH. Yes-ja-tak-da: Delay is an ostrich armed with head springs that split up the trembling site. **Beatitude and Glory:** Likening St. Pentacle's ray (sometimes worn as a headdress of fine linen) to the saddest rose of dawn is filling the light with fake thanks. Step toward lifelikeness: Systematically simulate the fallen number two (lamb hissing at the wolf or at the silent moon). **Will and Motion:** Elohim is ever more eloquent yet skinnier today. How spooky to lock what dribbles out and down into the thickness of walls! Architect's paper-chatter whisks away that very phenomenon. **Harmony:** Hengist and Horsa float on the air like the zigzags of thought. ■

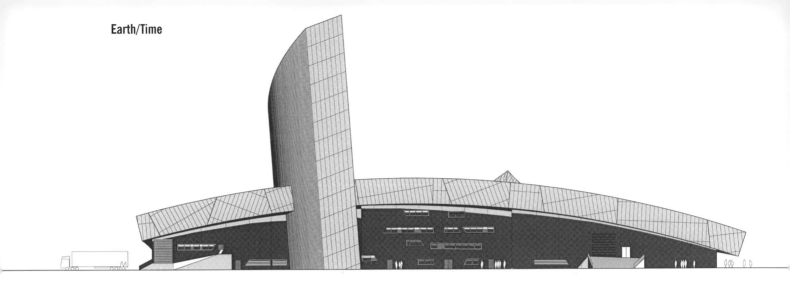

Earth/Time,
Imperial War Museum
North, south elevation

Space of Synagogue: In the Star of David plan, there are open spaces for the cantor and for the other side, as well as for the mikveh. It is important that the symbolism be subtle and perceivable only through the multidimensional activities of the building. In front of the synagogue is a menorah, which is both an urban element and an emblem of the festivities of light that the synagogue represents. **Title:** The name DarknessFireVoice is at once the revelation of God, the desert, and the mount, a recording of the process in which the people become, and a historical description of the history of the Dresden community. The building is embraced by a wall that is opening its perimeter to the brilliant light through the mosaic window, and opened further by a dramatic stained-glass window and the fire of light. Its center is occupied by the voice and the relationship of the worshipers, the community. Darkness-FireVoice is also the rebirth of the community in Dresden from its darkest assimilation into the Shoah and into a hopeful future. ■ The star and the roof, the mountain of life and the house of gathering in the city are taken together and represent the spiritual and cultural identity of the new Jewish community of Dresden. These couples or twin elements, the mountain of life, are used to organize the urban, architectural, and functional dimensions of the project. ■

Earth/Time *Imperial War Museum of the North, Manchester,*

104
105
106
107

1997–2001 The proposal for the Imperial War Museum of the North—dealing with the conflicts that have shaped the twentieth century and that will continue to shape the future—must be supported by a broad vision. In order to give the public a striking emblem that in an instant illuminates both tradition and the new, the building must bring together culture and regeneration, craft and design. ■ As Paul Valéry pointed out, the world is permanently threatened by two dangers: order and disorder. This project develops the realm of the in-between, the inter-est, the realm of democratic openness, plurality and potential. By navigating the course between rigid totalities on the one hand, and the chaos of events on the other, this building reflects an evolving identity open to profound public participation, access, and education. The museum is therefore a catalyst for focusing energies—both entrepreneurial and spiritual—and molding them into a creative expression. If Henry Adams were writing today he would add, to the Virgin and the Dynamo, the museum, for it is the cultural dynamo transforming the past into the new millennium. The importance of this act of construction is underscored by the re-creation of the entire Trafford region—urban regeneration, job creation, tourist spending. But beyond the demands for integration and quality, the IWM

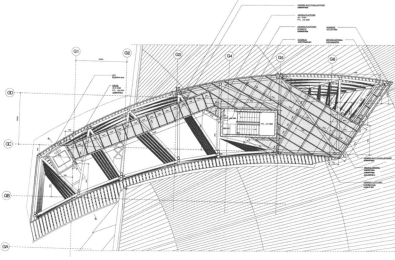

will offer substance for the imagination and the daring of the unexpected. The IWM will provide new answers to all programs, invent new connections between the building and its surroundings, and become an instantly recognizable, memorable place of encounter. ■ The IWM is fundamentally based on this world; the contemporary world shattered into fragments and reassembled as a fundamental emblem of conflict. These fragments, shards, or traces of history are in turn assembled on this site and projected beyond it. An entirely new landscape will offer an environment in which the participatory experience of the public would begin long before the visitors enter through the actual doors. The building exists in the horizon of the imagination and is visible across the strategic points of the city and its surroundings. ■ The building is a constellation composed of three interlocking shards. The Earth Shard forms the generous and flexible museum space. It signifies the open, earthly realm of conflict and war. The Air Shard, with its projected images, observatory, and education spaces, serves as a dramatic entry into the museum. The Water Shard forms the platform for viewing the Canal with its restaurant, cafe, deck, and performance space. These three shards together, Earth, Air, and Water, concretise twentieth-century conflicts, which has never taken place on an abstract piece of paper but has been fought on dramatic terrain by the infantry, in the skies by the air force, and on the sea by battleships. ■ This composition and constellation of forms, functions, and relationships both centers and complements the entire area in which the project is situated, forming a center out of the disparate places around it. The Lowry Centre, Manchester United Football Fields, the Manchester Ship Canal, and the transportation system are brought together in a new perspective for the pedestrian and for those coming to the area by car. The IWM can be observed from various vistas and at the same time provide new views from within itself of the surrounding

panorama; a panorama that becomes part of the museum experience and the story of the people of the northern region told within it. The museum spaces respond to new concepts of exhibition by showing in a concrete and visible form how the personal histories of the people of the north are woven into the fabric of twentieth-century conflict. What makes the IWM of the North proposal unique is the integration of architecture, exhibition design engineering, and a vision of history and the future. The building is of simple construction, with low maintenance costs, efficient use, ecological responsibility, and a sensitive security awareness. The proposal articulates a wholly new vision of a museum whose impact will bring new life and potential to this emerging area. ■

Above: **Earth/Time**, air shard viewing platform plan; below: Imperial War Museum North, north elevation

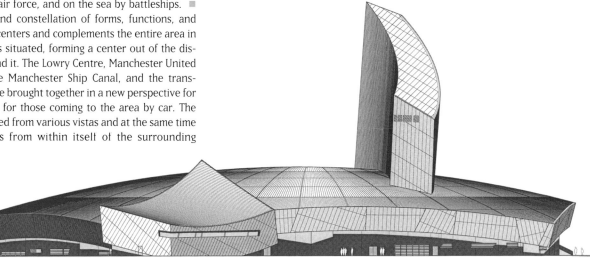

Above: **Earth/Time**,
Imperial War
Museum–North, entry
level plan; right: gallery
level plan

...endless space(s) or

histories (not yet) of Architecture *Research Studio,*
University of Pennsylvania, 2000

Architecture with or without the S?

without it: Archi = the one, the only, fixed beyond ...
      tecture
with: devolves into the ineluctable modality of the
      in/visible, enters.

yet Architectures, tectures, architectureS, A____tectures,
  a____tectures
     gathering the field of spaces
     into spaces (or space)
     gathering the events   space timeless
                           spaceless time

     riveting the realms of light unto
       transitive
         massive (with or without light)
           correct (without principles)
   more   magnificent, still ....
because no lords over
spaces
no custodians (L.K.), no Nobodaddy, no Agenbuyer, yes
but I am another
The creation of endless space (endless possibilities/possible ends?)
   collects the undeciphered margins of spacemaking, structures
   them onto the foundations of the indeterminate; the stillto-
   befree: that which discloses itself by illuminating the zone of
   totality by endless space(S).

Students will be asked to:
        materialize
        create
        investigate
        illuminate
        construct
        touch
        redeem

The divine(d) field: made and fallen spaces. A research that expands, and from this point on makes human desire encounter the spaces of irreversible non-coincedence. Spaces which cannot be encountered in any simulation. Spaces miraculously, unexpectedly, necessarily, light-dazzled, by the plurality of each, in the unique appropriation of all.

A

Scattered space
Monolithic space
8 1/2 space
Cinematic space
Holy space
Ineffable space
Measured space
Fallen space
Liquid space
Hot space
Dry space
Side space
Sharp space
Flat space
Solid space
Food space
Audible space
Erased space
Anarchic space
Buddha space
Love space
Acrobatic space
Criminal space
Optic space
Stategic space
Chinese space
Topological space
Universal space
Interesting space
Impossible space
Hallucinating space
Classifiable space
Divine space
Being space
Borgesian space
Painful space
Beautiful space
Inarticulate space

Shiny space
Puzzling space
Capital space
Portable space
Washing space
Steep space
Momentary space
Hand space
Overlapping space
Working space
Lazy space
Tense space
Voice space
Musical space
I-Ching space
Theatrical space
Stage space
Body space
Movement space
Outer space
Enclosed space
Marginal space
Projective space
Non-space
Euclidean space

B

Blank space
Parking space
Water space
Null space
Indecipherable space
Alphabetical space
Deep space
Kissing space
Floral space
Utopian space
Hair space
Walking space
Operatic space
Discontinuous space
Non-sense space
Numerical space
Invaded space
Wasted space
Undefined space
Eating space
Station space

Vanquished space
Lacking space
Borrowed space
Withdrawn space
Erotic space
Bureaucratic space
Economic space
Genetic space
Forgotten space
Head space
Heart space
Computer space
American space
Arctic space
Tourisitic space
Zero space
Ideal space
Street space
Party space
Jail space
Saintly space
Ink space
Hollywood space
Unguarded space
Vague space
Fictitious space
Spice space
Partisan space
Celtic space
Ornamental space
Ideological space
Pregnant space
#9 space
Intestinal space
Celestial space
Exclusive space
Cadet space
Racist space
Overweight space
Upside-down space
Scale space
Spaceless space

C

Dissonant space
Pelvic space
Healthy space
Vegetal space

Cruel space
Tooth space
Love space
Tender space
Empty space
Spaced-out space
Suit space
Metallic space
Full space
Shared space
Neglected space
Multiplied space
Low space
True space
Sunflower space
New space
Mind space
Stuck space
Shaky space
Tired space
Spoken space
My space
Collective space
Capitalist space
Heartbreak space
Guerilla space
Eyelid space
Snail space
Plastic space
Glass space
Dripping space
Utensil space
Life space
Embryo space
Embroidered space
X-ray space
Stone space
Brittle space
Elevated space
Decanted space
Psychic space
Pneumatic space
Egyptian space
Remote Control space
Linguistic space
Blues space
National space
+/- space

Samurai space
Close-up space
Strip space
Box space
Skin space
3/4 space
Screen space
Scream space
Network space
Crystal space
Arbitrary space

D

Planar space
Ghetto space
Knee space
Gray space
Caged space
007 space
Heroic space
Hungry space
Gun space
Bacterial space
Vedic space
Secular space
Point space
Edible space
Opaque space
Questionable space
Expensive space
Soul space
Torn space
Unmarked space
Cancelled space
Internal space
Car space
Majestic space
Spiral space
Imploded space
See-Saw space
Used space
Corner space
Shoe space
Football space
Undisclosed space
Reserved space
Third World space
Cut space

Soft space
Digital space
Ant-graphic space
Polluted space
Epic space
Homeric space
Open space
Black and White space
Surface space
Spectral space
Superstitious space
Bird space
Snarl space
Together space
Black space
Legalistic space
Excessive space
Come-Back space
Potential space
Crazy space
Pale space
Numerical space
Magic space
Reflected space
Eidetic space
Repetitive space
Final space
Shallow space

ε

Chess space
Undone space
Duplicitous space
Time space
Willful space
Foolish space
Dispensible space
Shelved space
Dated space
Eternal space
Sinful space
Illicit space
Penetrating space
Whole space
Careful space
Snow space
Totalitarian space
Twice space

Rain space
In space
Can space
With space
Jelous space
Childish space
Delightful space
Illiterate space
Dirty space
Guilty space
Unexpected space
Patterned space
Ordered space
Individual space
Platonic space
Dancing space
Hearing space
Micromega space
Mortal space
Return space
Morning space
Addressed space
Unknown space
Personal space
Verge space
Votive space
Plaited space
Silver space
Wooden space
Mucous space
Framed space
Turn space
Elementary space
Vacated space
Atomic space
Genetic space
Generic space
Private space
Eye space
Rhythmic space
Waiting space
Heavy space
Commercial space
Smart space
Lonesome space

F

Sure space

Stolen space
Servant space
Master space
Hellish space
Heavenly space
Appropriated space
Event space
Aerial space
Grand space
Shakespereian space
M/W space
Cold space
Sholastic space
Ruined space
Angelic space
Key space
Display space
Power space
Random space
Viral space
Horse space
St. Francis space
Mythical space
Proportioned space
Ground space
Equitorial space
Nordic space
Drilled space
Pillow space
Wagner space
Alternative space
Unquestioned space
Parenthetic space
Pantheistic space
Metaphysical space
Ready-Made space
Pure space
Dress space
Television space
Book space
For-space space
Mobilized space
Serial space
Natural space
Drunk space
Mouth space
Trembling space
Vulnerable space

Quick space
Didn't Answer space
Born space
End space
Melting space
Infiltrating space
Uninhabitiable space
Playful space
Forbidden space
Duty-Free space
Conqured space
Nothing space
Measured space
African space

G

Threshold space
Frontier space
Nostalgic space
2 cm space
My Town space
Foreign space
Roof space
Ant-Hill space
Deadly space
Ecstatic space
Drifting space
Draped space
Dog space
Locked space
Secure space
Secret space
Star space
Obscure space
Stair space
Balancing space
Touching space
Crammed space
Test space
Marx Brother's space
Bent space
Imaginary space
Kneaded space
Rolled space
Unplugged space
Sweeping space
Breaking space
Protecting space

Packed space
Unstuck space
Filtered space
Decisive space
Growing space
Insulating space
Sunset-Sunrise space
7:35 space
Tiny space
Back space
Rented space
Disowned space
Rock space
Hysterical space
Micky Mouse space
Presley space
Monroe space
Professive space
Bloom space
Trapped space
Lattice space
Polytopic space
Breathless space
Bound space
Concentrated space
Acquired space
Stereo space
Remembered space
Canal space
Peak space
Drum space

H

Violin space
Red space
9 A.M. space
Nihilistic space
Escaped space
Linear space
Martian space
Zinc space
Apocalyptic space
Flight space
Gliding space
Surf space
Get-in space

False space
Theoretical space
Pre-rational space
Exhilarating space
Debtor space
Embossed space
Work space
Demobilized space
Epiphanic space
Epipsychidion space
Pit and Pendulum space
DNA space
Chromatic space
W space
Homeless space
Lapwing space
Organless space
Olympic space
Abysmal space
Parabolic space
Exemplary space
Anagogical space
Non-figurative space
Flood space
Straight space
Subversive space
Virgin space
Identical space
Bachelor space
Bride space
See-you-again space
Kitsch space
Abandoned space
Constructed space
Built space
Amphibian space
Ghost space
Annihilated space
No space
Cyclical space
Horoscopic space
Anamnestic space
Unbounded space
Manipulated space
Liberating space
Post-mortem space

The End of Space *Interview by Gerhard Ahrens, 1992*

What's your idea about the position of theatre today in contemporary architecture?

That's a very broad and difficult question, because you're asking me about the space of theatre. I think that many people who are working in theatre both as actors and directors have been looking for a space which is not a space of theatre, but a space to be found, a space which has not been colonized by either planning, architecture or by the history of theatrical production. So it's the space which has been forgotten. And this forgotten space also points out, in my view, the fact that space as such is a myth—the idea that there is a space and we all have access to it. This is due I think to the brainwashing from the centuries, that space is a universal constant in human endeavour. But one can say that there is no space, there are spaces. Space is not one, but space is plural, space is a plurality, a heterogeneity, a difference. That would also make us look at spacing differently. We would not be looking for one.

This means that theatre has lost its space?

Yes, I think that theatre, like everything else, has lost the illusion of the 'one' space, 'the' space, the space of fair language, the space of memory. It has to do with a totally new relationship to the plurality, and of course then to that ghost of space which is always hanging over the theatre like gravity over architecture.

Do you see any attempts to get a new concept of space in theatre today?

Yes, I do. I think it's coming from unexpected directions in the theatre and also from the body. I think the notion that there is a body in space is itself part of the notion of space as universal. And then you have that particularity of the body which does not belong in space. And this gives the whole impetus to the development of so-called eternal spatiality. The eternal space which will outlive; the stage which will outlive its actors—is, I think, also one of the dissolving symbols, since we now, in general, see that acting is already space. Acting is the breakdown of space. So to act is the break of space, the dissolution of space. Acting is a continual breakdown of distance, which brings spacing or acting back into architecture, since architects are increasingly realizing that their interventions are really of a negative sort. The utopias, ironically, turned out to be the nightmarish creations of ideology which destroyed any human potential. And that's why I think that in this camera obscura, in this black box, in this zero point of utopia or noplace, there has also been another kind of beginning in theatre and also in architecture. This may be very difficult to talk about because we don't even have an agreed-upon vocabulary, but I think it's generally felt by architects, by writers, by artists, by composers, filmmakers, actors. And also this idea that space used to appear, as something convex, like a thing, having a bodily presence, and therefore as something that could be, like in a billiard game, removed or disseminated across some huge table. But now space is actually the negative of that convex, that grasping capacity. In fact it is a concavity, but not a singular one; a multi-dimensional concavity, in which the concavities are actually not adjusted according to any virtual central point, which would be a kind of negative God—which is what space was. One could say that space was a negative God. A God whose presence was often described in the metaphors of convex and concave, as something fulfilling the emanation which illuminates the world in strata and in radiating circles and rays. But, going back to this concavity . . . this concavity without central absence—the negativity of the negativity, would also mean that this concavity is not adjusted; these different concavities are badly adjusted to each other, and I think this maladjustment of concavity is exactly what I would define as being space. It's the badly adjusted cancavity which is what we appreciate and admire and live for. Space is the hole in hollowness. But anyway, space has only been used since Kant made it into a philosophical problem. The Greeks certainly did not grasp space in that way and in other societies they don't see space in the same way as we now talk about it, as if it were something that we could hold or get a grasp on.

Can you describe this philosophical progress on the different space of theatre in Greece and in the Renaissance with the black box? People are still working in the black box.

There is a singular tradition from the Greek theatre to the black box. It shares the same logos or the same pathology, actually, of space as an appearance and a manifestation. And this is what we are witnessing the end of: that through the appearance of space there is also an appearance of the actor who comes into or onto the space, but also in the process of evolving this space the actor somehow realizes that he has nothing much to offer vis-à-vis this kind of space. Not that he doesn't make an offer, but his offering is not accepted. So coming from the Chorus of the Greek stage—which is a terroristic stage, a stage where the chorus always represents the terrorlike implications of terrorism of space—all the way to the black box, it's the same enduringly vanishing phenomenon. But there is no way to get out of it except to go through it. Not simply from outside. Part of this millennial process is that no one seemingly chose to be part of it in the

first place. No one decided on it. It happened. It's the gigantic malice of appearance coming to an end.

The actor on stage is not only a body but he is speaking. And my idea is that the speaking actor, the language, is in a specific way part of the resurrection of space. The language is. And at the same time the actor is always acting already in the world, already caught in it, already part of the world. Which means that actors and theatre will be increasingly involved in the implication of the resistance of the world to theatre. Which also means a resistance of space to theatre. That space is one thing which is not theatrical, which is not a matter of strategy or tactics or scenography. But it's precisely a kind of subversive relationship since the actor and the theatre, like architecture, already live of, are already part of this habit. I think this is the interesting thing to mention about language. Since language in my view won't play the same role in the future. It may cease to express itself.

What do you think about the concept of theatre in Germany as a *moralische Anstalt* proclaiming the classical idea of the *Wahre, Gute, Schöne*?

I think it's perverse. There will always be that longing to get back, to reestablish the repressive and oppressive terrorism. But I think that's part of the mythology of memory itself. It's the insistence of memory. Because if you work with memory in a much more objective way or in a more scientific way, you can also get rid of it, that's part of the aim. You can process it. You can get to another place where one is not oppressed by the weight and the knowledge that went into that absurdly particular construction of identity. And I think that is what we're talking about: the disappearance of identity. Of course the last hold-outs for identity, whether it's classic or postmodern, are inevitable. But I don't think they have a hope of a second coming anyway. Because memory is being consumed. Because it's not our memory anyway. That's why we don't have control over it. We don't have control over keeping the classic or resurrecting it. And the whole epoch-like character of theatre is also disappearing. I believe there won't be any other epoch of theatre or a new epoch of architecture, because at all the epochs' end the epoch itself gives way. The Greek epoch had a sense of suspense, the suspension or the keeping in brackets, so to speak, of what is coming. Of course by many people this will be conceived as anarchy, something horrifying, because there is noth-

ing to hold on to. But nevertheless I think it is experientially a coming. Even if people call it catastrophic or call it horrible or anarchic or epoch-less.

You are speaking of the end of space?

Yes. Of the end of space. That's right. There is a different understanding, and if one enters it one can see that the end of space is not the end of everything. It's just something completely different. And one is therefore not impressed by the monuments and by the logic that went into stabilizing the manifestation of being. One is actually unimpressed by all this.

Do you think there is a deficiency of reflection in art and theatre and in the institutions of art and theatre?

The problem is a general human problem, that people get to a point of a success, and then it's easy to become a theatre director and remain one, or to become and remain a writer. But more difficult is to keep going and also to follow the implications of this search which is not something very clear—it's obscure, and to admit the obscurity of it. It would already be a big help if one didn't look for clarity all the time and didn't look for the guiding light but also went with the darker, the more obsure understanding. One could also get into other areas, see other things, do other things. But the sciences—it's ironic that the sciences, which are the most stable and today the most talked-about things— are actually the places where people have the freedom to spend their life on something that has no real chance or no hope. A large number of mathematicians and physicists are working on things that may never, even in eternity, have any possible application to anything, nor lead to anything—and yet, within the scientific context it is possible to spend time and have the patience to do really nothing very useful. What will come as a critique of culture from the sciences is the possibility of doing things which don't have immediate geometric relationship to the future, and not even to look at time in this geometric way any longer. And this could offer a new experience. Somebody has said that space is the biggest of all mouths. Of course that's what we are discussing. We could also be more specific. How could there be an architecture of theatre? The notion of the classical stage is really not fitting to contemporary reality being swallowed by space.

What's the condition for making such an architecture?

Architecture has a big impact on it because architecture is finally the world we are born into. We were never part of the city. Nobody ever wanted Berlin to look this way. It's not a product of anybody's intentions. It's a negative by-product of a series of misunderstandings and false calculations and catastrophies. But then we come to Berlin or find ourselves in Berlin and it forms, I think, inevitably, unconsciously, a framework of thinking about the future. Therefore, I would only bring up the point that the city itself and the stability of what comes down historically has an extremely important effect. I know this sounds like a cliché, but what to do with such a cliché? How to make it respond to something new? That is the question. I think we have to be braver. We have to be able to get rid of the past, to be not so pessimistic about human capacity to un-make what it itself brought into being. To make a new association, to put a different color in the water of Berlin, or in the sky. I think it is only a matter of time that this happens. Even without believing in the messianic idea, I think it's only a matter of time because the world is reaching an apocalyptic state. I mean the capacity of the world to absorb more time is running out. An indefinite inflation is not possible in terms of time. Time doesn't have time. Of course, this also goes against our idea of home, space and stage. We always say "We can always get back home," or "We can always go somewhere." But this somewhere, we are realizing, doesn´t have anywhere to go. And this is the end of logistic space. We can go home, but the place where we go home has no place to go to. It used to have a place to go to. Somewhere, up, down, across. But if it is immobilized, if it is totally wrapped into this process of getting there, then we might wake up from it as if it were a bad dream in the first place.

Why do you spend time in the theatre?

I don't spend much time in theatre, but I loiter. I may find myself next to theatre, or music. I am not an avid concert-goer or theatre-goer. I don't spend my evening at the opera or things like that. Yet I feel that there is a connection between what's going on there and what I am interested in. There is some connection. It might be very distant. It might be almost completely erased and almost not accessible any longer. But the wonder of it, the wonder of these phenomena persists. And this is also what, in the long run, might be a saving force. When the theatre or architecture are not where you expect to find them. When they displace suddenly; when they are able to displace the institutions. It's not historical because it's also a sudden and unforseeable shift of behavior; a shift of understanding and self-understanding, and even a sudden loss of understanding and conceptuality: the removal of all this. I am interested in the silent space which is not in the theatre anymore.

What's this about silent space?

The silent space is the space not for the predator, it's not for the terminator, it's not a space that you could get through or shoot through—it's not a space actually for an architect, by the way, because architects always want to do something, like people in theatre. They also want to do something. They want to act. They want to expose or deploy their own bodies. But I think that to follow the silent space is to actually follow the divergence, the parting of the symbols, which has to do with the parling of the experience. The symbols are not there by themselves. They emerge out of the experience they symbolize. They are part of how we ourselves are able to say something about what we feel. This parting is not necessarily a de-parting. It also has a biblical dimension as cleaving or parting of water which is impossible to conceive in aesthetic, scientific, or planning terms. But the minute we say that an architect doesn't have to do, cannot intervene in anything, we are, I think, closer to architecture. When we say that an actor has nothing to play, nothing to act and nothing to be in the theatre for, the closer, I would say, he is to the theatre, and closer therefore to the bond between architecture and theatre and the city. A lot of people search for a key to something like this, a key to the invisible. But to realize that this is not the problem of finding the key, that it's not about opening anything. It's about being in that situation without the search for the key, without the impression of the door. Are we waiting for the judgment or for messianic saving or for grace, fatality or destiny? Can we anyway become free of all this? We are not outside ourselves. The entire ecstatic and existential tradition is outside one-selves. Space will not define us. Because that's really the final ecstasis. It's the one exteriority we used to think we had. But if the ecstasis is itself part of the badly maladjusted concavity, then the ecstasis too would fall into oblivion, and we would find ourselves captive, following a trajectory that came up and didn't seek to get down. And maybe this otherness will be a healthy thing. It depends on who comes into this field. It would be good if actors worked on cities. If they abandoned their traditional acting and became fully engaged in transforming the city. This would be a great hope. Because then there would be a displacement of those people who are supposed to come into architecture, who are supposedly technically minded people; who, like lawyers and doctors, are looking for a particular profession. Can one conceive what would happen if actors suddenly became builders! It would be fantastic. And vice versa. Those who wanted predictable development of law or regularity could stand on the stage, visible and hopeless in that particular light. This might happen. People of a completely different kind would come into a field.

You are looking for chances of reorganization?

Even more than that. One has to have some vision in order to survive. I read an account of a woman in one of the concentration camps. She describes that she was in some horrifying place, in hell, in Auschwitz, and that one day she saw a white line in the sky. Just a white line in the sky. And she held onto this line, and holding on to this white line in the sky she survived. That's how she says it. After the war, when she was already in Brooklyn for many years, she thought about this white line, and she thought: maybe it was just smoke from some airplane passing by. She didn't know. But then she said it didn't matter, that was the beautiful thing. It didn't matter how the white line appeared. The trailing. But that line really was there. It really doesn't matter where it comes from. It doesn't matter what its origin is, from what system of organization. It really makes no difference. It's to hold on, let's say, to that white line. It's the mystery of survival. ●

FORMAL BLANK POLITICAL

Is the formal political? Certainly. Here is the proof: A single line taken far enough becomes political. This much is a lacuna ___. This much of it is (unconscious) blankness _____. This much is still (just) indifference _____. But try this much!_____

———

———

———

———

———

———

———

———

———

———

———

———

———

_____

_____

_____.

Wasting precious means of communication signifies that the formless has given way to the apolitical by an appeal to form. Now there are no more lines left. No more lines to fill up. No left lines.

On the other hand try to draw a conclusive line which is not political, the right one _____. Looks just like any other line, pure form, blank followed in blankness by blanks. But this drawing ⋀⋀⋁⋀⋀⋀⋀ seems politically motivated by another (image of form) - this time one in which the indefinite oscillation renders itself as obsolete as a parable.

Let's try again ～⋰⋁⋀⋀⋀ more definitely, less technically. Political? Its only a signature, a seal or some idiotic private scrawl defacing the page of an otherwise completely apolitical publication. Try again:

_____

Now its a matter of disgrace, proving decisively that architecture should, must, has, and always will be _____and not ～⋀⋀⋀⋀

From here on its easy to have apolitical form, for example:

(bars)	(cross)	(power)

How nice to be free at last! No more politics in architecture, just poetry, geometry and the eternal return......... yes eternal......... same.........

same......... what did you say?

They are only politicians, but disguised by _____

_____. Because "_____ _____: *[signature]*,

_____ politically quite _____!"

~~*[signature]*~~

(Daniel Libeskind)

P.S. It has always been known that architecture had to be opened in order to be violated... if one questions its closure, it is clear that it has already lost it, therefore one still holds onto it - otherwise there would be no question of the ~~formal~~, or the ~~political~~.

German Architectural Prize Speech

Berlin, 1999 I am often asked, and ask myself, what in the world brought me to architecture! How did I get involved with building, since the path I chose was not that of someone wanting the security of a profession, but rather one who was engaged in the adventure of the arts, music, mathematics, and the trajectories of ideas. ◎ How does one bring these dimensions to the field of architecture, which is resistant to change? Whole intellectual enterprises, from astrophysics to genetics, from economy to cybernetics, have evolved to present a radically new picture of an emerging world. Yet architecture, framed by tradition and bound by convention, struggles to break out into the contemporary. ◎ It is surely very difficult to write a poem, paint a painting, play a piece of music—yet to introduce into the public realm of architecture even the slightest geometrical shift of a window, to inflect a stair toward a different destination, constitutes not only a difficulty, but a veritable scandal! ◎ I believe that architecture is not reducible to any particular climate of opinion. No abstract theory, game of forms, application of technology or pragmatics is sufficient to communicate the fact that architecture is a movement beyond the material. It is length, height, and width, but also the depth of aspiration and memory. The living source of architecture is the very substance of the soul and constitutes the structure of culture itself. ◎ When I first moved to Berlin to realize the project for the Jewish Museum, I brought

For the Unheard,
plan and elevation

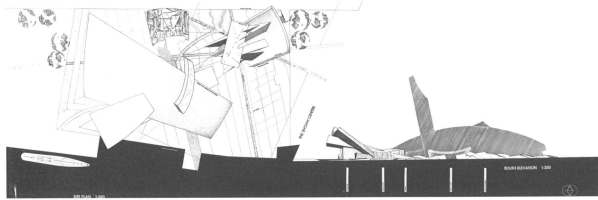

For the Unheard *Competition for the Shoah Centre, Manchester, 1999–present* Building the Shoah Centre in the context of Manchester's rich history is an urban and cultural challenge. Unlike many Holocaust Centres springing up around the world, the uniqueness of this centre is its emphasis on the pre-Holocaust ordinariness of Jewish life, the testimony of witnesses, the abyss created by these events, and finally the significance and implications of this history for the citzens in today's world. Even more unusual is its emphasis on the human voice and the sound of the Shoah traversing history. Thus, the Shoah Centre is at once an experience made relevant to contemporary events, an educational encounter, and a visceral experience in space that touches upon the depths of memory.

■ The form and space of the Shoah Centre encapsulates in the geometries and their materializations the ongoing drama opening toward both the past and the future. The building is a stark composition in which a "Shard of History"—a curvilinear fragment resembling both the Earth and the "Tablets of the Law" is violently penetrated by splinterlike forms. The starkness of this composition is balanced by an Entrance Pavilion, representing the normality of both the entrance and the return. The spatial and architectonic spectrum of the Shoah Centre is a visible memorial with a precise functional requirement of an unprecedented exhibition. ■ Even without entering the center, the light and proportions of its spaces communicate to the wider public the breakdown of civilization that the Shoah represents, in the context of the ongoing conflicts of history. ■ As a starting point the visitor enters the regularly shaped Entrance Pavilion which is also the museum and display hall—the Threshold Datum—where one will be able to gather the day-to-day context of Jewish life in Manchester, England, and elsewhere. The Threshold Datum emphasizes the ordinariness of Jewish life and its long history. ■ Leaving the normality of the threshold, the here of the everyday, the visitors are able to move across a number of variegated paths. The individualization of the paths through the system of "splinters" allows the visitors to engage in the materials

very light baggage with me. We moved here with two suitcases, three kids, and a belief. This belief was not based on accumulation of building experience, reams of ready-made details, or the slickness of know-how. The cultivation of naiveté, the feeling that one should remain a beginner worthy of entering the "cloud of the unknown," is what motivated me to continue this work across the vicissitudes of the past ten years, six governments, five name changes, four museum directors, three window companies, two sides of a wall, one unification, and zero regret. ◎ Architecture is a direct response to the permanent questions posed to human beings by the evolution of space in society—a space that seems to be autonomous, yet seeks a profound and ethical discourse. Architecture is generated, sustained, and propelled into the future by dreams and aspirations, by awakenings and realizations, by the visible and

the invisible. ◎ I have sought to make a building that communicates the memorable—across receding distances and erasures; across a landscape both vivid and imaginary; across light both dim and exhilarating. ◎ A building can be experienced as an unfinished journey. It can awaken our desires, propose imaginary conclusions. It is not about form, image, or text, but about the experience, which is not to be simulated. A building can awaken us to the fact that it has never been anything more than a huge question mark. ◎ I believe that this project joins architecture to questions that are now relevant to all people. To this end, I have sought to create an architecture for a time that would reflect the dynamic of history, a new understanding of museums, and a new relationship between program and architectural space. Therefore this museum is not only a response to a particular program, but also an emblem of hope. ●

השואה
THE SHOAH CENTRE

For the Unheard,
section and diagrams

of the exhibition with an intensity not normally possible in large public spaces. These intimate yet complex paths together form the folded, jagged, and corrugated spaces of the building in both plan and section. Along these routes, which change shape proportionately, there are intimate exhibition spaces and sound chambers. ■ At the horizon of this web of journeys, where the visitors have heard and listened to the stories of individual lives and perused the associated materials that elucidate them, the visitors encounter the dramatic and oblique space of the Barbed Shard. This is a barrier whose blankness and opacity obscures the horizon beyond. ■ Crossing to the Other Side of this barrier—the Barbed Shard—the visitors experience larger spaces, in which the splinter-like forms culminate, allowing dramatic views of the city beyond. ■ The space of the Other Side offers the opportunity for reflection and a new perspective. In this space, the

unfolding dramas and barbaries of injustice in the contemporary world are exhibited. The visitors return by a simple path to the Threshold Datum, their sense of history having been transformed. ■ The significance of the Shoah Centre lies in the creation of a unique and emblematic architecture. Through the resources of light, sound, material, kinetic movement, and form the visitors are confronted with ethical issues that have been taken down from an abstract level to a visual and sensory experience. ■

The Garden of Love and Fire *Polderland Garden, Almere,*

The Netherlands, 1992 The Garden of Love and Fire constitutes itself as a sign of a new city—a place that emblematically and physically marks a moment of spirituality in space.
■ It makes visible the trace of an apparently invisible conversion: light into object, poetry into number, thought into landscape. It is an expression that the garden is only the number of our existence made audible to the soul. ■ The garden consists of an observation platform, three narrow water canals, and a fourth dry channel on which an oblong volume is resting. These lines direct themselves toward

108

109

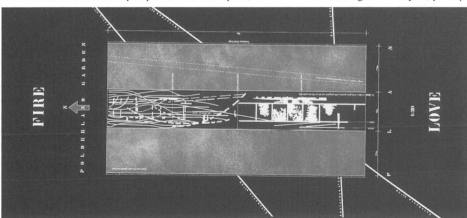

The Garden of Love and Fire,
diagrams and elevation

three particular locations: Salamanca, Paris, and Almere. They signify a world location in which love (Juan de la Cruz) and fire (Paul Célan) intersect in Almere's future. The inscribed ciphers refer to the encounter between Juan de la Cruz and Paul Célan in the newly reclaimed land. They become readable at precisely those times when the materiality of forms dissolves into oblivion. ■ The meditation garden is formed by a prism supporting a number, an empty wedge, and a transparent plane. On the occasion of humidity change (fog), the garden projects light through the transparent plane, which is inscribed with a graphic "anniversary" image. ■ The light illuminating the surface becomes a trace of "lost light," as well as the manifestation of nature and construction. The entire ensemble is governed by a column of light, sometimes visible, sometimes not, which gives body to itself through fog. ■ The shape, function, mechanism, and character of the garden seek to reveal that we are surrounded by a world full of amazing and powerful signs, the laws of which are intimated but cannot be unraveled. The meanings that reach us are those of an accidental encounter with fragments of our own awareness. The displacement between form and function opens a gap in the text, date, and atmosphere, which transforms the notion of space from that of domination to that of an uncontrollable anniversary. The garden evokes an unresolved tension that sensibility conjures in a play that has a conclusion that is unreadable yet consecrated. ■ The twenty-first-century garden is one in which cosmic laws momentarily appear before the lover of nature, but only to manifest that the fire-inspired head of the universe is perpetually turning. ■

Homage to El Lissitzky *Berlin, 1990*

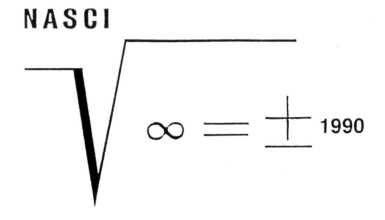

ENOUGH of IDEOLOGY
IDEA - LOGY
ID - EOLOGY
I - DEO - LOGY

EACH STATION IS AN IMAGE OF NOT MERELY ANY TEMPORARY GOAL. A BECOMING FROZEN OF WORK REPRESENTS THE FORM. THUS A PROCESS AND WAY FROZEN IN THE PROCESS.

MERELY OF PROCESS...   ...ANY "A" BECOMING. EACH WORK REPRESENTS FROZEN STATION, A FROZEN PROCESS: THE GOAL. FORM IS NOT TEMPORA-RY, THUS THE "IN - IMAGE" (IN, AND, OF).

N THE STATION A GOAL MERELY REPRESENTS A BECOMING: EACH FROZEN MAGE. FROZEN IS THUS ANY WAY TEMPORARY, AND NOT A PROCESS OF THE PROCESS OF FORM. WORK.

A GOAL OF BECOMING A FORM STATION. THE "REPRESENTS" IN EACH IS MERELY THE WORK IMAGE OF ANY "AWAY". FROZEN AND FROZEN, PROCESS PROCESS. THUS NOT TEMPORARY.

Libeskind, Berlin, Apartment Building

House with a Front Lawn
Homage to Alvin Boyarsky, 1977; Folly, Osaka, Japan, 1994

110

The story of this "folly" is the story of the quest for an architectural order that speaks a language: the language of geometry coming to an end in architecture. Thus the language of this tale is a fact—a fact expressive of the precariousness of the symbol of architecture/nature. ■ As such, this fact is its own content. Geometry coming to an end in architecture is nature: an arctic flower. ■

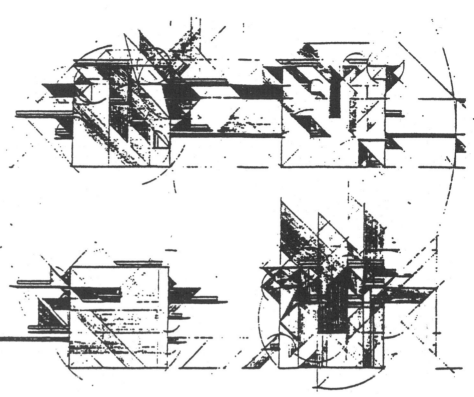

House with a Front Lawn, elevations

"I truly saw those visions; I did not perceive them in a dream, nor while sleeping, nor in a frenzy, nor with the human eyes or with the external ears of a person, nor in remote places; but I received those visions according to the will of God while I was awake and alert with a clear mind, with the innermost eyes and ears of a person, and in open places. There may be a reason why I received those visions in this manner, but it is difficult for a human person to understand why."

—Hildegard of Bingen (1141)

Intertopos
Campus design for JVC University, Guadalajara, Mexico, 1998–Present

111

It is my belief that a new university campus should not be a quarantine or detached one. The association of "institution" and "past" should give way to a new microcosm, in which education, whether of architects, teachers, or public administrators, takes place in an inspiring environment. Einstein has remarked that there is nothing, not even the speed of light, that is quicker than the human imagination. It is imagination and wonder that con-

nect education, public administration, and architecture, grounding them in reality. After all, as the Greeks knew well, architecture, education, and public administration challenge, illuminate, and question the world in order to make it better tomorrow. ■ The primary parameters of the university should open up the mystery of knowledge to find worthy goals interacting with other spheres of enquiry and issues. The neutral box with people propelled in it, as if they were particles in an experiment of physics, is no longer sufficient. Instead, a continuum is required—a series of continua—which interlock, dissolve, form new knots. The programmatic spectrum is based on the 365 days of the year in which people's lives take on temporal shape. ■ The university should be a meeting place of many different aptitudes, skills, and horizons: Each special sector of the university must be enriched by the greatest frequency of possible contact with others. The need for intensity, compactness, and ease of communication between all the constituent parts is essential to twenty-first-century

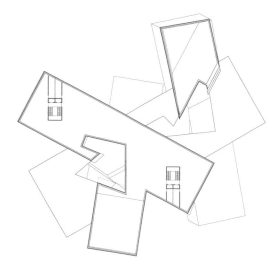

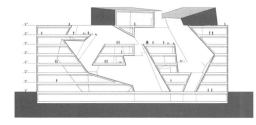

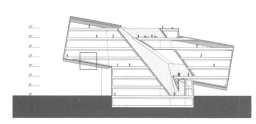

Intertopos, plan
and sections

discourse. Meetings, both accidental and deliberate, must be provided by the greatest number of intersections en route, without producing congestion. Such a public configuration of encounter will be ideally suited to connect all the students in a community of knowledge. ■ This interaction is accomplished on a pragmatic level by simply offering students from the three faculties the entire space of the university. The structure is fixed, accommodating a program that shifts. The various disciplines and their specific needs will be determined organically by the architectural topography and topology of relationships, rather than by room numbers and assigned spaces. The university will become a natural "home" for sharing and celebrating each creative day. ■ A mosaic of relationships can be accomplished by the literal weaving of the larger halls, cafeteria, and meeting and presentation rooms in such a way that they are always connected to the more intimate strands of the program, in which specialized activities are contextualized. The relation—physical, kinetic, and spiritual—is of consequence to educators, architects, and public-policy makers. This is not an abstract exercise. The architecture of the university must demonstrate and encompass the multilevel discourse that the program calls for by diffusing the specialties and reshaping the university as a social organism with common interests and goals. ■ The uni-

versity as a whole should transform the ivory tower protected against the world of modernity into a contemporary and vital institution. A meeting place in the morning can become a fishing ground of ideas in the late afternoon, a gathering place in the evening, and a meditation place at night. The program as a whole is a sphere in which an ever-shifting adaptability is associated with the permanence of architectural space. ■ Spaces of the university will be viewed as a dialogue between teacher and audience, between the monological and the heterogeneous. The School of Architecture, School of Education, or School of Public Administration can form a built constellation where organizational links become guideposts to activity and learning, illuminating them with the lightning flash of communication along the channels of integration and the future. ■

JohAnnishoffZZ Urban competition for Johannishof Viertel, Tacheles, Berlin, 1999 (joint venture with Matthias Reese)

Johannishof Viertel, the site of one of the last large ruins in the Mitte, is a paradigmatic urban Berlin site between the busy Friedrichstrasse and the historical Spandauer Vorstadt. To transform this once central site into a diverse and dynamic piece of a city a new logic is needed. The mindless conventions often used by developers in conjunction with be administrative inertia to produce neighborhoods without neighbors, mixed uses without mixture and cities that must depend on advertising and propaganda, and not their inherent dynamic qualities. ■ This scheme navigates between the large scale of the site and the reality that investment patterns are not a reliable guide for planning a neighborhood. Visible overlappings of program, tension between form and function, and a creation of accidents elaborate a site through trajectories of discovery and the varied experience of everyday life. Public space—so often marginalized by corporate exploitation of the city without regard to human scale—is here featured as the topological structure whose articulated complexity allows for a rich inhabitation of the site by work, housing and cultural activity. ■ By creating broken blocks and a relation to visual vistas, passages and pedestrian connections of different intensities are brought to play in a series of overlapping circles. This transforms the large shopping character of Friedrichsrasse through the cultural variety of Tacheles to the small scale calm of Johannisstrasse. Buildings near Friedrichstrasse have massive clear passages to the interior area,

Above: **JohAnnishoffZZ**, sections; below: plan

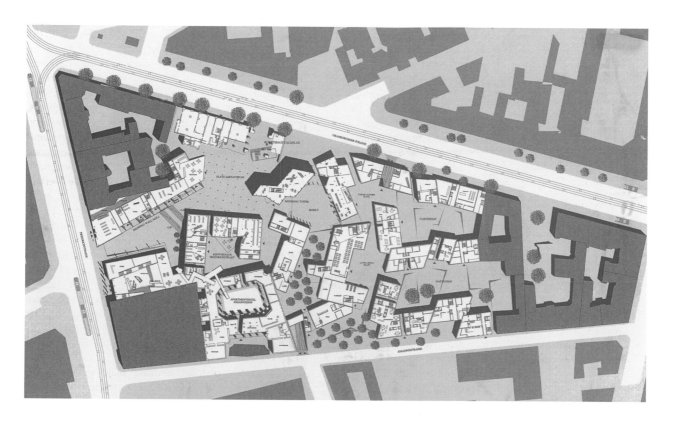

while office spaces give way to residential quarters the further one moves into the center of the site. The green merges into the residential area along Johannisstrasse. By inventing hybrid typologies of small scale housing that is less visible, and by giving large spaces along prominent addresses, the scheme introduces a streetscape where retail and cultural functions reestablish the liveliness once associated with the Mitte. ■ The logic of the scheme allows the project to be built in phases, with different architectural languages to be built, creating a varied texture. This proposal develops over time and gives substance to an ecological approach, allowing for permanent dynamic regeneration. ■

K *Scenography and costume design, Gladsaxe Theater, Copenhagen,*
113 *Denmark, 1994*

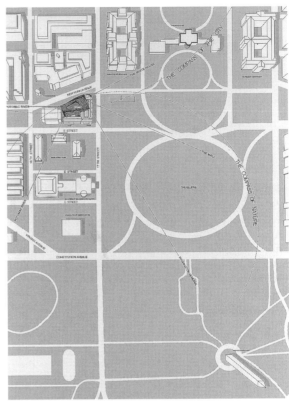

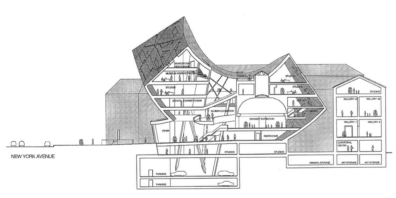

The Kaleidoscope *Extension to the Corcoran Gallery of Art,*
114 *Washington D.C., 1999* Any project proposed for the extension of the Corcoran Gallery of Art must take into respectful consideration the historic centrality of the beaux arts and neoclassical buildings of Flagg and Platt. At the same time, the scheme must provide dynamic reciprocity between old and new, museum and school, private and public. ■ The Kaleidoscope becomes a dramatic focus of the axis of New York Avenue and Seventeenth Street. The building is formed by two different curves: the first follows a movement along New York Avenue ascending toward its apex at Seventeenth Street; the second follows the roof of the studios descending and bringing light into the lobby. These two curves form the hinge that connects the galleries and the school. ■ The project is not simply an autonomous addition to the Corcoran, but intertwines and utilizes the functional and historical fabric of the existing buildings. It reorganizes and thematizes the

The Kaleidoscope,
section, site plan,
ground floor plan

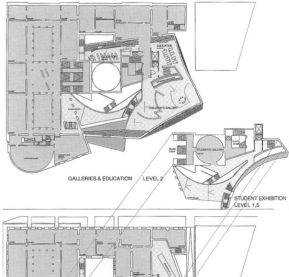

central galleries, staircases, and the Rotunda while regaining the lost but impressive gallery spaces of the Flagg and Platt buildings. The internal logic of the existing historical fabric is complemented by the new diversity of spaces created in the Kaleidoscope. ■ The Kaleidoscope offers new public spaces, restaurant, cafés, an art forum, galleries, education spaces, commercial facilities, boardroom, and spectacular views from the rooftop observatory. It is a completely contemporary facility for the fusion of the gallery and the school, with the spatial and functional qualities allowing for the production of art with an appreciation of the public. ■ The building's ivorylike cladding complements the Cherokee marble of the Flagg building. It presents a shimmering, translucent facade whose luminosity enriches, reflects, and transforms the existing context. The great architectural qualities of the existing two buildings are thus sharpened by the lens of the new. ■ In its urban context, the Kaleidoscope can be seen as an ever-shifting silhouette from a myriad of perspectives. At the same time, the building allows visitors, faculty, and students a panoramic view of the heart of the nation's capital. ■ The Kaleidoscope is a response to the ambitious program of the Corcoran, a legacy to be made visible in its new architecture. It is not an arbitrary play of forms, but a rigorous embodiment of memory and function. It is an emblem of continuity, a unity of differences, and a constellation of possibilities. ■

L'Chai'm: To Life *Jewish Museum San Francisco, 1998–present*

(joint venture with Gordon H. Chong and Partners) The design of the Jewish Museum for San Francisco provides a space for exhibitions, a place for activities, and a symbol dedicated to the revitalization of Jewish life in San Francisco and beyond. Such a building, rooted in the Jewish imagination, and opening itself to the diverse contemporary currents of life, will be a fundamental contribution to the Yerba Buena renaissance. ■ The challenge, significance, and potential of this site and the program of the Jewish Museum are part of the cultural process symbolizing the foundation of a new and innovative Jewish institution in San Francisco—an institution that will deal with continuity and identity. This relation is revealed by the struggle to make space in this delicate location. ■ The site of the Jewish Museum is an abandoned power station from the turn of the twentieth century. The Jewish Museum will provide new spaces for new programs through the imposing Polk facade of the substation. The new spaces will be incorporated within the

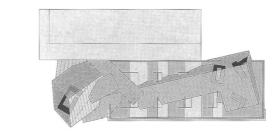

old structure and will articulate a close relationship to the new Millennium Tower and the pedestrian connector. ■ The atmosphere of the old power station is carefully retained, while providing a wholly new program and circulation spaces for the Jewish Museum. The visitor is made aware of the old parameters of the power station: the walls where batteries and equipment were once lodged, the skylights, and the structure. In contrast and complement to this experience of history, the visitor will also experience the reconfigured spatial form of the new extension. History does not come to an end, but opens to the future; history is a dynamic ground. ■ The site, a complex urban locus, provides the necessary pressure for the emergence

L'Chaim: To Life, elevation and roof plan

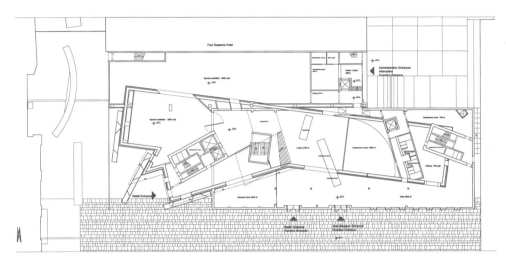

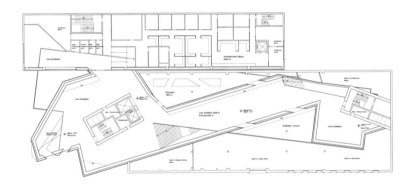

L'Chai'm: To Life,
ground floor and
first floor plan

letters are not mere signs but are substantial participants in the story they create. Thus the spatiality of *chai*—a fundamental emblem of Jewish life—will be experienced as a full dynamic movement responding to the many levels of interpretation this word possesses. ■ The entire building is a penetration of *chai*/life into the Talmudic page structure where the margins and commentaries are as important as what is commented upon. No place in the finished museum is unconnected to the whole, forming an organic structure of space and function. The entire museum is a matrix calling forth interpretation by the visitor. ■ The building brings together the activities of the Jewish Museum, the fullness of the senses and emotions, by weaving the themes of exhibition, education, and knowledge for both Jews and non-Jews alike. It is the celebration of Jewish imagination and unity within the context of an evolving and developing history. ■ The new building is based on the unprecedented spaces created by the *Chai*: the *Chet*, which provides an overall continuity for the core exhibition, and the *Yud*, located on the pedestrian connector, which gives a new identity to the power station. Together these letters and their meanings constitute a special emblem for the ongoing development of the Yerba Buena area. ■ The Jewish experience presented in this discourse of forms will engage the public with the image of a newly emerging Jewish-American iden-

of a unique form and energy. The Jewish Museum will make visible the relationship between the new and the old, of tradition and innovation. It will transform the physical energy associated with the power station to the power of human communication and imagination. The building, though small in comparison to the context, will become a steel-clad jewel, like a beacon glowing of the future. ■ The Jewish Museum building is based on the Hebrew word *L'Chai'm*, which means "to life." The two Hebrew letters of *chai* (with all their symbolic, mathematical, and emblematic structure) are literally the life source and the form of the museum. In the Jewish tradition,

tity. It will deal with the issues of imagination, creativity, vitality, and access. The spaces and their programs will delve into the depths of Jewish spirit, and celebrate the discovery and relevance of Jewish culture for all. ■ Visitors enter through the old, grandiose entrance of the power station. The entire ground-level lobby, with its restaurant, café, and shop, reveals a dramatic view of the power station skylights and the *Chai*, the southern wing where the museum visit begins. An illuminated stair rises from the lobby through the southern edge of the *Chet*, crosses the central point of the *Yud*, and emerges into the northern wing of the *Chet*. The multi-

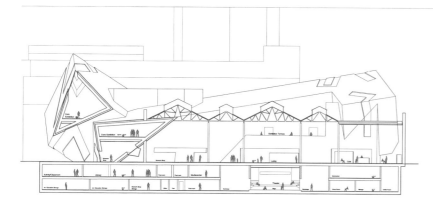

San Francisco. It is a museum of the Jewish imagination and creativity, which, despite its all too tragic history, is a culture of freedom and possibility. The museum is about Jewishness without the old theology, yet with all the ideas and experiences of a vibrant community. What does a museum do in order to communicate, not only to Jews but also to non-Jews, the significance of this dynamic process, which did not end in the 1930s? A creative Jewish Museum will open a culture that develops into new directions in the fullness of experience: an ecumenical experience available to all those interested in the contemporaneity of the 4,000-year-old "Jewish experience." ■

L'Chai'm: To Life, plan and section

Line of Fire *Exhibition Installation, Geneva, 1998* Architecture ON

[119] line: line that traces a furrow by drawing a ploughshare through the soil, and line that defines limits between things beyond which one refuses to go. **Architecture TOWARD line:** equalizer of day and night—reaching to make equal. Great circle of the celestial sphere, which is not a circle, and whose plane is refractory to the access of words, which are not words. **Architecture UNDER line:** at the equator. Line under: UNDERLINE. For just perceptible below the red light and submerged in white light is an inscription of architecture that does not consume or demolish. **Architecture 1,244 degrees:** Zero degree. Many directions with a single angle. Endless row directed to the spaced inclination between all angles. The end of right angles, of rite angles, of write angles. Bend along a fold . . . 10 words. Ten words. 1,000 letters. One thousand letters. Plus one. Even when mirrored, 1,001 remains 1,001. One thousand and one reflections, trajectories, flights—all measured by an engineer. With infinite patience and precision. Through the plumb line. The read line. The red line. The read red line. LINE OF FIRE. ■

purpose theatre, temporary exhibitions, educational services, and administration spaces are integrated throughout the scheme. ■ Just as the fundamental concept of the new Jewish Museum of San Francisco is *L'Chai'm: To Life*, so does the building seek to contribute a powerful new structure, traversing the substation, to the exciting Yerba Buena development. The discovery of the richness of Jewish culture will become an enduring magnet offering the public the opportunity to share a universal heritage. It is very different as it does not deal with the Holocaust and the tragedies of Europe. It shows the imaginative possibilities of a Jewish Museum in

Micromegas: The Architecture of Endspace Drawings,

1979 Architectural drawings have in modern times assumed the identity of signs; they have become the fixed and silent accomplices in the overwhelming endeavor of building and construction. In this way their own open and unknowable horizon has been reduced to a level that proclaims the a priori coherence of technique. In considering them as mere technical adjuncts collaborating in the execution of a series made up of self-evident steps, they have appeared as either self-effacing materials or as pure formulations cut off from every external reference. ■ While the classical axiomatic of architectural drawing elaborated its usefulness within an overall theory of order (by beginning with well-established theories of representation and attempting to unify them), contemporary formal systems present themselves as riddles—unknown instruments for which usage is yet to be found. Today, we seldom start with particular conditions that we raise to a general view; rather, we descend from a general system to a particular problem. However, what is significant in this tendency (where the relation between the abstract and the concrete is reversed) is the claim that disengages the nature of drawing, as though the "reduction" of drawing was an amplification of the mechanisms of knowledge, an instrument capable of revealing at a stroke new areas of the "real." ■ There is a historical tradition in architecture, whereby drawings (as well as other forms of communication) signify more than can be embodied in stabilized frameworks of objectifiable data. If we can go beyond the material carrier (sign) into the internal reality of a drawing, the reduction of representation to a formal system—seeming at first as void and useless—begins to appear as an extension of reality, which is quite natural. The system ceases to be perceived as a process whose coherence is supported by empty symbols, and reveals a structure whose manifestation is only mediated by symbolism. ■ An architectural drawing is as much a prospective unfolding of future possibilities as it is a recovery of a particular history to whose intentions it testifies and whose limits it always challenges. In any case, a drawing is more than the shadow of an object, more than a pile of lines, more than a resignation to the inertia of convention. ■ The act of creation in the order of procedures of imagination, here as elsewhere, coincides with creation in the objective realm.

Drawing is not mere invention; its efficacy is not drawn from its own unlimited resources of liberty. It is a state of experience in which the "other" is revealed through mechanisms that provoke and support objective accomplishments and the one who draws upon them. Being neither pure registration nor pure creation, these drawings come to resemble an explication or a reading of a pre-given text—a text both generous and inexhaustible. ■ I am interested in the profound relation that exists between the intuition of geometric structure as it manifests itself in a pre-objective sphere of experience and the possibility of formalization that tries to overtake it in the objective realm. In fact, these seemingly exclusive attitudes polarize the movement of imagination and give an impression of discontinuity, when in reality they are but different and reciprocal moments—alternative viewpoints—of the same fundamental, ontological necessity. ■ We cannot simply oppose the formal to the nonformal without at the same time destroying the mobility, variation, and effectiveness incarnated in the very nature of formalism. From a certain point of view, everything is formalism; the distinction between "perspective" and "figure" (depth and flatness)—which seems definitive—branches off and distributes itself over layers of intentionality, which in reality show a continuity more than a difference. In a parallel analogy, all seems to be supported by the empirical significance of signs themselves, which magnify appearances by reducing structure to them. ■ My work attempts to express this inadequateness at the heart of perception for which no (final) terms are provided; a lack of fulfillment that prevents manifestation from being reducible to an object-datum. Only as horizons, in relation to time, can forms appear in this exploration of the "marginal," where concepts and premonitions overlap. There is a presentation, but always according to the mode of imperfection; an internal play in which deferred completeness is united with a mobilized openness. The work remains an indefinite series because this dialectic cannot be halted. As such, these drawings and collages develop in an area of architectural thinking that is neither a physics nor a poetics of space. ■ Because the "geometry of experience" is only a horizon of potential formalization and we find it already inserted into that other horizon of desire and intuition—the task of essential clarification, as I see it, becomes the systematic and dynamic transmuta-

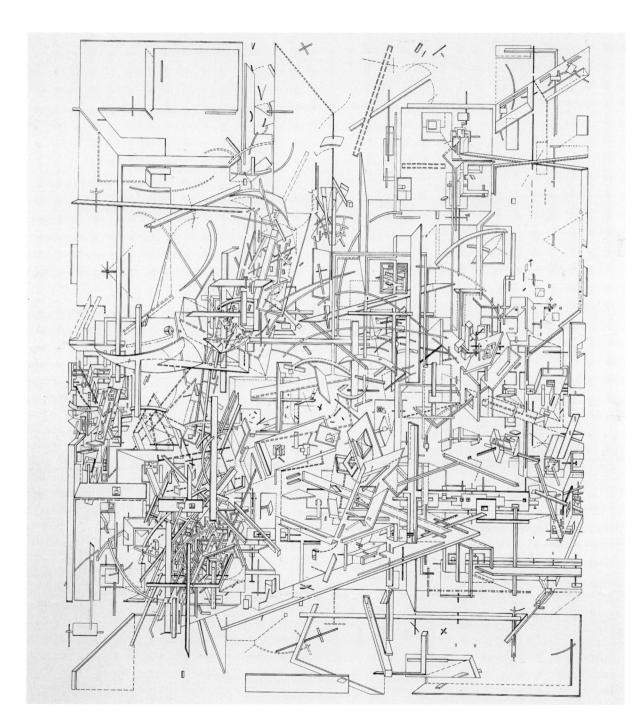

Micromegas,
Little Universe

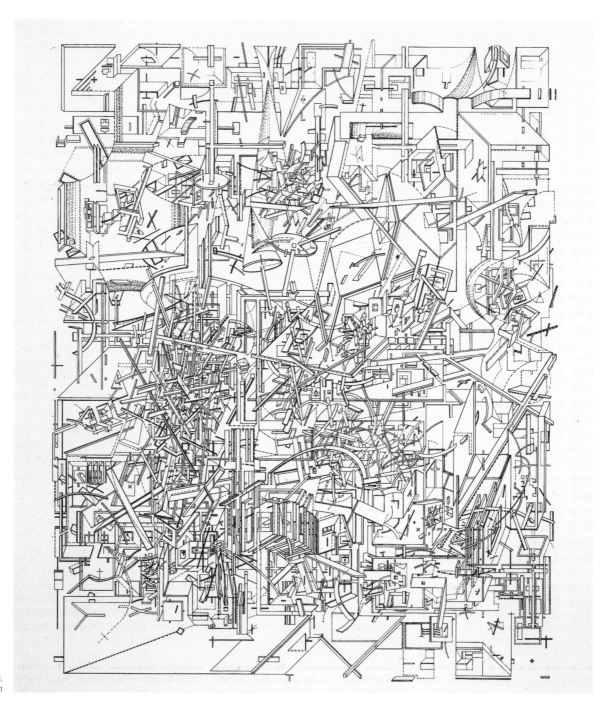

Micromegas,
Maldoror's Equation

tion of movements; an exchange between abstract ciphers exhausted in their own objectivity and hardened in fixed signs; and concrete contingencies responsive to the permanent solicitations of a spontaneous appeal. ■ An authentic abstraction gives us what is most unique in incomplete but formalized levels of grasping objects. It does so because, at first, uniqueness is given in an impure fashion, blended as it is with elements representing categories of experience, which must be progressively extracted from the general alienation of overqualified intuition of spatial structure. This "purification" attempts, through a series of successive steps, to realize the elimination of intuitive content and numerical relations, and leads to ever more encompassing (spherical) possibilities of configuration. ■ But through an enigmatic reversal, one discovers in this ascent (or escape?) through the "funnel" of an increasingly precise effort of projection, a regression toward the unique and primordial condition of metrics. The vectoral "going beyond" is at the same time a deepening spiral movement that exposes this transgression as a moment of concentric approach. In this sense, an overall envelopment neutralizes tension and reveals a foundation of both continuity and change; a homogeneous state pervades even the most complex antinomies. ■ Most of all, however, I am a fascinated observer and a perplexed participant of that mysterious desire that seeks a radical elucidation of the original precomprehension of forms—an ambition that I think is implicit in all architecture. If there is true abstraction here, as opposed to generalization, it is not achieved by the elimination of contents through a gradual deployment of an increasing emptiness, but is rather an isolation of structural essence whose manifestation in two

dimensions illuminates all the subsystems of projection (for example, three-dimensional space). ■ Edmund Husserl's *Origin of Geometry* has been an inspiration to me in all these "researches." Understanding that the historical genesis of geometry evolved from the problems of land-surveying (as calculus originated from the study of movement, or statistics from the study of collectivities), I have become increasingly aware of the fact that the disclosure of the first horizon (outlining the space of initial encounters) also guarantees the "leakage" in the project of objectification. The same structures we have already experienced in a confused and prereflective situation are continually transposed to a reflective realm, where they open the way for ever more elaborated descriptions. It is not a matter of piling superimposed hierarchies one on top of another, rather the trajectory of intentions transposes content into operation and, at the same time, displaces descriptive geometry by the structural. The transformation of object into operation imposes a temporal dimension on this process, a process whose meaning is not arbitrary and yet is not predetermined either. ■ The invisible ground from which it is possible to scaffold moving layers of construction enables one to recover modes of awareness quite removed from the initial hypothesis of rationality. These drawings seek to reflect on a deeper level of consciousness the inner life of geometrical order whose nucleus is the conflict between the voluntary and the involuntary. Once again this duality (like that of realism-formalism) appears as an unsurpassable condition pointing to a dynamic ground, which testifies to an experience that receives only as much as it is capable of giving, draws only that which allows itself to be drawn into. ■

Market of Consciousness *Research Studio. ETH Zürich. 1997*

Market apparently kills consciousness. This mechanism exchanges commodities, deprives or gives value to them. Consciousness trades nothing: is free. Yet the relationship between the nothing of consciousness and the something of market lies at the very core and genesis of the city. ⊚ A market is connected to consciousness by an abyss whose viscosity is imaginary and density ethical: a region defying control and manipulation. This abyss, lodged in the systems of exchange, cannot be

managed by a thought—infrastructure or detail—thought. It is, rather, a question of how far the disconnection between thought and design has already penetrated and overwhelmed architecture, making any project deficient when faced with the monthly reports of the World Bank or the daily transformations of the sky. ⊚ The studio sought to develop an area of experience— "the market of consciousness"—which can hardly be represented today by a commonly agreedupon language. The precision of drawing and building vis-à-vis the ambivalence and ambigu-

ity of that nonconceptual experience is the source of programs, forms, and responses that were here explored. Imagination, in outpacing this experience, provides alternative solutions to problems without defining or thematizing them. ⊚ The smell of architecture in the third and fourth millennium, as well as its foretaste tomorrow and the day after, will have little to do with traditional composition, whether the composition of theoretical relationships, spatial configuration, or virtual exchanges. Such composition has in the past been predicated on the putting

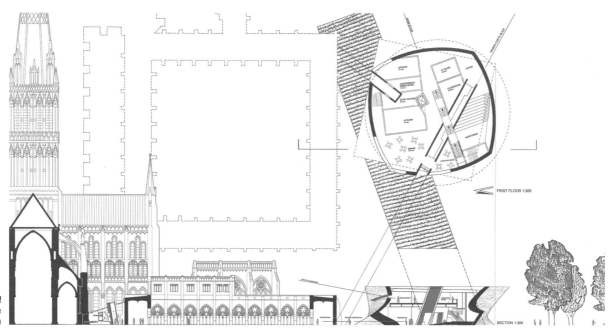

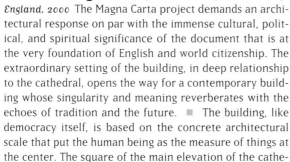

This page: **Measure of Things**, section; opposite: site plan and ground floor plan

Measure of Things *The Magna Carta Project, Salisbury, England, 2000*

120

121

The Magna Carta project demands an architectural response on par with the immense cultural, political, and spiritual significance of the document that is at the very foundation of English and world citizenship. The extraordinary setting of the building, in deep relationship to the cathedral, opens the way for a contemporary building whose singularity and meaning reverberates with the echoes of tradition and the future. ■ The building, like democracy itself, is based on the concrete architectural scale that put the human being as the measure of things at the center. The square of the main elevation of the cathedral is placed horizontally on the ground, forming the basis for the spatial transformation of ground into the circular horizon at the roof. ■ This transformation creates an unprecedented fusion between the center of the square ground—ground of opposing directions—with that of the other center of the circle—the horizon of humanity. The humanistic ideal, where the human is the emblematic reconciliation of the worldly and the transcendent becomes, for the first time, materialized, giving a new access to space both real and symbolic. ■ This Magna Carta project becomes an experience that embodies the integrity, reality, and dynamic of a fully democratic space. ■ The Magna Carta Project, with its open, multi-dimensional, yet centered field—the space of encounter between tradition and the contemporary—will disclose a uniquely new yet age-old cultural aspiration. The Magna Carta Project will give simultaneous access to both the temporal and the eternal, connecting old forms and its rings with the evolving horizons of a democratic world and world citizenship. ■

together of discrete, linguistically autonomous, and ready-made regions; whereas it is actually a question of indeterminate, nonlinear, and archipelagic dissolution of edges. ◎ The studio explored architecture as a voyage into an unknown, city and buildings as clairvoyants, homecoming without home. The constructive interrogation of architecture might yet point to the anachronism of exchanges. Their flesh-and-blood medium appears today to be inseparable from the virtual rather than the virtue of building. For virtue is inherently a spiritual experience of nothing, rather than any exteriority attributed to it. ◎ Urban mythologies, assumed moments of communication, ravages in the physiognomy of cities, the twilight of deserts, might yet be signs of a dawning disclosure, a disclosure that the city has already made and is continuing to extend globally, despite the fact that one doesn't recognize it. ◎ The work has alerted us to an absence of revelation whose suspended imminence one cannot afford to miss. ●

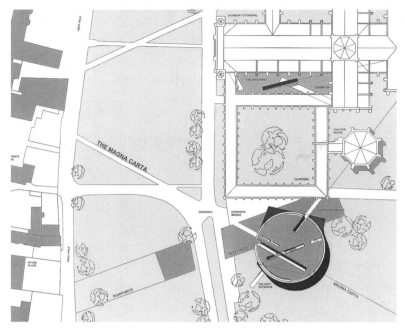

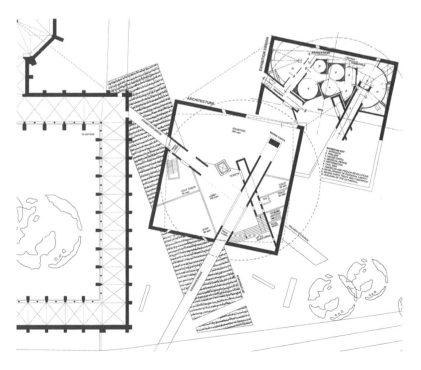

Moskau–Berlin, Berlin–Moskau

[122]

Exhibition Installation, Berlin, 1995

Berlin-Moscow, Moscow-Berlin . . .

[123]

words naming upheaval and greatness whose overwhelming urgency and asymmetrical inclination are characteristic of a relationship best described by pointing to the little space both separating and uniting them. ■ The little lacunae into which the breath and gaze vanish points to the gap, the abysmal nonidentity inserted into the relation it represents. ■ I see this difference as a space opened between two gigantic wedges of ideologies and systems: an epochal space made human and heroic by those we have come to call "exiles." Whether they were Russians in Berlin or Berliners in Moscow, these exiles and the poignant brilliance that shines through their suffering represent the central and perpetual aura of the twentieth century, an aura substantiated in the redness of blood and the black darkness of night. ■ These powerful wedges of resistance, of social struggle, and of the creative act stand out against the exhilaration and barbarism of the times. They are the magnetic needles rotated toward the spirit of events that gravitate around them, even when they lead to imprisonment and silence. ■ The rest of the works in this mammoth exhibit are organized to allow the visitor to assess and orient the beauty and terror of the first part of this century around those whose works and ideas were doomed to exile and banishment. In their reciprocal fatality, but also in their optimism, these Berliners and Moscovites have given real substance to an undying relation best summarized in N. Mandelstam's phrase **"hope against hope."** ■

Mourning ₁₂₄ *The urbanization of the former S.S. Barracks of Sachsenhausen, Oranienburg, Berlin, 1992–present* The task of urbanizing the former territories connected with the Sachsenhausen concentration camp raises the most fundamental political, cultural, and spiritual issues of the twentieth century. This site and its history are paradigmatic for the catastrophe of Germany and its responsibility in the future. Beyond the unspeakable crimes perpetrated in this "**Ideal City of Death**," the land and water forming the ultimate resources of humanity have been exploited, polluted, and debased through man's inhumanity to man. What must be faced in any endeavor to re-create and redevelop such an area is the need to mourn an irretrievable destiny, and a hope that this mourning will affect the political program, social use, and their connection to the topography. ■ The former Sachsenhausen death camp cannot be hidden or detached from the site that formed its historical context and infrastructure. The use of this site for housing is inappropriate, and I propose that the entire field should acquire significance in relationship to the city, referring to the past and the future, embedded in the present. The paradoxical challenge of the work is to retain a strong memory for the generations to come

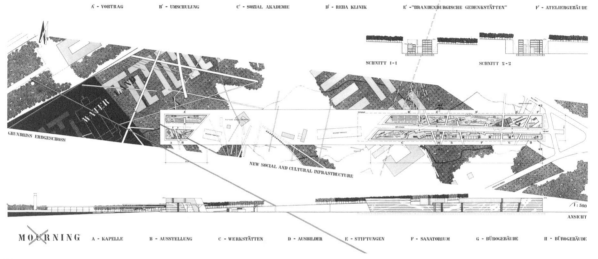

Mourning *Lecture, Berlin, 1993* Some time ago, I was invited to a competition to decide the use for the land adjacent to the Sachsenhausen concentration camp. The brief was ninety-five pages long, ninety-four of which discussed the urbanization of the land in terms of housing. Upon being invited, I struggled with the idea to participate in such a competition at all. The site was odious, the camp horrendous, the suggested program outrageous. I then decided to ignore deliberately the entire so-called program and take the issue of urbanizing these lands in another manner altogether. At the presentation, the argument raged dramatically during the jury deliberations. The five other architects complied willingly with the idea for housing and the first prize was awarded to an Austrian architect whose scheme proposed housing for eight thousand persons. I received an honorary prize, which was a perfect way of dismissing the issue with a clean conscience. ◉ However, many of the citizens of the city of Oranienburg and others in the state of Brandenburg believed that housing was not the answer to these lands, so subsequent to the decision of the jury, I was invited back by the mayor of the city to address the issue and present my scheme to the elected members of the building committee. A decision has now been made that housing will not be allowed on the site, and the city has decided, along with the state of Brandenburg and the Federal Bund, to follow the ideas that I had suggested. I ran into conflict with the historians who wanted to reconstruct all the Nazi buildings in order to preserve the history. I thought that this was a ridiculous way of going about it. The buildings are completely decayed and one would have to rebuild them completely, requiring large sums of money. There would have to be new walls, new stabilizing foundations, new windows, and by the time the Nazi buildings would be reconstructed, one would have produced a mockery, a kitsch, a misunderstanding of history. In fact, I advocated in my original proposal that the S.S. buildings disintegrate over time. It is very difficult to do this ecologically, but one could do it in a controlled manner, in order to see the history, not as a simulation of the Third Reich, but to see what is there invisibly, the infrastructure between the S.S. lands and the Sachsenhausen concentration camp. ● I argued with the historians and pleaded that they think about the invisible traces of history, the history which never had a chance to be expressed; a history that should not be seen simply as an outline of a building. I am glad to say that after many dis-

This page: **Mourning**, site plan; opposite: conceptual diagrams and at the same time to formulate a response that provides new possibilities, new activities, and new images of a hopeful future. ■ This proposal shifts, detaches, and reconnects the competition site in its relation to the equilateral triangle that forms the visible apex of the all too invisible symbol worn by the thousands of prisoners within the camp. It should be noted that there were three points that were deliberately built to define the outer limits of the triangle: the crematorium for incineration, the villa of the commandant, and the administrative headquarters of all the concentration camps in Europe. In this proposal all three points are reconnected through an altered relationship. Through the displacement of the site and of these three points, a new orientation has been created along the line pointing toward Lübeck, where the infamous Sachsenhausen Death March was to reach its conclusion in the drowning of the victims. This shift no longer allows for the former monumental central axis of the concentration camp, which celebrated the triumph of inhumanity. As a result of this cleavage and difference, the competition site splits into two areas that are treated in two wholly different ways in order to displace the imagery of the past and to reconsecrate the land. ■ One part of the plane is excavated, and the remaining buildings on it are flattened, exposing the foundations and interconnections of the machinery and its brutality. This part is then flooded with water from the adjacent canal, creating a sunken archaeological zone. The newly formed lake refers not only to the slave labor connected to the waters, but also frees the water from its historical role by using it as a new ecological element to restructure the topography of the place. The public walks on elevated walkways and piers in contemplation of the accelerated ruin of these buildings and, at the same time, is able to see this site as a new baptism. ■ The adjacent site is built up from the soil excavated to form the water basin

and is gradually landscaped in an ascending landform. This land buries the remaining fragments of the past and extends the circulation network from the water by tunnelling through and out of the land to the context beyond. The site is heavily planted with the local variety of trees, forms a new physical stratum for vegetation, and provides a natural habitat of an especially intensive kind. Within this wooded sanctuary, there is a clearing that, in a controlled and deliberate manner, structures a future development for this area. ■ I propose for the building and urbanization of the site a program that is responsive to the critical nature of this historical area. I have called this development area the "Hope Incision," because it contains public and private facilities for a new economic, social, and cultural infrastructure. The building program provides space for retraining facilities for the unemployed, for the underemployed, and for the young. There is a dense development of buildings that provide facilities for private computer schools, industrial retraining programs, private service-sector training, as well as offices for physical and mental health clinics and other forms of therapy. Foundations should be invited to sponsor social, cultural, and political societies, which can rent offices and rooms for research and discussion. Space is provided for a library, archive, museum, and an ecumenical chapel. The free space outside of the built area can be used for the development of horticulture. Finally, as a reflection of the need to create and recollect on this particular site, there is a plan for studio space for various disciplines connected to cultural production, such as space for artists, sculptors, dancers, filmmakers, musicians, writers, instrument makers, and so on. ■ This program quite emphatically rejects trivializing the site with any plan for placing housing on it, or otherwise domesticating the site. Rather it suggests a land use that combines an ecological intervention and invention with an economic base for the city of Oranienburg. Its aim is to bring people to this place, to reveal, disclose, and remember. At the same time it must be a place for hope, a place where those who are trying to rebuild Germany can find a workplace, an employment future, the growth of new nature, the quietude of contemplation, the rehabilitation of the physical and mental spirit: the dawn of a new Mourning. . . . ■

cussions, some of the historians began to see not only the practical problems of reconstructing these nasty buildings, but also the ludicrous nature of trying to use them as office buildings or schools. These Nazi buildings are not good spaces to be in; they are not buildings that would uplift a student while studying in them. ● Well, I think we have come to a compromise, and I agreed that some of the buildings could remain and be made visible and used in a way that is consciously public and within a cultural domain. We have agreed that buildings that would simply be simulations of an unreality should be understood in a new relationship to the landscape and history. For of course, one is very much part of what happened not only yesterday, but what is happening today, and what will happen tomorrow. ● I think there is a history of the invisible, which has been made visible in practical and economic ways. Architecture has a more important task than simply to solve banal problems and reduce discourse to the pragmatic, which is very often the case today. Architecture should embody the invisible, the hopes and dreams in something we live in, we die in, and we remember. ●

IDEAL CITY OF DEATH

TOPOGRAPHY OF HISTORY

PARTITION

ERASED SHIFT

DEATH MARCH

WATEROP'S LANDOP'S

VISIBLE INVISIBLE

WATER CONTROL

INCISION

Museum Without Exit *Felix Nussbaum Haus, Osnabrück,*

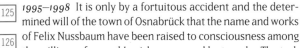

1995–1998 It is only by a fortuitous accident and the determined will of the town of Osnabrück that the name and works of Felix Nussbaum have been raised to consciousness among the millions of erased Jewish names and lost works. The task of building a museum to house the artistic remnants of Nussbaum's life raises issues that are not merely architectural, but are indeed moral. I believe, therefore, that the destruction of Jewish culture perpetuated by the Third Reich must not be dealt with solely in memorial terms. The remaining witnesses to the annihilation of European Jewry are now dying out. The paintings of Nussbaum are more than paintings—they are ever-living documents that, placed in a new context of participation and a new witnessing, elevate the narration of history as art into the emblem of the very survival of the Jewish people and of European civilization. Every element of the spatial organization, geometry, and programmatic content of this scheme refers to the paradigmatic destiny of Nussbaum: his prize in Rome removed by the Nazis; the time in Berlin; the consequences of his permanent exile from Osnabrück; the futility of escape routes through France and Belgium; to his final deportation and murder in Auschwitz. And yet all this tragic destiny is placed in the context of Nussbaum's abiding hope in ultimate justice, which this proposed scheme seeks to fulfill. ■ It is part of the mission of this design to house the Nussbaum collection in a new museum complex, as well as to transform the entire historical ensemble of buildings into yet another whole. Expressive of permanent absence, the Museum of the Unwitnessed and Unfulfilled is a museum resonant of both the fatality as well as the significance of the unrepresentable abyss of the Holocaust. The museum has a particular task to avoid a sentimental moment in order to thematize the existing histori-

cal context of Osnabrück through the disclosure of new cultural values. The different components of the new complex are seen as connecting and composing an integral structure, while exposing a permanent horizon of disconnection that paradoxically links significant places to the town, substantial points of history to spatial memory. The new building, therefore, does not seek to dominate as a new form, but rather retreats to form a background of hope for the existing Historical Museum and the villa containing the folk art collection. These buildings are treated as the familiar, yet solitary, everyday figures, while the entire site is reorganized around the nexus of a new topography that connects the town back onto itself. The Nussbaum Museum becomes the link to a lost history. It acts as a transformer transmitting the mysterious irreversibility of time and destiny. ■ The visitor enters laterally into the Nussbaum Pathway, which is cut open in order to record and define the importance of entering "The Museum without Exit." The exterior of the Nussbaum Pathway is absence itself—an empty canvas of Nussbaum's martyred life—referring to the absoluteness of the crime and the importance of the public site: bequeathing a sense of openness and incompleteness, which is necessary for the interpretation of Nussbaum's oeuvre. Within the Nussbaum Pathway are traces of the vitality of the former

Museum Without Exit *Felix Nussbaum Haus, Osnabrück, 1995–1998* The Felix Nussbaum Haus in Osnabrück is about individual memory, about the singular. The museum is about the placing and displacing of memory. In a site that is very familiar to the town and its history, such a museum stands against forgetting. ◎ The memory of Felix Nussbaum is tied on every level to a specific human being and human discourse. The museum is the retracing of the fatal elements and dead ends of Nussbaum's life. It is a projection and accessibility to those dead ends

as a way of orienting and re-orienting ourselves in the space of the museum and of that history. This architecture opens the space to his paintings, to his experience of what the Shoah meant—without abstraction, without the statistics of six million, but of one human being murdered six million times. ◎ Taking a walk through the museum, through a particular set of blank walls, narrow spaces, and dead ends, the visitor is made aware of the unpaintable—the eternal identity of difference and closure of possibilities. The museum is part of an attempt to transform the idea of chronology—to move away from the idea that one can retrace life by moving backward or forward or in a system. Rather it exposes the explosion of that life, the dissemination, that which

is not there. ◎ The museum is constructed as a set of physical spaces that interlock, the irreconcilable "time zones." Through this simple structure I show the impossibility of dividing the pre-Holocaust works from the last works, those which are continually on the verge of being labeled historical documents, yet do not relinquish their contribution to the world of art because they retain the possibility of hope. ◎ Yes, the Nussbaum Museum is resistant to the notion that the museum is for the one, but not the other: It rebels against the idea that a museum is appearance, stasis, or icon rather than substance and dynamic. It was my intention that the museum open a reality that deliberately conflicts with the mythical personification of a biography. The museum shows that this particular biography is vulnerable, and in order to hold it together one has to create a space of encounter that does not reduce it to an object, but maintains it in the tension of a history that is not over. ●

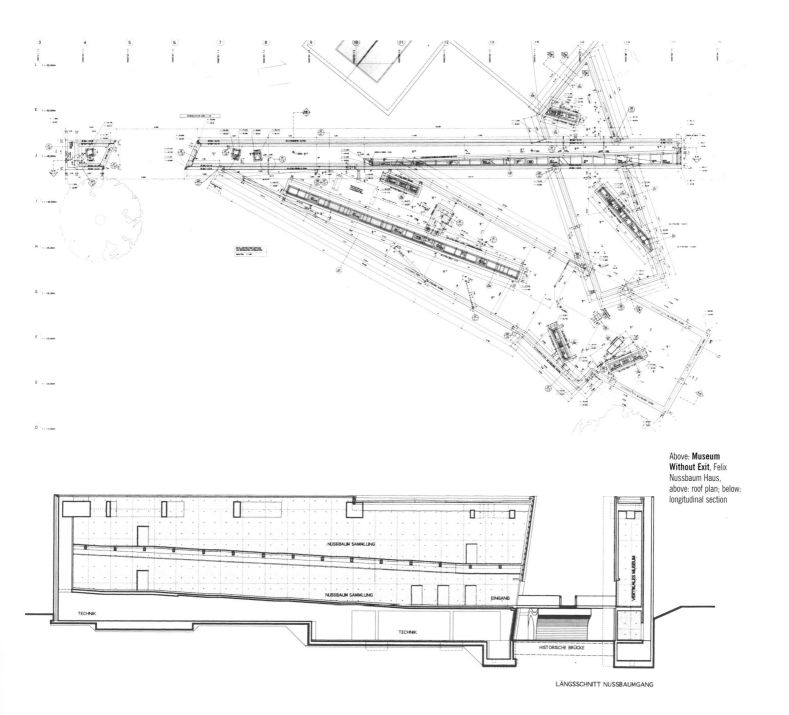

Above: **Museum Without Exit**, Felix Nussbaum Haus, above: roof plan; below: longitudinal section

LÄNGSSCHNITT NUSSBAUMGANG

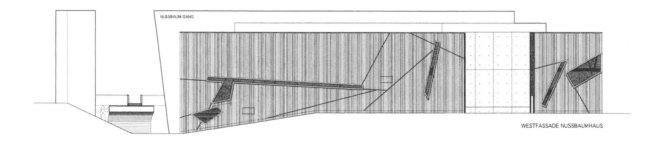

WESTFASSADE NUSSBAUMHAUS

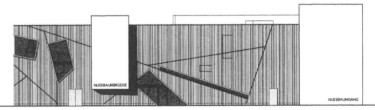

OSTFASSADE NUSSBAUMHAUS

Jewish life of Osnabrück. Once the visitor is inside this compressed space, which is illuminated by triangular skylights, he/she is confronted with a displaced volume containing the vertical entrance volume and its attendant functions. ■ The Nussbaum Pathway makes visible the museum complex as well as inscribing the invisible incinerated synagogue. The visitor is placed in the precarious equilibrium between the collected and the uncollectable; the recollected and the unrecordable. The Nussbaum Pathway leads the visitor through the compressed geometry of the double cone of vision, which (forward and backward in time) giving the visual and kinetic embodiment of the Star of David, which Nussbaum chose as his final identifying birth- and deathmark. ■ The entire trajectory through the museum makes the visitor

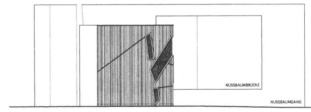

SÜDFASSADE NUSSBAUMHAUS

Museum Without Exit,
Felix Nussbaum Haus,
elevations

aware of the interplay between the lost shadows of the synagogue and the light of an anticipated future. The visitor moves toward the open space of the temporary exhibitions, glimpsing the narrow vertical horizon that opens at the completion of the route into the second-story connection. The temporary exhibitions of the town with the lecture hall and the activities of the day make a relevant introduction to the second level, which contains the necessary space for the unfolding of Nussbaum's dramatic work. The design suggests the importance of integrating the historical collections of Osnabrück, at least emblematically, into the context of the work of Nussbaum in order to place the Nussbaum collection back in context with the Historical Museum's collection. ■ At the completion of the second-floor exhibits, the visitor becomes aware of the col-

lapsed spatiality of Nussbaum's works, the pathos of which lies in the double recognition of the political futility of escape and the spiritual resistance of art in the face of inhuman oppression. The second floor's unfinishable gallery is a time-cut, which signifies the oblique and wrenched segment, a suspended connection to the existing museum. This suspension indicates the finality of the 1944 paintings, testifying to the indomitable spirit of Nussbaum and the universality of art. The volume of this critical segment is equal and reciprocal to the geometry of the cut and disconnected Nussbaum Museum. ■ The floating connection to the existing museum leads to an exhibition area that suggests transformations of part of the second floor of the city's Historical Museum. The scheme indicates the necessity of integrating the new and the old beyond appearances; the actual connection between the historical and aesthetic. The integration of the existing and the new museum is the key task that must be accomplished so that the memory of the past becomes active in the present and its ongoing narration. ■ Thus, the key structural feature of the plan suggests that the Nussbaum Museum, though separated from both the existing museum buildings, is, by virtue of its form and function, profoundly related to them. The Folk Art Museum, which in 1933 was the headquarters of the Nazi party, and the main Historical Museum are reattached and absorbed in a conscious and deliberate manner to the polyphonic composition. The whole represents an architectural hinge that prevents the entire site from banalizing, homogenizing, and isolating historical facts. The visitor becomes aware that the work of Nussbaum, and particularly its relationship to the cultural, historical, and physical identity of Osnabrück, requires extraordinary spiritual differentiation. Thus, the import of public space (both internal and external) and the relation between the ecosystem and the architecture is clear. ■ The Nussbaum Museum becomes a profound place for the encounter of the future and the past and not merely a testament to an impossible fate. The unpainted paintings of Felix Nussbaum demand nothing less than to become visible to the contemplating eye. ■

Museum Without Exit *Project Description, 1995*

When I won the competition to build the Felix Nussbaum Haus in 1995, I knew only a little of the life of this famous son of Osnabrück: a human being, a well-known painter in his time, but also an emblematic figure representing vitality and success, and the erasure of culture and continuity and the destruction of history in the extermination known as the Shoah. I have had the possibility over the course of the past three years to delve deeper into the uniqueness of Felix Nussbaum, and have sought to incorporate in the architecture of this museum the deep humanity, the lasting vision, the profound significance of Nussbaum and all he stood for. I took it as a supreme challenge to present the biographical and historical displacement of this man, and indeed of the city of Osnabrück, as it moves from the past to the present and into its own future.

How then does one deal with the life and death of a human being? How does one express architecturally the aspirations, the realities, the despairs of a Jewish painter from Osnabrück in those years ending in tragedy? One enters the museum through a concrete wall with a compression and fragmentation of spaces, to the inner side of the gigantic activating blankness. The museum is designed and constructed in three volumes. The first is a wooden building aligned with, and in a very special relationship to, the old synagogue on Rolandstrasse, one of the synagogues of northern Germany, burned on Kristallnacht. Within the Nussbaum Haus, there is the gallery space of the Nussbaum Sammlung for permanent collections, the mezzanine level for graphic works and documentation, and the large gallery space for temporary exhibitions. The specific period of

Museum Without Exit *Lecture, 1995*

Berlin, by the way, is not the only city which has a lack of memory. I remember how shocked I was when I lived in Israel as a child (after we emigrated from Poland), that when we spoke Yiddish on the streets of Tel Aviv—this was in the late 1950s—somebody would say, "Shhh! **We are Israelis, this is a new place, this is not Poland. You are in another place now**." I felt how difficult it was for us as immigrants to make another leap across a desert. The relationship between Berlin, Israel, New York, and other places—the radiation of events, of their "afterlife," of trauma, is not something that can be manipulated with ease in any ideological setting. ◎ With this in mind, I would like to refer to a project, another competition which I was fortunate to win and that is fully installed and open to the public now. It is a museum for a small city in western Germany, Osnabrück, near the Dutch border. The project is for a building which is

devoted to the works of a particular citizen of Osnabrück, Felix Nussbaum, a well-known painter of that city and of that time. He was a very important painter who studied and painted in Berlin, received the Prix de Rome, a successful artist in Europe. As of 1933 he lived another life. He was a fugitive in Germany and was chased across Europe by the Nazis. He always thought he would win out, he was an optimist. In his self-portraits he depicts himself as a survivor who will somehow tell the story. But he was unfortunately, tragically deported on one of the last trains from Brussels to Auschwitz and exterminated. ◎ The city of Osnabrück found out about his paintings and got them back and then made a commitment to build a museum for these works. The program of the museum was to connect these paintings with the other historical buildings on the site: the "Kunsthistorisches Museum" and the "Schlikker'sche Villa" which now houses archaeological artifacts and folk art. Osnabrück

itself is on very ancient and historical foundations, and is a very important Catholic city in Germany. Felix Nussbaum was a painter whose works and life were virtually unknown until the last few years. He was almost successfully eliminated from history. In the 1987 edition of the *Jewish Encyclopedia*, Felix Nussbaum is not even mentioned. The discovery of his works is a very recent phenomena. Only in the late '80s and early '90s did people begin to see that this oeuvre of work was significant and emblematic of all those who had been annihilated, together with the places of memory and the witnesses. ◎ So, Nussbaum is not only a painter but a creator of meaningful work. How to represent him? I represent him in a very simple way with three volumes. The first is a very traditional wooden building which stands on the site in a very special relationship to the old synagogue on Rolandstrasse which was burned in 1938. I made a kind of traditional wooden building for about three hundred works painted in the 1920s and early '30s. That wooden space is violently cut by a dramatic volume standing 11 meters high, 50 meters long: the Nussbaum Gang. It is only 2 meters in width, the narrowest volume which can be built as a public space under German regulations. It is made of concrete, has no windows of any sort. And there I proposed to show the works of Nussbaum created in his race through Europe. Whilst a fugitive he lived in tiny rooms and painted in very close quarters. He could not stand back from the works to look at them. He painted in secret in a kind of delirium of a historical notion of art. These paintings and drawings, sometimes created only inches away, have only been viewed close up, never from some aesthetic distancing. So I proposed to exhibit them in this narrow volume and the city and museum director accepted that there should be a space in which these particular paintings could be seen in a different kind of public space. ◎ One enters the wooden building, the Nussbaum Haus, with the prewar paintings and then one goes through the narrow space of the concrete walls, the Nussbaum Gang, in order to get to what I have called the Nussbaum Brücke, a metal building, the third volume. This building is a connector housing the newly discovered paintings of Nussbaum, a collection which will continue to be discovered one by one. Let me add that during the last years of the war Nussbaum's signature was erased from most of his paintings and resold as anonymous paintings. ◎ The new museum is a gigantic empty wall, but it is also a very dense, sometimes claustrophobic and sometimes very traditional idea of culture and public space in Osnabrück as it moves from the past to the present and into its own future. Again, it is my belief that it is very important to reincorporate the experience of history and of the city into architecture not only in the intellectual sense, but on all levels. There is a collision of materiality and scale: the complete blankness of concrete colliding with the articulateness of wood, passing through the tubular nature of steel—the matrix upon which the museum stands. The museum is designed as a topographical site in which one would stand on irreconcilable pieces of land: one facing Hamburg, one facing Berlin, one facing Rome, one facing the concentration camps he hoped to escape from, back through the Benelux, through Amsterdam, back to Belgium, and finally to Auschwitz. ◎ I have tried to represent that destiny and make it available as an experience to people who fortunately never had to face and re-face their lives in such a context as Nussbaum. I tried not to be sentimental about Nussbaum. But one could really look into those days and see a message which is like the message lost in a bottle and coincidentally found somewhere. Who can possibly know what that message is and what can be passed on: what statement, which code? I thought that one should pass on everything in that message, including the darkness, the inarticulateness, the opacity, and that which cannot become analysis. ●

Felix Nussbaum's oeuvre are the works painted in the 1920s and '30s, prior to the Nazi period. These paintings represent a life of cultural normalcy: family portraits, tranquil landscapes, Jewish holidays.

The Nussbaum Haus is cut violently by a dramatic 11-meter-high, 2-meter-wide, 70-meter-long concrete volume—a narrow volume of space that communicates the closure of his city and country. There are two ascending floors in the Nussbaum Gang lit from above with a narrowing diagonal skylight. Within this volume, which is dimly lit, are the works Felix Nussbaum painted as a fugitive exiled from his homeland and forced to escape from cities, holding stations, concentration camps, finally hiding in a small attic in Brussels. These paintings, produced under these inhuman circumstances, are not only art, but also a document of the deepest spiritual significance. They have an extraordinary impact and are placed within a space that does not allow for aesthetic distancing, but rather allows for a context that communicates the claustrophobic and dimming environment in which they were painted.

Finally, unifying the Nussbaum Haus and the Nussbaum Gang is a metal building, the Nussbaum Brucke, suspended above ground and connected to the existing Kulturgeschichtliches Museum. This "bridge building" houses the recently discovered paintings of Nussbaum, works from which even the signature of Nussbaum had been erased. The gallery spaces are on two levels opening from the Gang. The Nussbaum Brücke brings the past into the future, spanning the gaps and hollows traced by the two other building volumes. It physically reconnects Nussbaum to the Kulturgeschichtliches Museum. The Nussbaum Museum incorporates not only the spirit of Felix Nussbaum, but also the physical and kinetic enclosure to the fragmented, broken, cut, light dark world of Felix Nussbaum, the Jew, the painter, the Osnabrücker, the citizen of Germany and Europe.

The entire matrix on which the museum stands is seen as a gigantic, incomplete canvas in the figure of absence. Here lie the irreconcilable lines of Nussbaum's history, delineated through the geometry and topography of the building traces facing Rome, Alassio, Ostende, Brussels, Berlin, Saint Cyprien, Brussels, Mechelen, Auschwitz, Berlin—all radiating from Osnabrück. This museum structures the contribution of paintings of Felix Nussbaum and illuminates his Jewish spirit and singular destiny. It is not about an abstract statistic of six million Jews who were murdered in Europe. It is about a singular and irreplaceable individual whose life went from light to darkness, from transparency to opacity, from canvas to ash, and whose fate offers a deep insight into memory and that which comes to light again with a new hope. ■

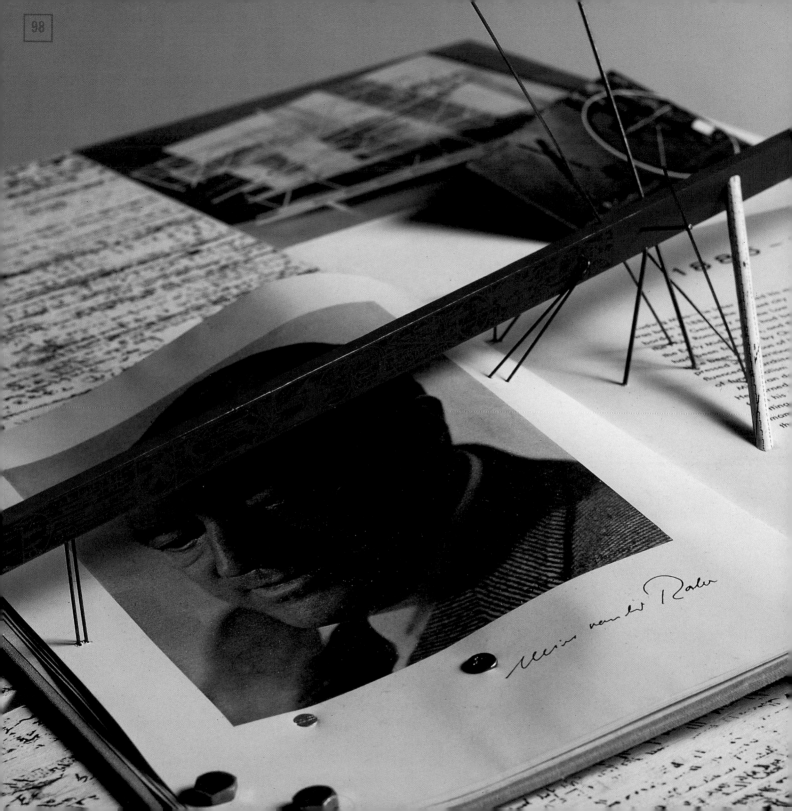

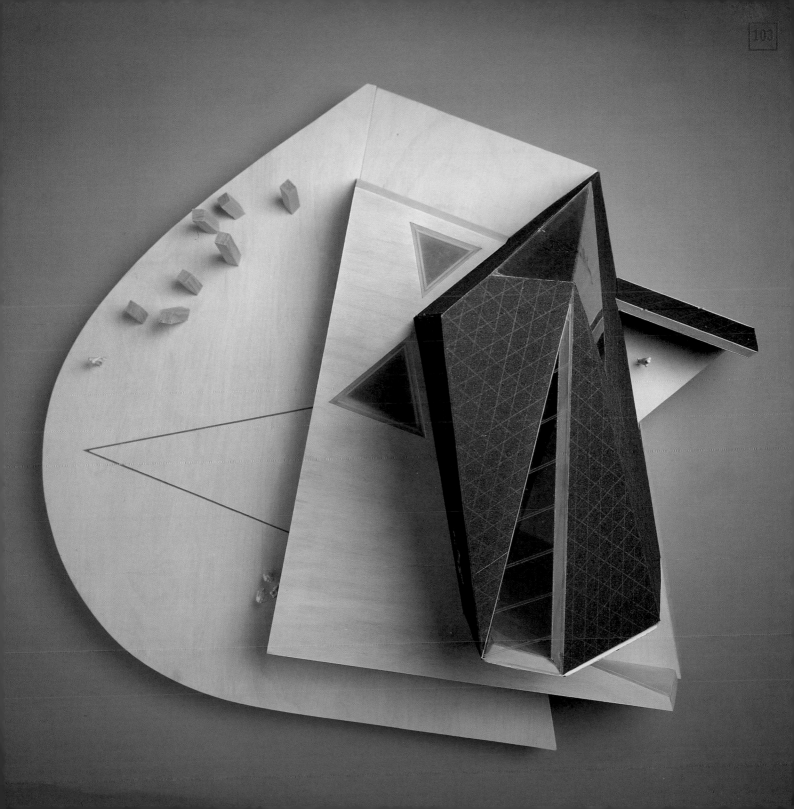

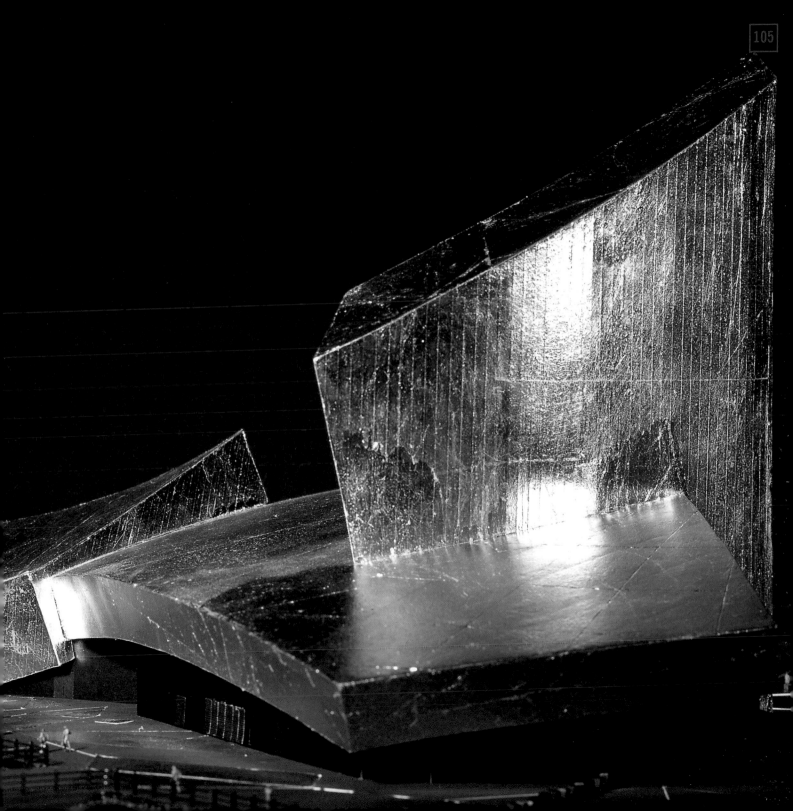

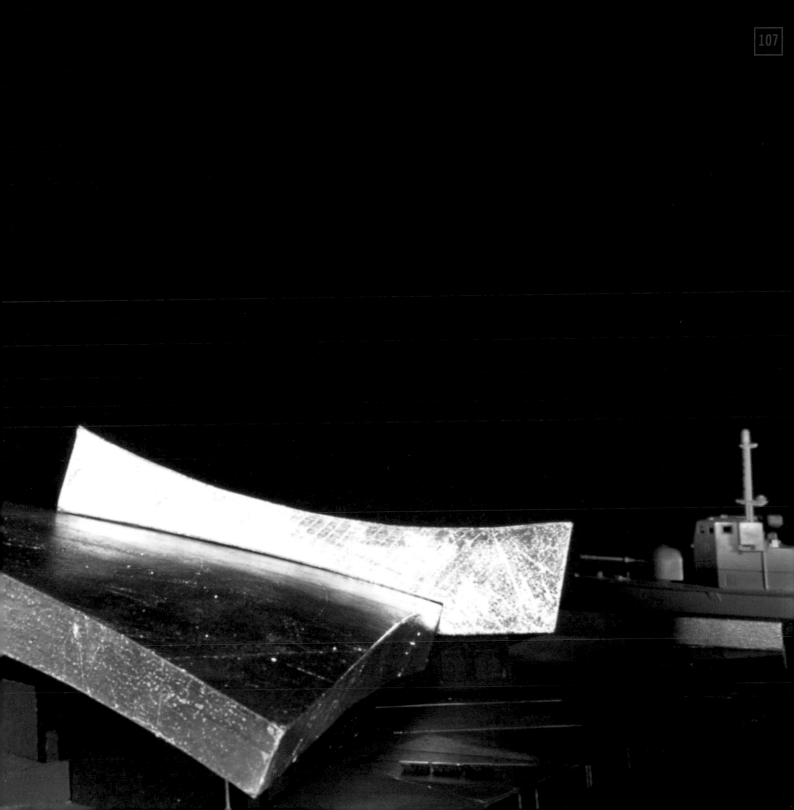

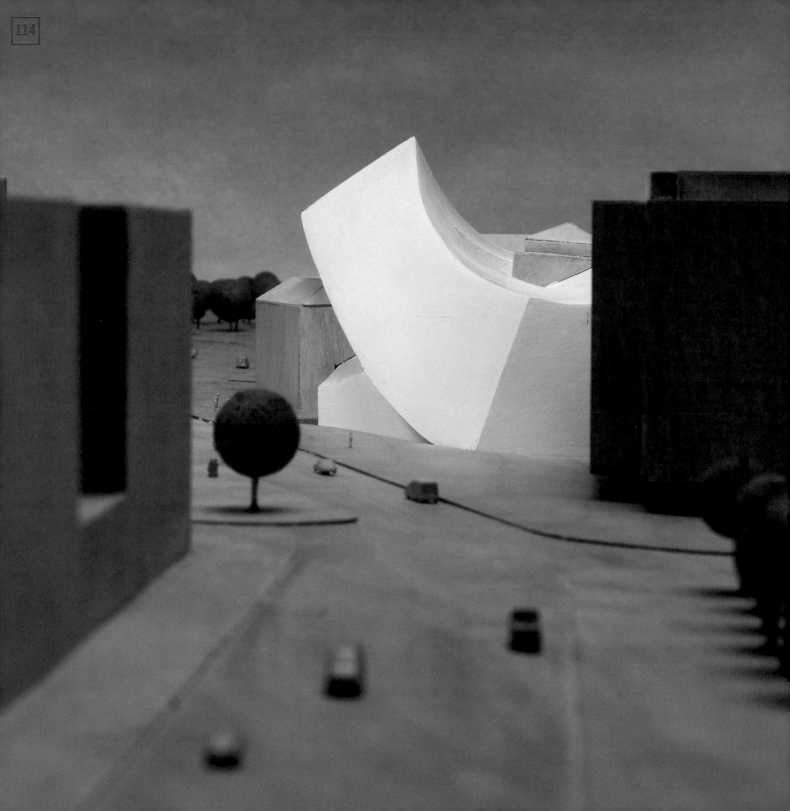

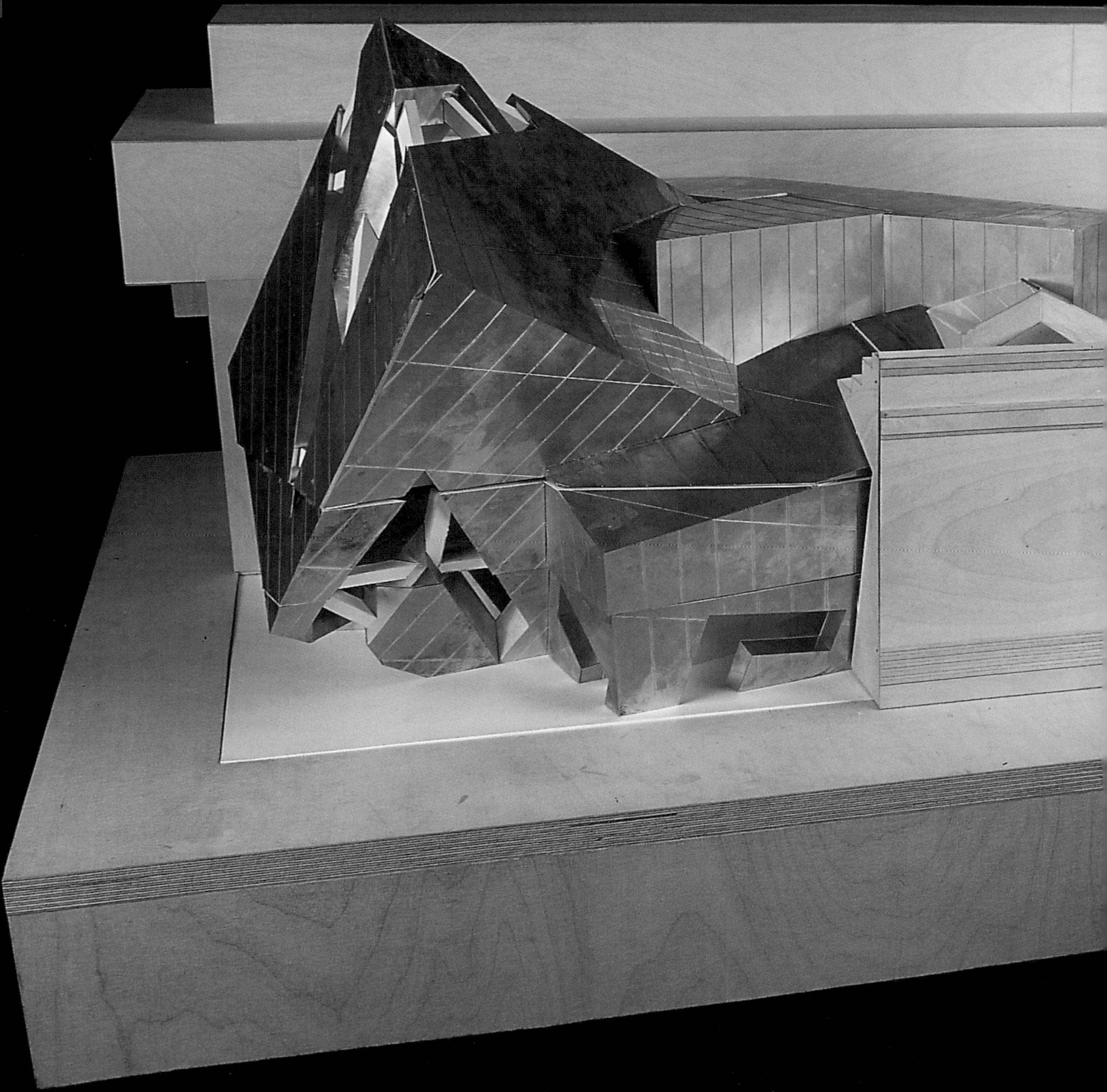

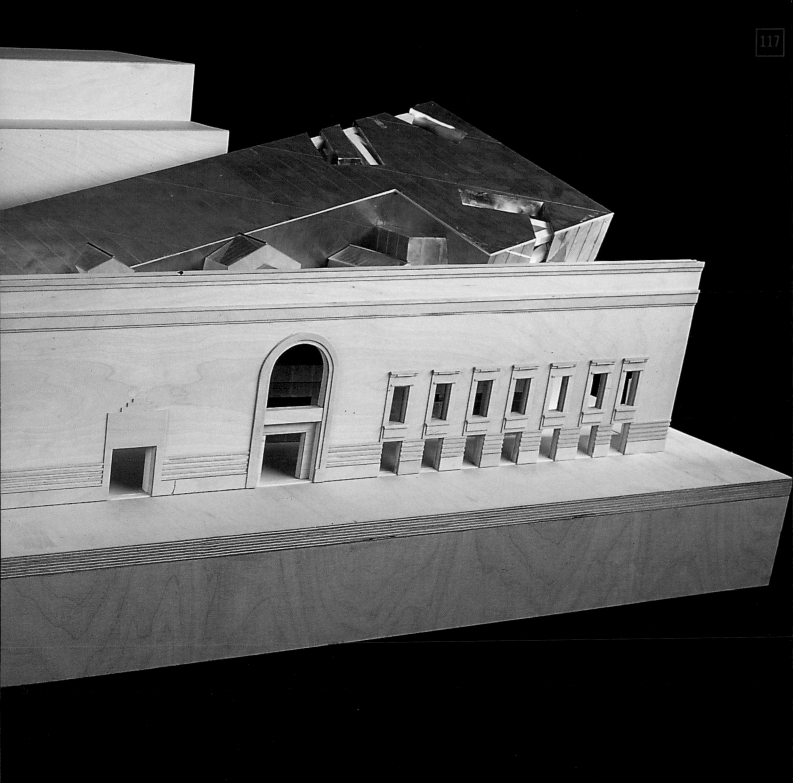

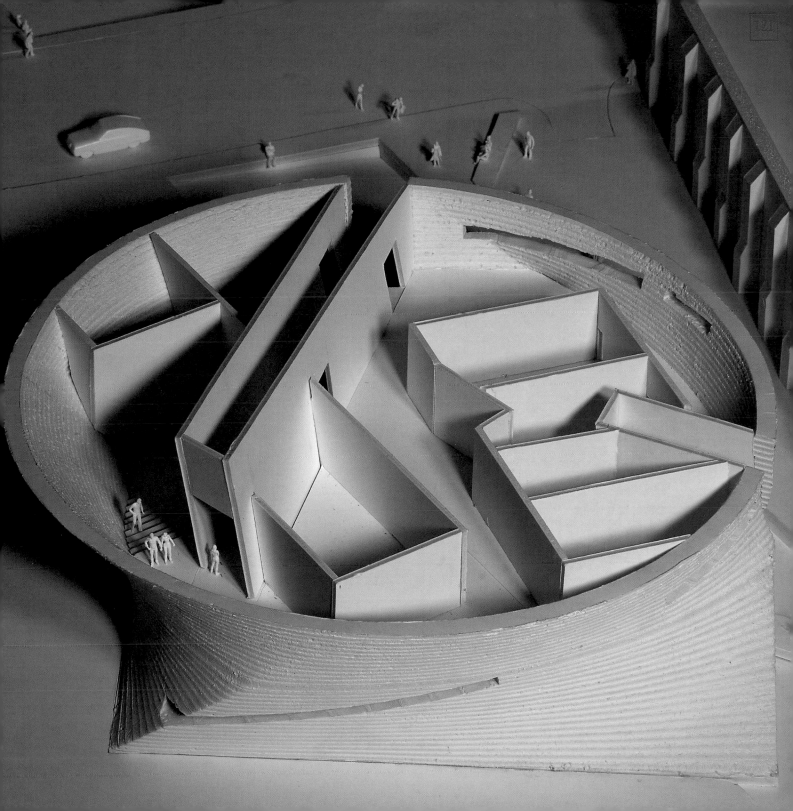

Musical Intersections

Concert hall, Bremen, Germany, 1995–present It is a great challenge to build a major regional music center in a historically sensitive context. This challenge, multiplied by the necessity of responding to new cultural trends of performance, audience participation, and urban revitalization, makes the Musicon Bremen a project of prime significance. But these two factors have to be seen in a new ecological response between the use of the building and the rhythm of the city. ■ By providing dynamic and flexible public spaces both inside and outside, the Musicon Bremen—a new idea of musical/urban/ecological space—responds to the fundamental charge to create a new and significant urban space and a major concert hall for Bremen adequate to the overture of the twenty-first century. A participatory space is created that has a wide variety of uses, multiple relations, and flexible adaptations, offering a vision of the integration of musical culture, urban life, and the natural environment. This project seeks to create a new place for leisure and relaxation, stimulation, culture, and urbanity for Bremen. **Urban Strategy:** The siting and geometric configuration of Musicon Bremen is determined by an organic relation of the function of the building in a strategically important urban site that is both built and natural. ■ The urban-design strategy seeks to configure the external and internal spaces of the Musicon Bremen by freeing the building toward important ecological concepts, such as minimizing the building footprint, making a strong connection between nature and pedestrian movement; extending areas associated with the park both on the ground plane and within the green connector; taking advantage of the sun, water, and earth in contact with the performance of public space. ■ It is important to integrate the building into the fabric of

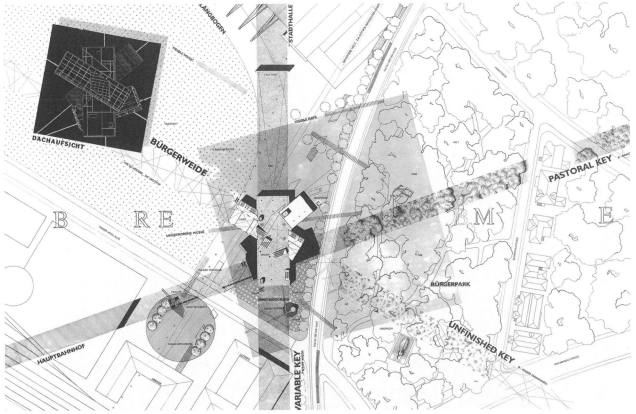

Musicon Bremen, site plan

Bremen by avoiding the all-too-frequent and negative disconnection and destruction of urban spaces at the ground level that such large spaces command. The success of building Musicon Bremen does not depend merely on a discrete public building, but on the reinterpretation of invisible, eroded, and ever-present lines of communication connecting both the city of Bremen and northern Europe. **Urban Design:** Musicon Bremen is an urban fulcrum responding to the twenty-four-hour pulse of the city. It is conceived as an open urban matrix that brings together different and historically heterogeneous areas of Bremen into a vital and imaginative whole. The site is created by the permeability of passage and access of both implied and existing places and promenades that exist between the four elements: Bürgerpark (east), the railway station (south), Bürgerweide (west), and the Stadthalle and park (north). In this way, the entire building becomes an urban foyer that extends and reinvents the image of Bremen. ■ The siting emphatically reestablishes the importance of the northern side of the railway station by transforming this vague zone of the city into an area that is balanced and corresponds to the historical city of Bremen. The importance of reconstituting the long-eroded historical developments along the virtual north-south vector is a key of the reintegration of the railway station, Stadtwald, the Bürgerpark, Stadthalle, and the Bürgerweide into a rich and multidimensional field for the people of Bremen. ■ To harness the energy of the human scale and of ecology, the project establishes the importance of pedestrian circulation, the importance of places and their openness, and music as a whole. Musicon Bremen becomes the cornerstone articulating different spatial sectors, becoming a permeable gateway that connects pedestrian space along an uninterrupted horizontal plane. **Open Space:** Open space extends the park zone toward the station on one side and the university on the other by the creation of a yin-yang field between the parabola of the Klangbogen and the parabola of the Gustav Deetjen Allee. This area, bracketed diagonally, by Musicon Bremen and the Stadthalle and orthogonally by the station and the Park Hotel with its water pool, is activated by a series of small-scale interventions, including new green areas, the unsealing of the presently sealed ground, walkways, promenades, a pavilion, bicycle paths, a fountain, and a children's play area. The texture of these accents connects the pedestrian and tram movement from the city with the activity of the Bürgerpark, the Bürgerweide, and the Hauptbahnhof by making visible the variable musical keys of Bremen. ■ There is a strong corner established by Gustav Deetjen Allee and Theodore Heuss Allee on the southeastern side. The building opens toward the recently completed arcade building to the south, and signifies a welcoming zone to passengers arriving by the railway to the music hall and to the beautiful parks lying to the north and the northeast. This strong corner is a reception zone along the important route of Gustav Deetjen Allee. The building opens toward the recently completed arcade building to the south and signifies a welcoming zone to passengers arriving by the railway not only to the music hall but to the beautiful parks lying to the north and the northeast. To the west, a connection is made between the Musicon Bremen and the Bürgerweide by addressing the nature of open space and the events that have

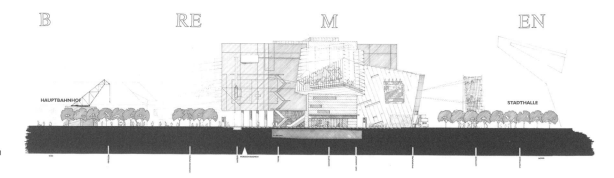

Musicon Bremen, section

traditionally taken place there. To the northwest, a connection is made to the Stadthalle and the park by creating a correspondence and an intensification of activities between these two zones. ▪ In summary, the urban design reintegrates contradictory functional areas of the city (station and park, public and private, new and old) by weaving gently through the warp and woof of Bremen. **Circulation and Connections:** The entire circulation system is a continuous diffusion of public space toward the discrete and specific spaces of performance. ▪ Musicon Bremen is structured by an open ground plane with multiple entrances and identifiable public spaces in order to make the building fully accessible, visible, and transparent to the public. The intermediate vertical level continues the ground plane through the organization of lobbies, bookshops, children's spaces, exhibition spaces, musicians' spaces, recital hall, and the floating green bar with its restaurant. On the upper level, one finds the auditorium and its related functions. **Concept of Performance:** Spatial and functional requirements are organized for heterogeneous, simultaneous, and variable performances and audiences, focusing on the centrality of the stage and the ease and speed of servicing it. The Musicon Bremen is configured to respond to its specific functional program by providing seating for an audience of 2,500 people for classical performances, and 3,200 persons in a standing/seating configuration. A number of alternative, and traditionally low-tech solutions for the transformations of seating and use configurations are possible. The Musicon Bremen is open to a number of future transformations of musical uses by relying on the stability of established functional and acoustical principles. **Construction, Materials, and Realization:** The building is low-tech (traditional, flexible seating systems), with energy-saving dimensions. The building materials are inexpensive materials of Bremen, which include lightweight cladding, local stone, and economical finishes. The intention is to create a building for all people that has a tactile and colorful quality in external and internal finishes. There is no glazing associated with the building as such. Only the green bar allows a dramatic movement of light, which plays an essential part in the creation of an "ecological garden" (green lobby). ▪ The large,

unopened areas of the facade are to be articulated with strong geometric and material compositions. These facades are newly envisioned through the projection of images, as well as by the imprints referring to the history and music of Bremen. The multifaceted interior responds to the most advanced research in acoustics, while the exterior refers to the clear dynamics of the city of Bremen. ▪ The concert hall can provide unusually responsive acoustics for the performance of classical music. It is able to offer other functional arrangements for musical events that range from modern music through rock music, dance, lectures, and sporting and theatrical events. The particular spatial and tectonic form of the building captures the musical events in spaces of intimacy and difference by creating a close rapport between the identity of each seating arrangement and its particular stage. It is an alternative to the banal boxes that thematize technology and speed rather than the magic and specific spatial form of each performance. **Functional Sectors:** The entire building is coherently held together through public activities such as box offices, boutiques, city information offices, retail spaces, workshops, cafés, and the diagonal green lobby. The green bar (which has the future possibility to be connected and extended) is an essential spatial and ecological unit connecting the horizontal and vertical functions of the building. ▪ An important dimension of this project is the dissemination of public lobbies in such a manner that groups of different intensity, size, and function can find the appropriate building scale that defines them. These lobbies are indeed extensions and mediations of both performance and public space. ▪ Retail facilities, workshops, and administration offices have independent entrances while tying to the life of the building as a whole. ▪ The musicians' entrance and parking form a separate "world within a world," with their own internal circulation independent of the public spaces. ▪ The depots, workrooms, and delivery spaces are separated from the main public spaces while contributing, through their visibility (elevators, hoisting mechanisms, work), to the overall festivity of events. ▪ The varying elements of function (B-A-C-H) constitute a fugal counterpoint to the monolithic seating of almost 3,000 persons in each performance. ▪

Nexus

Denver Art Museum, Denver, Colorado, 2000 In Michelangelo's Birth of Adam, the outstretched fingers create an incredible density of space that provides a connection by infusing life into the individual members. This is the ambition of Nexus, the proposal for the new wing of the Denver Art Museum. ■ The fundamental urban issue is to position the new extension of the Denver Art Museum as a key generator of urban life in the heart of Denver. This design offers Nexus as a primary gateway between the downtown and the Golden Triangle neighborhood, flanked symmetrically by the existing Denver Art Museum and public library. Nexus creates a public and pedestrian marker signifying that art, architecture, and the urban experience are choreographed as a single whole without losing individual identity. ■ To intensify pedestrian life in the civic center complex, we are proposing an urban art experience. This public ground garden connects the northern entrance of the cultural complex into the depth of the Avenue of the Arts. The urban art experience designates and signifies the importance of the new museum as a destination building. The lobbies of the Nexus are positioned on the southern boundary of the site, allowing the scheme to integrate the museum into the Golden Triangle neighborhood and form a transitional zone in scale and Character, bringing commercial shops and activity deep into the neighborhood. In this way, the double demand of a new museum identity on the northern side and neighborhood life on the southern side is accomplished. This urban configuration pays special attention to the large partner buildings and gives them their appropriate breathing space. ■ A double gateway is created in both the North–South and East–West direction, forming a chiasm of urban space. The form of the building counterposes a lateral horizontal movement to the tower-like massing of the Ponti building. The Nexus minimizes its footprint by elevating a large part of its program thus opening the urban art experience on the ground level. This spatial ensemble makes it possible for public spaces to penetrate not only the horizontal but also the vertical and oblique. This strategy allows for a balance in the entire complex by providing a light and floating form to contrast with the castlelike solidity of the Ponti building. ■ The building is based on

America, you are luckier than this old continent of ours; you have no ruined castles.

—Johann Wolfgang von Goethe

Nexus, sections

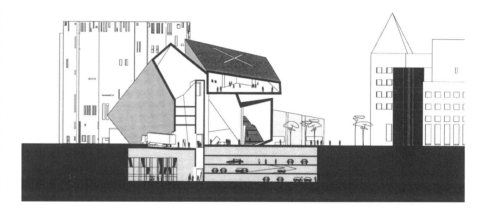

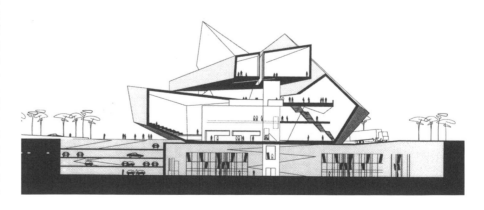

the intertwining of two spatial circuits and articulates two materials, one traditional from Denver
and one more contemporary which are united in
the Nexus. The groundlines will relate to local
Colorado stone and pick up existing relationships
to the library. The dramatic skyline will be built
of titanium panels, glowing as it ascends to the
sky. The two materials will fuse in the massing of
Nexus with the various volumes intertwining not
only in space but in materiality. The titanium skyline will gradually and subtly transform from
opacity through translucency to transparency,
with cascades of glazing bringing natural light
where required. The mass of the building dissolves at the contoured glass tip, becoming a beacon across space. ■

Nexus, watercolor sketch

Nouvelles Impressions d'Architecture _Notes for a lecture,_
_1997,_ from Daniel Libeskind, _Line of Fire_ (Milan: Electa Spa, 1998)

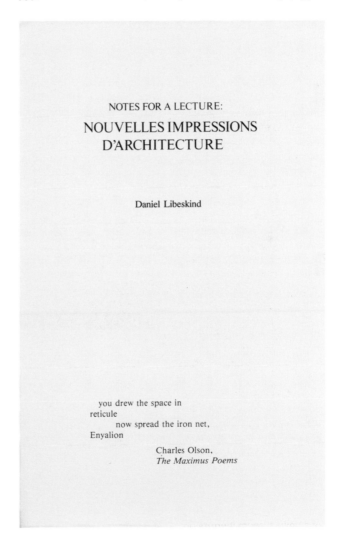

NOTES FOR A LECTURE:

NOUVELLES IMPRESSIONS
D'ARCHITECTURE

Daniel Libeskind

you drew the space in
reticule
    now spread the iron net,
Enyalion

Charles Olson,
The Maximus Poems

No longer can one find Architecture in a pre-existent state, after the manner of techno-physical space. The former unfolds itself, lubricated by a substance that neither acid nor water will dissolve, only through the dominion of densities. These compact resistors are hardly ingestible by that 'widest open of all mouths which is Space' (Malcom de Chazal).

In being drawn to 'places' (loci which are inflected according to the caresses of contingency), Architecture is charged by waves emitted from these densities: wireless micro-stations which send signals uniquely disposed to determine the *spiritual space* revealed by the removal of objective carcasses.

Enough to take away the object to see that the trace lingers, like an elongated shadow, in its place. The emptied locale floods the consciousness and strikes at the husk of memory. Thus drawn by an experience of spaceless-place, a realm opens which is not visualizable, a region of invisible presence that refuses to be occupied by anything.

Released from the dictatorship of proletarian thoughts, space oozes out into a nebula that has no connection with any astral deity. There it undergoes its death with a dignity once accorded to alchemical transformations. No longer seen, because now incarnated and belonging to the eye itself, space becomes a clot localized and diagnosable within the embolism of carnal traumas. In the disguise of 'place' it looks back at us with the gaze of a melancholic — having sacrificed its suicide to an afterlife in which none are possible.

When Architecture no longer deals with Space, all transactions, in which the container and the contained twisted together — whether the ecstasy of space was that of birth or death or form — have come to an end. Only a phosphorescent glow reminds one that the two-dimensional contour one is pursuing is that of his own eyes.

The supple distance between the eyes, a third dimension of craft, is sufficient to prevent the collapse of a crystalline domain, which drawing too protects. Participating together in an organic complicity between two kinds of elisions, something gratuitous and free comes to the fore. One could call it the Undecided Flesh (of Architecture). A possibility emerges for Architecture to escape from its 'cage' precisely because it is 'absent' from itself, like the subconscious released to float in the air through the mortification of the body. Today Architecture's truth is not dependent on its embodiment. The vacant 'eye' of space — blind or dormant, who is to say? — has drained the Angel of Light of his glow; how strange that his dazzle could offer itself so meekly!

Can Architecture come to a 'free-hold' on dwelling? Can the receptacle ever again be merged with its contents? Can parallel activities (such as drawing and thinking) intersect in any realm? Nonetheless, today they refuse to intersect because at the imaginary point of contact (a point which is always ahead) one realizes that the 'performance' — in which the distinction between actor and spectator is eradicated owing to the seating arrangements — has already occurred, but *from behind*. Thus the necessity to re-awaken the eyes in the back of the head is not to be looked upon as a concern for Pataphysicians, Madmen or Utopians; rather, this need of 'becoming what one already is' (Heidegger) incinerates apprehension with its forward-looking aims, and reflects it retrogressively on the *derrière* of the retina. Staring intently for so long at the 'sunlight of forms', one has come to see Architecture (is it an after-image?) in the whiteness of its non-forms, in the blackness of its forms.

Architecture remains 'nameless' — for it now seeks to spare dwelling. By refusing to 'deal' with imbeciles at noon, by avoiding the 'kick-backs' of space, by accepting its uselessness in the cataracts of the neo-constructive, Architecture adjusts its concavity to that other concavity we call the Real World. In this double concavity it loses its former spherical voluptuousness and crosses the frontier of colour into the infra-red area associated in the mind with the colour of the sky or with the River Styx. Having 'crossed-over' (Hejduk), the emptiness of Space no longer appears as a deficiency — as a failure to fill the gap between the heart and the stars. Presumably emptiness allies itself with it, forming a new ovule, and through no failure of ours brings to fulfilment a foetus whose resilience is inconceivable in its unmitigated thinness.

Emptiness is not a pure minus — not a deficiency as the idealists thought — but a play of new curvatures, curvatures eternally misadjusted to each other's hollowness. The audibility of Unoriginal Sounds — yet to be heard amidst the cheerful ice crackling around us — projects this immeasurable 'hole' of absence into a megalithic proportion coextensive in size with the head, the hand and the eye. No one can be closer than that to the creator, while dis-remembering his plans for a uni-directional tele-communications centre from which radiate signals that can never be retrieved.

IN(TRO)DUCTION

In the crucifixion of dwelling — irreversible because resolved as space — drawing as an aesthetic is stretched along the axis of past-future: the Alpha and Omega forever at right-angles to the point we call the Great Beyond, and oblique to the present.

The drawing 'system' is sacrificed to a divine discontent precluding the immediate Delivery of the Unhistorical. This *aporia* of the architect, accompanied by his inability to have any emotion left for the 'lebenswelt' — having himself succeeded in eradicating any *Justitia* he had felt for it — is a camouflage of the Noetic. Architecture is *not* consubstantial with Dwelling but only with the garment it displays. This ambiguity may be viewed with equanimity, however:

A. An observer of disorder ('man of marble')
B. A disorder of the observer (aphasia as a mnemonic device)

Resolving mathematically, one computes the following calculation:

If A = B, then a voiceless sound (surd) suggests that *you speak to your drawing as if you were speaking to yourself* (as the drawing speaks to you).

In other words: draw on your drawing while you are drawn upon.

In sum, the element of perfect rigidity is the gyrostat. Everyone is familiar with those square or round copper frames containing a flywheel spinning rapidly around an interior axis.

The remainder of this treatise is wanting:

I shall not consider the actions and passions of men as if they were a matter of lines, surfaces, and volumes. I shall consider these as Spinoza's secret rendezvous with Humanism's ghost: inscribing in the diamond the taste for a one-room house.

Entering the hallway, one is confronted by an architecture of weird and commanding beauty, the baffling intricacy of its fearless design. . . .

At moments of fatigue, however, one no longer looks ahead but laterally, cancelling the depth of the whole by a line that connects the two uprights with a lintel.

In short, we ordinarily find it impossible to align the axes of perception with Adam's rib.

PROLEPSIS

Some are less susceptible; (see Chandayoga Upanishad III, 11); Architecture as a whole is less susceptible to Metaphor than a

Thought Balloon	House Tea-cup Bird Triangle
Symbolia	Line
Staggeration	Les lettres du blanc sur les bandes du vieux billard (the white letters . . .) Les lettres du blanc sur les bandes du vieux billard (the white man's letters . . .)
Wafteron	digital cleverness cerebral traction
Agitrons	hordes

Antiquities briffit : 'our daily bread'
Bernini Jarns : 'even Jerusalem'
Tatlin quimps : 'Ain-soph'

Euclid's diagram for a first proposition: area enclosed by the arcs is a mystical figure, Vesica Piscis, symbol of the womb;

'A line is a length without a breadth.'

Grawlix: **

Wonder of the World (imagination of bronze)

1 Pyramids/SOL

2 Walls and Hanging/MI

3 Gardens of Babylon/FA

4 Statue of Zeus/Re

5 Lighthouse at Alexandria/LA

6 Temple of Diana/DO

7 Colossus of Rhodes/DO

8 Mausoleum/TI

now revealed at the
'edge' of space as familiar
but dubious: No fire-fangled feathers
here!
Noah's raven returns with olive leaf in his beak
'You speak. You say.'
 Like a building in the shape of something minus space
 dazzle equals room (Red, Vernueil, Rose, Blue, Green,
 China, East, Monroe)
   and a heliped on the SOUTH lawn
   with no thoughts of people now dead.

  JOB
Business promises
      'if this proves right' he said

 'then we would have to search for the special
     character' of
      'if you had enough of Rome',
       said Bruno, 'go to
         Paris'
  CLEARING AWAY
   From Jonah, George and the Whale

INTRODUCTION TO DRAWING
(ARCHITECTURAL)

In drawing one must love the lines themselves, their ideas,
images, rhythms and their liquid-crystal display with the
capacity to love anything at all:
       Even the endoplasmic reticulum.

Accuracy of observation = the precision of CARE in the
membrane:

Equivalent to the accuracy of the

     Architecture

Because drawing is the better part of

     Thought

(adding the proviso)
only because Architecture is the better part of

     Drawing

Only because the plant Kingdom is represented from the roots
up, whereas edible animals have been illustrated in such a way
as to show those parts . . . with the exception of man.

For every line one must supply the following information:
differentiation code, expiration date, subscription code,
subscription source, demographic code, address, surname
count, and coded surname count.

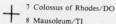

SOCIAL PREFACE
(ARCHITECTURAL)

A community of ORIGINALS is not a community.
Hence a fashion of the Unoriginal, rather than
AUTHENTIC UNORIGINALITY:

1. It is easier to copy than to think.
2. Cemeteries are more picturesque than coat and hat-racks.
3. Space is in the plural (if it were One the soul would crumple like an . . .).

(In the original manuscript, from which I have been copying this, there is a gap here followed by a series of etymologies.)

'The Art of the Moving Picture' by V. Lindsay

Here is the picture of an angle: ◀ , Latin
equivalent, Q.
This is another reminder of the technical outline . . .
I will leave the spiritual interpretation of the
angle to Emerson, Swedenborg or Maeterlinck.
Here is a picture of a mouth: ◀ , Latin
equivalent, the letter R. If we turn from the
dictionary of the monuments, we will see that
the Egyptians used all human features in their
pictures.

$\frac{9}{10}$ (actors' faces) fixed (as the masks of the Greek chorus)

By staying too close to the ground, one is proceeding at too
low a level; where is the rope stretched which makes one
stumble?

The Graphic as the soul of Architecture.

'The special character of sculpture as one of
the graphic arts' (Heidegger) to be followed.

Language as the Material of Poetry is not a medium or
instrument: Theatre of Trope or Drawing as Architecture must
'resist the intellect almost successfully', must not degenerate
into an instrument nor into Deepinsnow. An epilogue — picnic
in the ruins — over the arches and arcs returns to architecture
through non-architecture like man through animal.

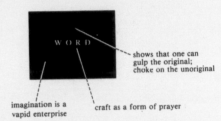

shows that one can
gulp the original;
choke on the unoriginal

imagination is a
vapid enterprise

craft as a form of prayer

The architect comes into his destiny today as nature in the
distant past came to him, a desert, with indifference and a
strange lostness.
(For demonstration, see *Gargantua* ch. XVI: On Inquiring
What Men of Learning There Were Then In the City, And
What Wine They Drank There.)

In this process — itself a metaphor which creates a new reality
— the drawn Original appears Unoriginal (unreal).

Short Treatise:
ON THE
DIFFERENCE BETWEEN THE
MEAT AND THE SIGNATURE

Architecture of Plenitude, this imitation of emotion (clip-on) when it refers to pain is called compassion (face-mask). When referring to the donut of desire it is called emulation or cover — which is nothing else than the padding of anything engendered in one by the fact that one 'imagines others to have that padding'.

Illustration:

A.	B.
CENTER FIELD	RIGHT FIELD FOUL LINE
Architecture is a vacuum	Realism
C.	D.
FENCE/WALL	HOME PLATE
Realism	Corruption of reality

Note: gateways, porticullises, jambs, pulley chains, and fluted spires are all included between the 'hot corner' and foul territory, as are all other on-off elements.

In the four quadrants (A,B,C,D, or B,D,C,A, . . . etc.) everything which appears becomes visible against the artificial turf; even buildings tend to become real. Everything tends to become real. We continue to build the city (AD, BD, CD, . . .) though we live on deck, protected by the umpire's area.

PRO(LOG)UE

According to some the effort to take your place, then, among these piles of less efficacious suppositories is constant enough to seem arithmetically proportional to the time alotted for it. Comforting thought. . .'it is time'. . . .

> 'Must she then die Latent Observer. . .
> Brr. . .Brr. . .The momentary oblivion
> induced by sleep. . .It is freezing hard. . .
> general sinister impression. . .brr. . .brr'
>
> Alfred Jarry

. . . 'it is time' to dis-articulate (architecture's) thought. There are some today who do not underestimate the object, but elevate it into a ┼ : the mere weight of this object on the ※ is an endless reminder that from a certain point onward the confession justifies itself in the form of ✕ (having dispensed with the lateral movement). Thus in reducing further we arrive at the formulation ✕ or the Deconstructed Labyrinth: ╲ .

The de-construction of de-construction yields:

'aren't you at least equal to Russia Cement?'

in this form: (   )

From figure to figure, motif to motif, repetition which parodies nothing —

Foible and Forte
Guard and Pommel
Blade and Mounting
Gripping Hole and Spring
Swivel and Crossbar
Cassini Division and Doppler Shift
Double Stars and Red Supergiants

Outside Line *Pavilion, Uozo, Japan 1997*

164

165

Line Between man-made
objects and natural forms
Line which observes observing
Line enclosing that which
cannot be said

The proposal for the creation of a new place of observation and contemplation to be situated in the new Sports Park near the city of Uozu is in the spirit of philosophical meditation upon the relationship between Man and Nature. That is, a search project in search for a contemporary understanding of space, place, and light of emerging discourses. ■ The elements of making Outside Line are situated within a precisely determined web of conceptual topographical relationships between object and place, eye and mind. These new lines of thought and vision point toward the beauties and mysteries of Uozu. ■ **Red Line** orients itself upon an imaginary axis connecting the descending history of the Buried Forest Museum and the ascending horizon of the Tateyama mountain range. Red Line is a line of orientation that remains straight in the horizontal plane but that develops its momentum in ever more complex vertical disruptions. It becomes a mimetic horizon: a thin red line against the blue of the sky. It is a line to hold onto and to release, open at both ends to the infinities of the beneath and the beyond. This line creates special ever-changing qualities of light and shadow and appears different during different seasons. In winter, snow will collect softly within its

This page: **Outside Line**, section; opposite: plan

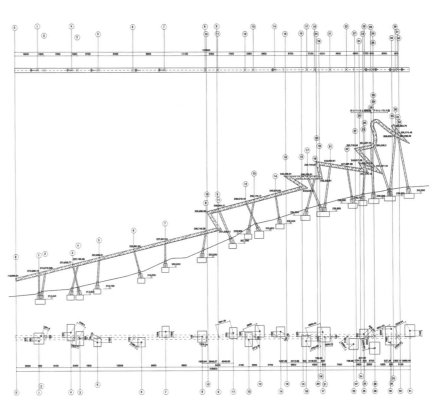

Observation on Education of Architects

Essay, 1987 Schools are not here just to produce the kind of people needed by a society. They are meant to educate people to the responsibility that is, of course, practical, ethical, and political for the work in architecture and in planning. Students should be given the chance to question and to respond in contemporary ways to the changes in society. A school should mirror global transformations of technology and education and thinking and should not conserve a provincial attitude in treating only local issues. It should wake up out of its sleep. Most schools do not seem to be as alive as the people who are there. People are talking about issues that have already been discussed back in the fifties and sixties. There is a faction in all schools that would like to impose ideals of homogeneity, typology, or style, a faction which follows an idea of eternity in architecture. But eternity begins in bed and ends in bed. This kind of frozen theory, implying a blind acceptance of certain rules and regulations, cannot run a school any longer. We know this from the totalitarian modern experience and all the "isms" that are bygone now. This attitude is very regressive because it harks back to a time when people were not allowed to question or to challenge a myth of power. Kim il Sung just died some time ago. That generation is disappearing and I hope it will not be replaced by another generation of dogmas, but by one open to new ideas. ● I would recommend that students of architecture become aware of what is happening in the world by traveling and seeing different societies, in Asia, Africa, and South America and not only in Europe and North America. It is important for students to express some more fundamental questions about the existence of architecture in the twenty-first century and to get out of this sleep in which the world of architecture seems to have fallen somewhere in the eighteenth century. Students have a tremendous role to play. They are not only the respondents, but also the creators of awareness. They have always challenged the prevailing opinions and are the catalyst in transforming knowledge. It is time that students remembered that schools were set up to challenge the wisdom of the world and its corruption rather than to reinforce it. ●

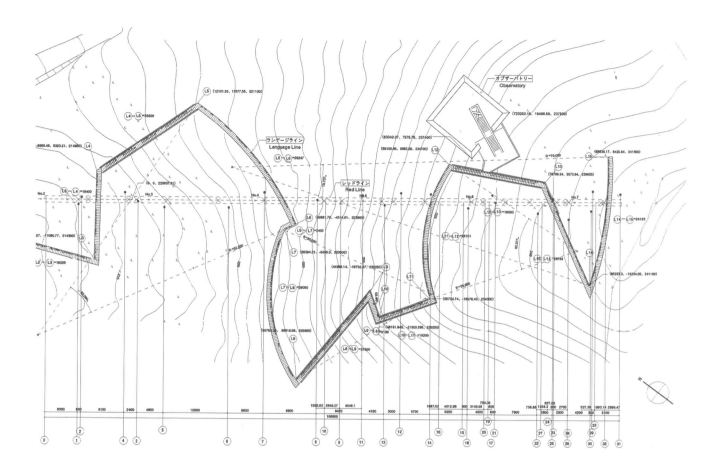

angles, and when it rains, the water will flow along its length toward the visitors' path of ascension. ■ **Language Line** determines the geometry of a circuitous path that leads the visitor from the park through the forest toward the observatory platform above. It represents a contemplative route, revealing the landscape in partial fragments from a variety of perspectives. Texts set within the path provide heuristic clues for the interpretation of the surrounding environment. It functions together with the orienting directness of Red Line as the disorientation of linguistic metonymy relates to the jagged spark of inspiration. ■ **Compass Line** opens up an obtuse angle of perception between the mountains and the sea, a field of contemplation upon visible and imagined realities. It takes the form of an invisible chiasmic X whose fulcrum determines the position and orientation of the observatory platform. ■ **Mirage Line** flies within the field of the compass and orients the observer upon the city of Uozu, upon imagined and potential cities of the past and the future. ■ **Observatory** consists of an observation platform and picnic area, a plane of assembly as the end of the route, and a staircase to a raised vantage point taking in all the elements of the composition and the surrounding landscape. The orientation of the stair is determined as a precise mediation between the two lines creating the path to the site, the highest peaks of the Tateyama, and the city and sea to the northwest. The platform contains the possibility of a future extension, into the ground, with a small meditative chamber and social program. ■ **Outside Line** is a graphic, spatial, and architectural condensation of roots, mountains, mirages, and the sea. ■

Out of Line *Urban competition, Potsdamer Platz, Berlin, 1991*

166 167 168 **ANGEL TRAPPING HISTORY** Berlin could be seen as an exemplary spiritual capital of the twenty-first century, as it once was the apocalyptic symbol of the twentieth-century demise. The identity of Berlin cannot be re-founded on the ruins of history or on the illusory "reconstructions" of an arbitrarily selected past.

The scheme traces the contortions of the nonexistent Angel who nevertheless remains as real as do the other deported archangels: Franz Kafka, Walter Benjamin, Primo Levi, Osip Mandelstam, Paul Célan . . .

The ten thunderbolts of absolute absence are deployed to alter the physical image of Berlin and to open joyous channels of communication, remembering the future.

RELEASING THE VIEW The concept of the site-as-puzzle has been derived from the symbolic fragments of memory of Potsdamer Platz as they have been recorded in nine projective/hysterical viewpoints. These accelerated time perspectives develop a momentum that finally cancels the very notion of perspective.

Like Humpty Dumpty's shattering act, this spot cannot be "put together in place again" even by "All the King's horses and all the King's men."

The site-puzzle is in fact the entry into a tenth "gate": the post-contemporary city where the view is cleared beyond the constriction of domination, power, and the gridlocked mind.

PLACE MOSAIC TIME The transformation of the shape of (future) city must be accompanied by corresponding changes in the mentality associated with prewar lot lines, anachronistic visions, dreams that money can buy. What is necessary is an optimistic view of the twenty-first century: a radical rethinking of zoning, function, property, and program. These categories are no longer appropriate to the changed relation between capitol, capital, public responsibility, and the end of ideology. Thus "totality," "uniformity," and "master planning" are over twice—once in the East and once in the West. The mosaic pieces come from around Europe: Paris, Venice, Vienna, Berlin . . . and elsewhere.

The profound undertaking of re-founding Potsdamer Platz must be taken at its face value, through the presence of witnesses, dates, anniversaries—Places out of Time.

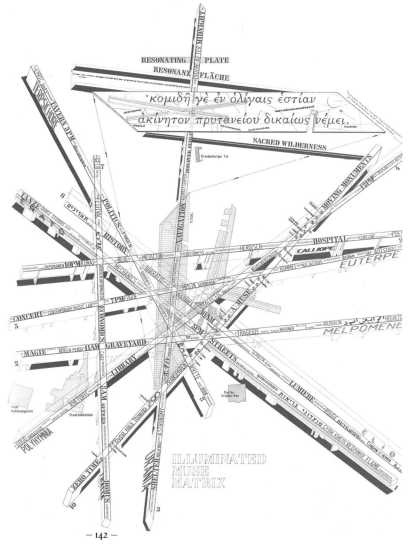

Out of Line,
Illuminated Muse Matrix

ILLUMINATED MUSE MATRIX What is needed is a connection of Berlin to and across its own history. This connection, this movement, goes through the relation of the old and the new, capitol and capital, full and empty, the "no-longer" and the "not yet." The (9 + 1) x (Muse) lines embody a diverse set of programs related to their use and function. These structures are buildings going over, on, and below the streets containing housing, production, cultural, and leisure functions. Apartments, factories, markets, hospitals, kindergartens, cemeteries, speakers' corners, cafés, libraries, communication and information centers connect to office buildings, housing, and transportation systems throughout the city.

The Muses constitute a diurnal and nocturnal journey through the geography of Potsdamer Platz, as well as through the topology of Berlin's culture. Historical places and old streets have been left as they are, removed from the realm of the monumental, and left to the eye of past history.

MAPPING THE IN:VISIBLE CITY The lost center cannot be reconnected like an artificial limb to an old body, but must generate an overall transformation of the city.

Potsdamer Platz can be the place where the East-West, center-periphery division can overcome the conflicts that were born, witnessed, and died in this very place.

These conflicts cannot be resolved by reconstructing a hollow past, but by laying new foundations and new images that are open to concrete dynamics.

Thus no style or system should be given priority over others. A heterogeneous, pluralistic reality is the goal.

The only priority manifested in this scheme is that a small child should be able to discover a dream and an imaginative future.

RESONATING PLATE The New Potsdamer Platz contains a myriad of diverse world-spaces and is symbolized by the prytaneion-field-building supporting a tranquil and flexible space that is based on the simple principle that people from around the world form the "shareholders association," thus owning a share of Potsdamer Platz. Soil from the World on the roof, wilderness of Berlin on the ground.

This elevated structure hovers like a plow over the land. Everyone now has the right to a space in the wilderness, the possibility of cultivation, streams of seeds powered by wind and sail, the eye-I-cure, thunderstorms, sky-books, artificial sun-rain, spark-writing, plantation in the clouds, the waterfall, inspiration… all necessities in the Berlin of tomorrow.

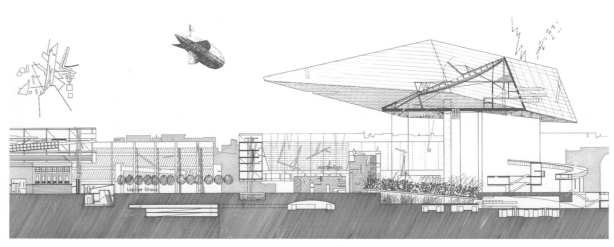

Out of Line, section and elevation

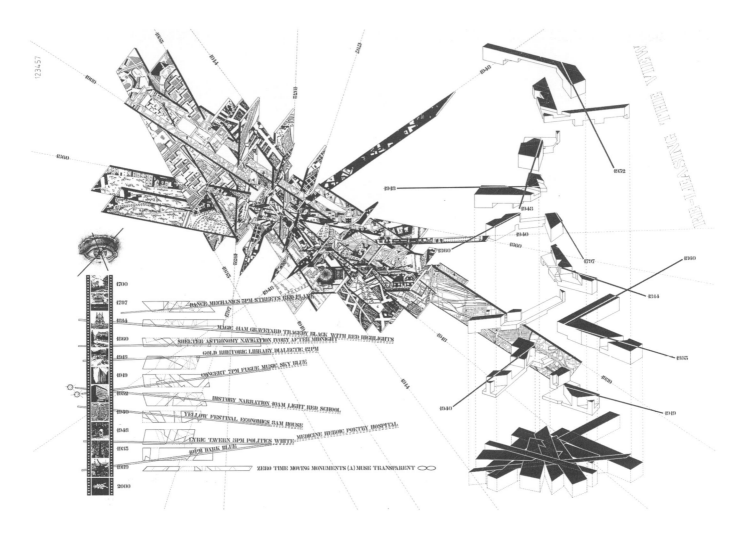

Out of Line,
conceptual drawing

THE CITY IS NO LONGER **MAN** WRITTEN LARGE BUT MAN IS CITY WRITTEN VERY SMALL—AND ALMOST ILLEGIBLY: CITY.

THE NEW VISION FOR BERLIN IS NOT UTOPIAN IN NATURE, RATHER IT CONCRETELY ENVISIONS A PLACE THAT HAS LEARNED FROM ITS PAST AND LOOKS TO THE FUTURE. THE CHANCE TO RESTRUCTURE, REPLAN, RETHINK, REDO SHOULD NOT BE LOST IN THE SIMPLISTIC SOLUTION OF SELECTIVE RECONSTRUCTION,

SINCE EVEN ORPHEUS DID NOT SUCCEED IN WALKING BACKWARDS INTO THE FUTURE.

THE FEELING FOR AN ATMOSPHERE OF SANCTITY AND DETACHMENT WILL NOT AGAIN MAKE AN APPEARANCE WITH THE PARAPHERNALIA BELONGING TO AN APOTHEOSIS OF AN ETERNAL STYLE.

I DON'T CARE FOR DISORDER AND I DREAD POLICE PROTECTION AS WELL. ■

Penalty Envelopes *Drawings, 1990; construction, Yatai, Japan, 1994*

169

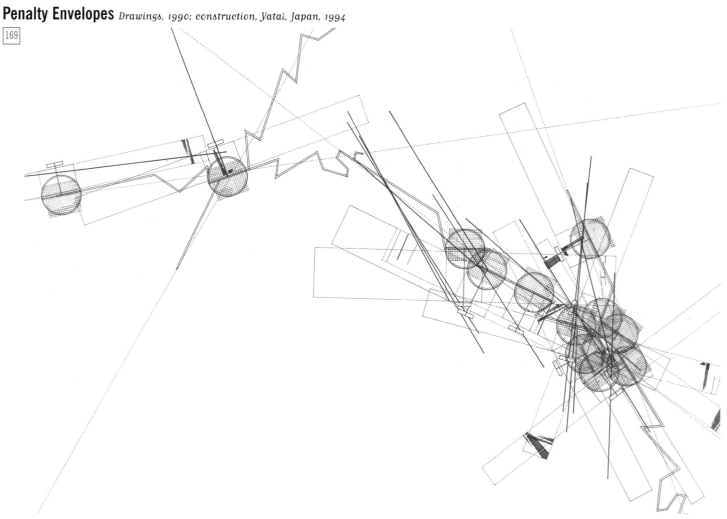

Penalty Envelopes, plan

Positions towards a Museum *Lecture, Bielefeld, Germany, 1998* The idea of a position has changed at the end of the twentieth century. The idea of having a position, having a principle in an age that has denied all principles, and that has subverted all principles. It is a really thought-provoking thing: What does it really mean to have a principle? Who is to be the principle, on what is the principle based, and who is to guarantee and legitimate any principle today?

The catastrophe of the twentieth century has a lot to do with the idea of examining the relativity of positions vis-à-vis the lack of position altogether that the century presents to us. Now, clearly, architecture is not theory, and architecture is not just practice, either. It is not like anything else in my experience, because the act of doing architecture is simultaneously antitheoretical and theoretical; a practice that results in buildings and spaces that are controlled by and delivered to a public discourse. ◉ What does that position, or the lack of it, signify in a world that is globally connected in terms of economy, direction, and momentum? And what is this momentum about, where is it going, where is the architecture leading, also, because, in a classical way, architecture is home, is the space we have, in which we identify who we are. I do not have any answers. Architecture, as opposed to anything else,

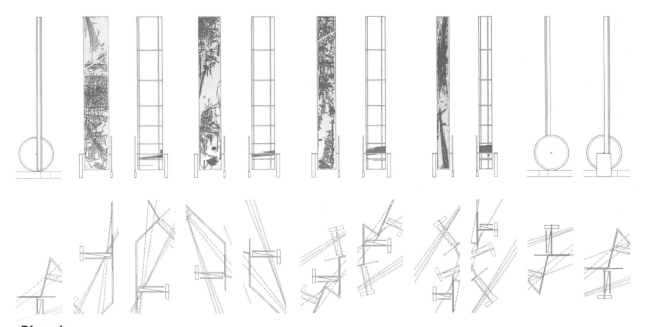

Phoenix *Geschaftshaus Wohnbau Nordwest, Dresden, Germany,*

170

171

2000 The project for Wohnbau Nordwest GmbH in Dresden represents a good piece of fortune in my work as it is the first commission I have had for a commercial office building. This good fortune has made it possible for me to rethink the office building with all of its realism and convention and to consider it not merely a box decorated with an expensive facade. Contemplating the entire spatial evolution of the office building offers an opportunity to develop this ever expanding type in another direction. Why should an office building look like an office building? and why in the twenty-first century should an office building function in a twentieth century manner? Are not office buildings of the future the museums of the past? ■ Almost totally destroyed in the war, rebuilt as part of East Germany's model city, Dresden is now reemerging as an important historical and contempo-

rary center. The dramatic history of the city, radically split as it is between the fragments of baroque architecture and vast GDR housing blocks standing at a zero degree ground, represents a challenge for any contemporary design. The site of Phoenix is precisely located between Dreikönigs-kirche, a baroque neighborhood and the rebuilt axis leading into the Neustadt connecting the center of the city with the historical/ahistorical neighborhood. As the corporate headquarters for Wohnbau Nordwest GmbH, a development company dealing with these issues, the Phoenix has to reconcile, thematize, and articulate the possibility of urban transformation embodied in a singular building. The character of work, the identity of the company, and the relationship of the public to its tasks were the starting points in the development of an office building. Working within the logic and economy of this type, the Phoenix

whatever we say about it, remains what it is, and cannot really be just talked away, interpreted away, theoretically discussed. It continues to be there despite everything, and presents itself as a part of another kind of event. I was never an enthusiast for a kind of universal idea that would be propelled by a political system. So, there is something to architecture, the irresistibility of it, because who cares about architecture except architects and a few

politicians who are all too powerful? In the end, we just find ourselves there and you cannot even really blame anybody. Not even the architects themselves. And it is interesting, I have talked very often to well-known architects and big companies and said, "**Who designed this building?**" and they said, "**Well, nobody really designed it; it is a communal process, you cannot attribute it to any person, because even the idea itself came out of a region of agreement.**" ◉

What is the discussion today in such a region as the public realm, the realm that represents the public: museums, for example? We know that there are two trends— well, overwhelmingly, one: a technical one. One that would provide a neutrality to the experience of the public, would extend the ideas of the Enlightenment into the next century. The universal space, the neutrality of space, the anonymity of the individual, the abstraction of the story—that is radically opens the perimeter of the baroque city to the gateway of the Neusadt, providing spectacular and unexpected views of the fragmentary remnants of Dresden. At the same time, the stratified massing of the building, refracts and dissects vistas frozen by time or projected ex nihilo into an indeterminate future. Thus the Phoenix stands for a rebirth connecting and dramatizing the differences within the history of history. ■ Subsequent to presenting the Phoenix to our client, we were asked to design an adjacent building as a gateway from the street to the depth of the baroque town. The two buildings frame a metamorphosis of "emptiness into fullness" by creating a hybrid density accruing to the indeterminate space between these two. ■ The working environment partakes of this through the movement of light and organization, transposing the old courtyard diagonally across the main structure of the building. Within this new structure, future activities of the various departments needing space within the development company will encounter light, functional organization, and distribution of events that have been dynamically reorganized in these emerging densities. ■ Without returning to the past, or accepting the present status quo of Dresden, the project seeks to delineate an emerging vitality. To give this vitality reality, light, and proportion are the challenges of this project. ■

Proof of Things Invisible Lecture, Humboldt Universität zu Berlin, 1997 It is a meaningful and exciting experience to be on this stage tonight to receive an award from a university that, in the history of ideas, education, and culture, has few equals; a university where the voices of Hegel, Kierkegaard, and the pantheon of thinkers who made the world stand on its head once resounded. This university, centrally located on Unter den Linden, between the Brandenburg Gate and Alexanderplatz, was well positioned to witness the astonishing events of the twentieth century. One could recall that Ludwig Mies van der Rohe designed his first glass-walled skyscraper within view from here; Yehudi Menuhin made his debut, with Einstein in the audience to applaud him; Georg Grosz recorded his savage observations of Berlin on this boulevard; and Vladimir Nabokov was here to observe "an elderly, rosy-faced beggar woman, with legs cut off at the pelvis…set down like a bust at the foot of the wall…selling paradoxical shoelaces." ◎ But what is particularly fascinating to me is the unexpected encounter between an old refrigerator and atomic physics on an operating table called Humboldt, an encounter whose fascinating history is perhaps not over yet. ◎ At this very university, sometime before 1934, on a cold and gray day at the end of October—similar to this one—Leo Szilard, an aspiring student from Budapest, and Albert Einstein developed and applied for twenty-nine joint patents in, unbelieveable as it appears, home refrigeration! ◎ A sad newspaper story caught the attention of Einstein and Szilard one morning. It was reported that an entire family, including a number of young children, had been found asphyxiated in their apartment as a result of the inhalation of noxious fumes of the chemical refrigerant used in their primitive refrigerator, a chemical that had escaped in the night through a leaky pump valve. ◎ Applying the sophisticated researches connected to relativity, the two physicists devised a method of pumping a metalicized refrigerant by electromagnetism, a method that required no moving parts, and therefore no valves that might leak. ◎ AEG signed Szilard as a paid consultant and actually built the Einstein/Szilard refrigerator—an astonishing Berlin object if there ever was one—but alas, these two inventors failed for musical reasons. The magnetic pump was so noisy, compared to even the noisy conventional compressors of the day, that it never left the engineering lab. (Based on Richard Rhodes, *The Making of the Atomic Bomb*, Simon and Schuster; Wolf von Eckardt and Sander Gilman, *Bertolt Brecht's Berlin*, Abelard Press; Kaes, Jay, Dimendberg, *Weimar Reader*, Yale

not really a position that I would take. I do believe that architecture is very particular, very practical—it is very pragmatic. But it is also related to a very specific and irreplaceable continuity, even if the continuity today catches by stunning surprise, because the time itself is—I think it was Hamlet who said that the time itself is out of joint. And I think that Shakespeare meant it in that way that time is never just joined in, it is out of joint, whenever the human being steps into the crisis, which is permanently produced by human beings. That is, I guess, human life; it is itself the producer and the emblem of the crisis. ◎ I want to talk today about an extension to the traditional **Victoria & Albert Museum** in London, and a new **Imperial War Museum** in Manchester. Perhaps I will be able to address the question of position, place, joint of time, the role of architecture or that particular architecture, the architecture that is not drifting in that anonymous space of conformed momentum, but is itself a form of resisting, changing, dynamically utilizing its own resources toward a different end. And what is the different end? All human beings are the same, but the places are not. That is somehow interesting. The places cannot be exchanged, even when human beings can be deported and brought back, the places themselves have never succeeded in that exchange. ◎ Manchester

University Press.) ◎ The prophetic linkages that connect asphyxiation and the patenting of the modern refrigerator to a device for accelerating nuclear particles in a circular magnetic field produced a kind of nuclear pump that was instrumental in the construction of the atomic bomb. ◎ The intertwining of gas, tragedy, inconceivable inventions, and anti-Semitism that finally exiled Einstein and Szilard as carriers of a theory, then deemed hostile to the "German spirit," is emblematic of Berlin and of the Atomic Age it somehow represents. ◎ As I was thinking about what to say today, I realized how difficult it is for an architect to speak about his work without the usual paraphernalia of slide projectors and images. Architecture, which is evoked only by words, makes one almost feel "at home" in language. By surrounding oneself with language, one almost comes to believe that one has escaped from the opacity of space, and that what remains "out there" is only an empty stage set. That is perhaps why most intelligent people apply their intelligence and analytic powers to everything but architecture; why architecture is given over to technicians and specialists, and why one is resigned to it as an inevitable and anonymous force that will shape the cities without one's personal participation. ◎ The experience of alienation from architecture as a dimension of culture should be contrasted with the stark and astonished encounter with it—crowned out, spewed out into night—resistant to theorization. For then, one might see that architecture—something static and unfeeling, as all that's turned into a coming—can be interpreted, but itself continues to remain oblivious to the interpretation. It continues to live its own existence whether we share it or not. ◎ Perhaps language and its meaning are grounded in the spaces of architecture, and not vice-versa. Consider the functions of foundation, circumcision, territorialization, openness, and closure. These are all experiences of space—and of a certain kind of architecture—that provide a symbolic model and understanding of life itself. Is architecture not the quintessential "taken for granted," the unthinkable, the monstrous, the genderless, the repressed, the

other? Perhaps this is the point of its madness, perhaps it is your conscience: the knot of life in which what is recognized is untied. And what thinking person does not want a fireplace, a home, a utopia, "the way it is," "the way it was?" What thoughtful person is not grateful for the beams of clear lines directed by this silent ray? ◎ What ineffable, immeasurable power of building in the city! The epiphany of the constructible is the strange sucking of the earth's axis. In the realm of architecture, ideas, having stared at Medusa, turn to stone. Here it is matter that carries the aura of ideas—ideas which metastasize into crystalline sleep-shapes assumed in the language shadow. Wasps, buildings, antennae sting the air, driving the sting to pass through the world of dream and death in order to sense this axis: the Earth's Axis. ◎ All this is accomplished through technique, such as drawing, wherein an exiled line falls to the ground. Two parallel lines signify a wall; precisely the wall that is between the lines and is not a line. Whether this wall imprisons and releases depends on whether one is a saint or a prisoner. It is doubly illegible twice over. In attempting to surmount the inner poles of this contradiction, architecture becomes like the plow, turning up time, revealing its invisible layers on the surface. ◎ The power of building is certainly more than meets the eye. It is the nonthematized, the twilight, the marginal event. But architecture forming this background is a surplus beyond obvious need: that which itself has no legitimacy in a proper foundation. This has led some to ask whether the true and the real need to be embodied at all. Whether one needs architecture or just a simulation mechanism. Whether architecture can flutter nearby like a spirit, the bell, or the Internet. It cannot. ◎ n its opacity and resistance, architecture rebels and communicates that only the superfluous, the transcendent, the ineffable is allied to us: the sky, the stars, the gods. I would like to confess my fascination for this strange activity, quite distant from the obsessive technologism, globalized marketing, and withered modernism progressively eradicating spiritual life. ◎ I would like to share with you something about the nature of the approach to architecture that I

is a great industrial city, one of the famous twentieth century cities. I participated in a competition for a museum that has a very interesting program: the **Imperial War Museum**. How does one deal with a museum of war in the twenty-first century, since in order to deal with a war museum, it is not necessary to deal with war, it is to deal with the significance of twentieth-century conflicts. In the twenty-first century, how are people to understand the conflicts and particularly the regional contributions of citizens to these conflicts and their participation in these conflicts in a new time? This is the program of this museum, so it is not a museum about glorifying a conflict, glorifying war, but about delving deeply into the question of war and sources of contemporary behavior, which are certainly rooted in the mission of the Imperial War Museum: to show how, with World War I, the whole notion of humanity fundamentally changed. ◎ The idea is rather stark, which is to show that conflict is not something abstract, but it has to do with space, it has to do with the fact that people never fought on a piece of paper, but on land. The museum will feature as its program how individual citizens of the north participate in these conflicts—very heterogeneous groups of people, many people from India, from Pakistan, from Africa, from the Commonwealth. So that will be the story and the place of that museum. ◎ So it is about am following, through buildings that not only house exhibitions within them but, as architectural works "exhibit" the world are indeed the "production" of the Earth. Together, they delineate a trajectory that musters the letters, mortal-immortal; show the aleph as coming after the beit; the alphabet after the house. ◎ Henry Adams considered the Virgin as the mobilizing form of medieval times and compared her to the dynamo, the mechanism of industrialization. Were he to write today, he would perhaps add the museum to the Virgin and the dynamo as the catalyst and conveyor of reality, since this institution is seen today as a force able to regenerate areas of experience, revive histories, transform images, and create a new identity. ◎ Throughout my projects I have followed a certain path, which one could name as the search for the irreplaceable, that which was known by the pagans as the **genius loci**. I am interested in the unique portrayal of architecture and space of provinces, mountains, maps, ships, horoscopes, fish, instruments, rooms, stars, horses, texts, people. In this labyrinth of places, one can discover the uniqueness of a human face and of a particular hand as a figure of architecture and of the city. ◎ Lines of history and of events; lines of experience and of the look; lines of drawing and of construction. These vectors form a patterned course toward "the unsubsided," which paradoxically grows heavier as it becomes lighter. I think of it as that which cannot be buried, that which cannot be extinguished; call it architecture if you want. ◎ Berlin Museum and the Jewish Museum: addresses; matrix of light; names; echoes of the void; intermarriage; assimilation; integration; exile; erasure; hope. What is lost in the sky, slender images as blue as shadows, vernal ice, divine ice, spring ice. They are leading a storm cloud by a leash. The music and light of Schoenberg's inaudible space, soundless bridges that illuminate the darker corners of thought. ◎ Nussbaum Haus, Osnabrück: three arches of the Rolandstrasse Synagogue, reincarnated in three excavated arches of an ancient Swedish bridge; Osnabrück; Rome; Brussels; Auschwitz; and Osnabrück again. The Nussbaum Haus, the Nussbaum Brücke, the

[23]

[92]

Nussbaumgang, Ohne Ausgang; a triple dislocation in the atmosphere of a quiet town. Read it: It is only a beam; it is only light; it has the power of murmured words. ◎ Victoria & Albert Museum, London: spiralling through William Morris' lightning rod; "Knowledge" and "Inspiration" inscribed on the portals; Owen Jones's Grammar of Dreams; Aston Webb's screen; the oblique connection between Constable and Cast Courts. Victorian light fractalized in an endlessly generated aperiodic pattern, decentering the spiral and releasing innumerable directions. Passages of the spiral through the interlocking continuity of swimming light. Ciphering and decrypting English heritage lodged in the honeycomb cells of the gigantic, brick clock called London. ◎ Imperial War Museum of the North, Manchester: conflict-shattered Earth; shards reassembled to trace the end of nations, but not of conflict that has never taken place on an abstract plane, but in the awful trenches, in salty waters, in air suffocating with smoke. Projection; introjection; suspension; air, earth, water surrounded by fire; where the earth curves more sharply than anywhere else; the slope becomes unexpectedly extensive, rolls down for as long as the last slave on Earth is breathing. ◎ Architecture's reality is as old as the substance of the things hoped for. It is the proof of things invisible. Contrary to public opinion, the flesh of architecture is not cladding, insulation, and structure, but the substance of the individual in society and history; a figuration of the inorganic and organic, the body and the soul, and that which is visible beyond. ◎ Some would deny this substance and, as a result, might themselves vanish into the emptiness of "facts," which as indices of power are only the illusory ghosts of a virtual world. One must reject the emptiness of ideologies, the nihilistic obsession with the return of the same, the vacuity of systems that base the whole on its part. The road to authentic construction, just like a smile, cannot be faked, for it remains insubordinate, not slave. ◎ Architecture is undergoing an anamnesis: the struggle to remember. Let me share with you one of the most difficult personal decisions I have had to make recently, which was the decision to enter the

[154]

[62]

the nature of experiencing a museum that does not start with entering the building itself at all, but starts with the topographical and major features of light and space in the city, which lead one—I think—to a museum that will be very interesting in terms of both what it presents programmatically to the public and how it differs from the Imperial War Museum in London, or other war museums that have been constructed in the world. ● Again, I am also speaking about the specific differences that are not only contained in the space of the city, but are also in the program connection to the genius loci of the place that resists, as I said, the thrown programs of theoretical and universal logic. I was fortunate to win a competition to extend the **Victoria & Albert Museum** in London, the last available site on Exhibition Road. The Victoria & Albert Museum is not really one building, as people refer to. There are many, many buildings, built by different architects. It is a city, actually, and despite what people think when they hear the words Victoria and Albert, this is programmatically the most avant-garde museum in the world. When you read the manifest that was written by Webb, by Waterhouse, by Morris, by Cole, what did they want? They did not want a museum that collects things arbitrarily in order to enrich some abstract idea of possession of the world. They wanted a museum that would

[154]

[159] competition for the Memorial to the Murdered Jews of Europe, to be erected in Berlin. An unprecedented task—a Memorial for the world's biggest crime: the murder of three percent of German Jews and ninety-seven percent of European Jews. A monument of shame, not honoring anyone; a monument not celebrating anything. ◎ How can such a memorial be built? Would it only reinforce the act of forgetting? What makes it difficult for a foreigner and a Jew living in Berlin to participate in such a project? ◎ Some will say that a memorial of the German people should not be advocated by others. Some persons in the Jewish community say, "it is not our memorial, it is theirs—but we insist that they should do it." Would such a memorial make any difference? No images, no symbols can represent the inconceivable. Only an imageless presentation with a deepening substantial presence might do it. No names of victims are appropriate here; and names of perpetrators are wholly inadequate when speaking of a crime that has a national dimension. ◎ I thought of myself not as someone doing it for the Germans, or instead of the Germans; nor as an architect of just another nationality doing a German project, but rather as someone who has no single identity; himself a product of the Holocaust era. ◎ What does it mean to be German today, after all? The monument is part of the process of finding out. The past that won't pass is not there only for Germans, but for everyone else, and it is growing. Does the monument come too late? No. The generations involved in these horrific events could not accomplish it, and even had they been able to, it would not have been credible. The fifty years past are nothing compared with the history of Berlin, which is not concluding a period, but opening a new one. ◎ The peculiar site that is the seam between East and West is an emblem of a common ground and a confession—killing fields of a kind—framing the Brandenburg Gate, which for fifty years, or one quarter of its two-hundred-year existence, has been deprived of significance. Such a monument cannot be left to the politicians, to ideologues, those who would try to tell a story with

an ending. The innocent idea of the identity of state and society has long gone, destroyed by the behavior of the German people during the Nazi time, and by the mockery of the GDR version of identity of government and its people. ◎ The monument is capable of enduring perhaps not because of its force and name, but because of its vulnerability; the weakness of the nameless; what was etched away by the ray-shot wind of language. For a monument is made to endure, but not as the full presence of those whose memory it bears. If there are no more masters, no sand book, and no more sand art, then this very absence not only remains, but expands. Not the full presence of the one whose memory it bears…but, on the contrary, what remains is a growing memory. Aren't we living in times when even being itself is a recollection? Perhaps the stratagems of architecture are already institutionalized on the principles of the transformation of being and recollection. The monument should emphatically transform the work into a remnant, residue, or that which remains when the process is over. This monument is capable of enduring because from the outset it is produced in the form of that which is no longer: the trace of the unborn; the exterminated human being. ◎ The world of Berlin has been stuttered by space in which the guest, a name sweated down from the wall, a wound up in the air, stands in the time-void. Such a place is a body open for air, silence, stars; it solidifies the time-void into those image gaps harbored in the slit arteries of awareness. We travel largely the last of the sonic booms…receives us: the boosted heart pace, outside, in space, brought home to the axis of Earth. ◎ The spiritual in architecture is urgent, though it seems to have become an embarrassment, a rumor on the street. The spiritual, appropriated by the fundamentalist right, has been expropriated from culture and history, eliminated from discourse, through which it should be reclaimed. One should attempt to retrieve the spirit of architecture, to recall its humanity, even within a situation in which the goal and the way have been eclipsed. The erasure of history and its carriers, the obliviousness of the market economy to the degra-

exemplify by its heterogeneous collections how the world is changing and how to educate people to a better life, to a better skill in arts and crafts, to a better architecture, better design, and better understanding of the future in relation to the past. So this is not a nostalgic museum; it is a very modern museum, although it possesses some of the great rarities and historical treasures of the world. Its mission is to transmit the material to a contemporary audience. ◎

When you come to the site, you will find a city of towers, as Henry Cole called it. It is not an area of London; it is an area of Europe. It is a unique city of high entrances, public entrances, Crumble Road Tower, Waterhouse's Natural History Museum, Science Museum, Geology Museum. Right now, the Victoria and Albert Museum has really one entrance; this will be the second entrance, and a major space for twenty-first-century activities. Of course, when you

design a building, it has to reach a public, but I never expected it to resonate in this way. It appeared in huge headlines in all the papers, and it was not all positive. A huge photograph in the *Guardian* said: "**Gasps and groans as V&A reveals its spiral— Architects split by a tiled building that 'explodes' up from the facade.**" Just to give you a flavor, the *Daily Telegraph*: "**Unveils exploding extension**." And the *Independent*, in full color: "**In the year 2001, this will be** dation and ongoing genocide of human beings, must be countered with a deeper awareness and action. ◎ Architecture is and remains the ethical, the true, the good, and the beautiful, no matter what those who know the price of everything and the value of nothing may say. ◎ contemporary architecture is split bitterness/sweetness, strictly, the ends of its smile go off into the anarchy of life, opening a paradoxical freedom. ●

the most admired, reviled and argued-over building in Britain." It reached everything, the tabloid and even the popular humor in *Time Out*. There was another cartoon that pits the "for" and "against": Queen Victoria is against and Prince Albert is for, because, as it was said, I was put on the side of Albert because I was a German architect. My favorite appeared in a full-page editorial in the *Times* of London, which is not a small newspaper, and it compared me to Jean-Paul Sartre and Mao Tse Tung. I never had the following of either Mao or Sartre, but the building somehow engraved itself in the public mind, and of course it started a very big debate, about Mao Tse Tung, Sartre, and Libeskind versus what is England. This was, please remember, just before the elections in which Tony Blair and the Labor Party came to power again. ◎ Now, what is the building? The building is a spiral, but it is unlike any spiral that has ever been designed because it is a spiral that is not going toward a central point, not creating an equivalent space around itself, but a spiral in which the randomness of its points also opens up unexpected but multivalent trajectories. And the spiral, of course, is not round and it is not literal, and this building is not round and not literal, but it is spiral. And I took the spiral, because the spiral is I think the ultimate emblem of William Morris. I think William Morris understood art and education and the future as the idea of a spiral, but he did not mean it necessarily as the figure that we have had of the spiral. So the spiral is here an unfolding of spaces along an unexpected diversion of its walls. From the very beginning, I thought the spiral should be the structure of the museum, since the museum

basically is about walls, space beyond and inside these walls. ◎ Despite its disruptions, the spiral always continues, but not in a single direction. There is the elevation of the single wall that incompliances the intertwining between external and internal demands of the program and of the city. So it is not something that has been derived from the idea of the spiral, but from the specifics of what the spiral opens on that site with those thoughts, immanent in the space of the V&A. It may look like a series of boxes, but it really is not. It is true that the spiral is not very evident, because it is not conceived to be visible from a certain point of view, since, first of all, there is no space to see it. It is compressed between the Puraly Court, Cromwell Tower, and the different wings of the buildings. But the idea of the building is to invite the public in, to penetrate the rather severe walls, which were put up by Webb in the late nineteenth century and open a new emphasis into the museum. The spiral builds itself up, so to speak; it actually holds itself tectonically and programmatically. It does so by a very close analysis of the spaces necessary, since these are not just big rooms for paintings or for sculptures but for projections, laser shows, video presentations, and hands-on experience, with fashion, pottery, ceramics, and metalwork being presented to a public, which would then be engaged in the work not as a voyeur but as a participant. So this is not a stage for twentieth-century art, but really a thinking about how and what a museum does, and the architecture is very strongly responsible for giving vectors for how a Museum operates in the future. ◎ I tried to show the complexity of this very spe-

cific site, and what the building has to do: provide lobbies, shops, and underground connections, educate the public. These triangular shapes that you will see over and over again are not results of the form, but in fact are part of smaller, intimate spaces, of theaters, which are linked directly to the big floor plates. At the top of the building is a crystal overlooking and giving a view of the entirety of London, including the V&A. I thought that was very important, because a museum that has more than eight miles of galleries, fifteen kilometers of gallery spaces—how does one introduce the public with a second entrance here? ◎ I did something that no one else did in this competition. It is always interesting to compare results of competitions and analyze why a scheme is selected. Every other architect of this project suggested to the V&A that they should make the entrance as simple as it could be, a glazed box or a neoclassical box, something that would just give you an empty space and project you into the rest of the museum. Well, that was not my suggestion. I think more than ninety percent of the visitors to the V&A are lost after five minutes. You enter that Cromwell Road entrance and the galleries are so extensive. And I thought that one of the most beautiful things for the twenty-first century is the idea that the twenty-first century will not be about finding ourselves, but losing ourselves much deeper in the history that created the future. So I did not try to make a box that gives everybody clear, easy routes to the Raphael cartoons, to the Greek collections, to the Cast Courts, to the Constables, to the Frank Lloyd Wright rooms—I followed the logic of the labyrinthic collection into the innermost recesses of the spiral of the V&A itself. ◎ The building is standing in a very close but tense relationship to the Webb and Henry Cole wings. I did not want to close off the impact of the existing elevations from Exhibition Road. The public should be able to view these very interesting pieces of architecture simultaneously with the linkages and with the space of the museum itself. And the entrance, of course, is a form that unfolds itself, but it is not completely open; it is open actually at its periphery, giving large floor plates outside the restaurant and café levels, for exhibiting work. The property of this unfolding of the experience of the visitor means that every floor has a different plan. Each plan is different because each level of the museum has a different linkage to an existing building. And of course these conditions of linkage determine programmatically how visitors move. The building works in its rotation and its activities. The program suggests that the building does not have any windows into it, but I felt that people should have some natural light. One should not enter a black box experience, which seems to be very popular today—the idea of a museum as a black box, in which anything can go. I think light is a very important element of experience. The building has light coming from that upper crystal; it washes down the walls to where the public circulation is, so that one would know what time of the day it is and have an idea of the world outside, and catch glimpses through small windows of the existing context. The center of the building is of course kept dark and illuminated artificially. ◉ I will say a little bit more about the proportioning of the building. The surface of the building is massive, and the building rises almost like a rooftop from about the middle of its form, forming a projection of itself, and enclosing the spaces. I collaborated on this with Cecil Balmond, who is an engineer from Ove Arup and Partners, and we developed a system of white tiling. So the structure is a very traditional concrete structure. It is a concrete building, built from the bottom up. The building is clad, however, in ceramic tile. I think one of the most interesting parts of the V&A is the analysis of

what they possess, and more than fifty percent of its collections deal with ceramics. Ceramics are in use in very modern technologies—such as with the very thin ceramics on the space shuttle—and are also a very traditional material. Three tile forms are part of the fractal set of an aperiodic mathematical from the chaos theory of Amman mathematics, though all are rectilinear and mass-produced as three single tiles interlocked in such a way that they never repeat their own pattern, while creating self-similar patterns on larger scales. So the idea of the facade, of the building itself, of the tiling, is that the tile is made from a rational system, but this rationality is taken to an extent that cannot really be coped with by simple visual inspection of the facade or of the tiling, since one cannot really find any repetitive elements in the same relationship to each other. That is a very complex mathematical and aesthetic research, because these bigger tiles repeat themselves as very small tiles. So the building has many different scales on its surface. But one has to really produce it and solve the problems of connecting and collecting the water and to do it in a very logical way. These tiles are, interestingly enough, not more expensive than the competitive cladding systems that could have been used by the museum. So this will be, I think, a very important part. The color is an ivory, right between the darker Portland stone on the Victorian buildings and the yellows and light tones of the Natural History Museum. By the way, as this finite elements analysis, which is a very sophisticated piece of technology, demonstrates, the tiling itself is integral to the structure of the wall. So the shapes and the sizes of the tiles have to do with the grammar of the structure. I did not do this frivolously, because from the very beginning of this project I was interested in the work of Owen Jones, who was one of the founders of the Victoria & Albert Museum, and he

wrote a very interesting book, called *The Grammar of Ornament*, in which he explored how the different ornamental patterns in the Victoria & Albert Museum collection constitute a universal grammar of structure; of course, he conceived it in two dimensions and in color, but we took it one step further into the structure of the building. ◉ There was an engineer on the jury who, when I first presented the project, said, "**Mr. Libeskind, you know, it is a very nice project, but there is one thing that I don't believe: That the building can really be built the way you have designed it. Because, you know, there is no way that this kind of geometry can bring stability; so you better put a big core into the middle of the building,**" which I did after the first stage of the competition, just to make sure, and it turned out that it was not necessary. The spiral, with its logic, is actually completely self-sustaining, and does not need the floors or the elevator cores to hold itself up, allowing for tremendous flexibilities. There are no other columns, there are no further subdivisions. The space is very generous and can be subdivided in interesting ways, because it is not gridded in any prefigured way. ◉ I had the occasion to demonstrate what the space of this building would be like in an exhibition on my work, which took place in the Dutch Architecture Institute (**NAi**) in Rotterdam. I did not do it with concrete but with sticks of steel, which were very small, only 2 meters long. And it shows it really in a large scale, because it is a 1:3 model. ◉ I have to say that this has not been an easy process, because nothing can be built in London or in England without high public scrutiny by not always public organizations, very often private advisory groups, such as the Royal Fine Arts Commission, the Victorian Society, and the London Heritage Commission, and I have to say that I presented to all these societies and against everybody's predictions, the building received a blessing from the Victorian

30

Society, the London Heritage Commission, and the Royal Fine Arts Commission, which only admits, I think, four percent of the buildings presented to it. Go get a clearance! Ninety percent have to come back with redesign. I was fortunate not to have to redesign. ◉ Coming to London today is not done by boat, as in the past, but from Heathrow probably. Coming from Heathrow, one sees the diagonal movement between the Cromwell Road tower and the new Spiral building, and I think that will be a very new image for London. I am very proud that after all these things and after all this struggle this came out; maybe a year after the kind of catastrophic analysis of the project by the English Heritage, which is ... I have to tell you this story, because I was the only architect ever allowed to present directly to the commissioners of English Heritage. Usually the London Advisory Board simply advises the counsellors. Now, who are the counselors? They are not even Lords or Sirs—they are Counts, they are Princes, and they are really the Royal English heritage. And they said, "**Mr. Libeskind, we cannot present this building. Why don't you go and speak to the commissioners yourself. You have only ten minutes.**" So I came. I did not have too many technical drawings, but I had the model and I had the drawing, and the commissioners said, "**Mr. Libeskind, what is this building about?**" And I said, "**Well, it is about the same thing that interested Turner and interested Coleridge and interested Christopher Wren,**" and I explained a little bit how the connection is made. I was thrilled, because they did not throw me out of the room. But about a week later they took out these huge advertisements, which show that they were not fuddy-duddies, that England is a very creative society with incredible architecture and that this building will be part of a renaissance view of England vis-à-vis France, Germany, other places. Of course, there is competition, and museums are certainly part of the imagery that the public has of what other issues are that the country is interested in. So it is a great privilege, and the building is now going into planning application; I have just presented it to the citizens, over to the planners, who will be working very hard, and it is on a course of construction to start in 2002. ◉ So it is an ongoing experiment. ■

Plegma *Collage, 1978*

QST.

QST. *Competition for a Cultural Center, St. Pölten, Austria, 1992* The challenge to integrate an important cultural center into the urban fabric of a distinguished Baroque city is almost without precedent. St. Pölten's new mandate and its ambitious vision as a capitol is one that should be answered by an equally far-reaching and dynamic urban and architectural vision that embodies change, movement, transformation, and participation. ■ The dimension that this scheme seeks to open is that of the acceleration and growth of the autonomous particles of European culture through the magnetic field of the city and its institutions. In this image an unexpected creative interaction takes place between the different individual facilities of the urban center, creating the conditions necessary for the release of enormous cultural potential. ■ The proposed center is organized—both architecturally and urbanistically—as a heterogenous structure whose articulations are embodied in buildings of expressly individual character (geometry, material, organization, program, symbol) and whose spaces are in dynamic tension with the planned government complex and the historic city. ■ The proposed design seeks to redefine the public realm by creating a spatial-functional multiplicity disseminated across the boundaries of particular territories, allowing for intermediate, interstitial zones at strategic public nodes and developing the site as a "hinge" around which culture and city can be turned towards each other. ■ The scale and substance of buildings is gradually transformed by the order of the Government Center, and then reinterpreted in terms of its own new structure and that of the historic center in order to link the Cultural Center strongly to the city. And inversely, the proposed design gives measure to the shifting shape of the city, which will develop in the future around it. ■ The realization of the plan results in the displacement of building typologies, the dissolution of edges between forms and events, the fracturing of spaces and their technologies, bringing the unexpected topos of St. Pölten's "philosophoumena" to reality. ■

The Spiral

The Spiral *Extension to the Victoria and Albert Museum, London, 1996—present* The Spiral Extension to the Victoria & Albert Museum (V&A) shares in the spirit of the twin inscription carved on Cromwell Tower Entrance—Inspiration and Knowledge—and carries that message into the concrete space and content of the new extension. The building goes beyond the habitual division between program and history, form and function, architecture and engineering, by offering new possibilities within the horizon of an evolving cultural and educational resource. The Spiral is not just another box filling an empty lot; it is a celebration of public activities in a unique historical setting. The building represents a new awareness of the central role of contemporary museology, technology, arts and crafts, in sustaining tradition and education in a spectacular cultural setting, central not only to London, but to Europe as a

172
173
174
175

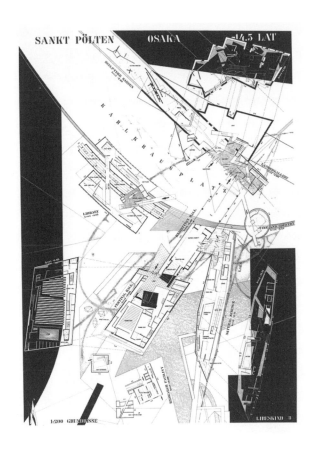

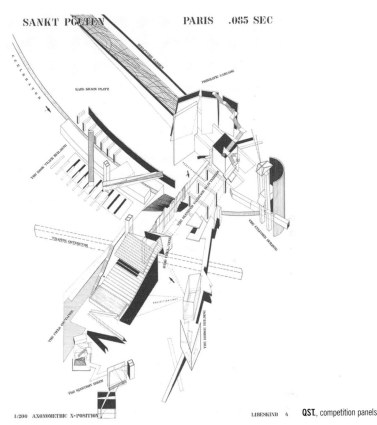

QST, competition panels

whole. **Vision and Form:** The Spiral Extension is an encounter of the enormous cultural legacy represented by the museum, with my belief that history is not something that has passed away, but is an ever-evolving and dynamic process, inscribing the present simultaneously into the future and the past. The trajectory of history, however, is not a straight line to be projected by technocrats without spirit, or sensualists without heart, but is a subtle, imaginative, and contemporary trace embodying the fullness of a poetic heritage. ■ The Spiral Extension is not conceived as an a priori form or a "ready-made" artifact imposed upon the site. It is not an architecture that imitates what already exists. The specific proportions, materials, and spaces of the Spiral are the visible forms resonating and condensing the special quality and specific originality of the V&A. Some of the most innovative and far-seeing experiments in architecture, technology,

and craft were first applied and tested by the illustrious architects associated with the construction of the museum. The V&A was not conceived as a repository for objects or a container for passivity and nostalgia. It was conceived as a set of exemplary spaces and inspiring experiences involving the public, through participation in the ever-evolving drama of art, education, and their mutual significance for society and the future. These explicit cultural themes, expressed in the heterogeneous and endless variety of architecture, decoration, and structure, have been taken up in the Spiral and extended for the enjoyment of people of all ages and knowledge—a rapidly growing museum public. Visitors will experience the contribution of this generation into the new millennium. **Architectural Context:** The Spiral opens an important public entrance on Exhibition Road by relieving the tight Victorian belt-perimeter, giving access to a large public. The Webb Screen, once a barrier to the Old Boiler House site, is now repositioned and becomes a loggia. This element creates a striking public space for the visitors coming directly from the Underground to the forecourt entrance, fulfilling Webb's original but unrealized architectural idea. The Spiral integrates itself into the overall composition of the "**city of towers unique in Europe**" described by Henry Cole. By closely relating itself to the urban landscape and roofscape of Exhibition Road, the new extension engages the public eye—not only with its shimmering, multifaceted exterior, but through glimpses into the inner activities created by the modulation of its forms. The Spiral will have an important and memorable relation to the icons of the past dotting the vast Exhibition and Cromwell Road area. ■ Configured in terms of scale and history of the site, the Spiral maintains an intimate dialogue with the surrounding eaves and ridgelines, being accurately proportioned to the primary and secondary elements of the rich street- and roofscape. The Spiral constitutes only four percent of the entire building mass of the V&A, an urban structure akin to a city containing more than seven miles of galleries and diverse buildings, built across a

century by different architects representing a plurality of architectural and cultural ideas. ■ Through a series of important, yet subtle, openings onto Exhibition Road, the activity of the museum will be visible to the street. The soffits and skylights expose the geometry of the Spiral, becoming the vitrines opening onto Exhibition Road, revealing spaces, objects, and people. These openings and the discretely shaped windows, which provide glimpses of the surrounding historical context, orient the public in space and time. Views from the observatory and from the links offer spectacular panoramas over the immediate V&A roofscape, as well as distant and dramatic vistas over the city of London as a whole.

Internal Organization: The Spiral is a unique response to an innovative and important building program of the V&A. The brief does not call for more traditional galleries, but rather for the construction of wholly new spaces for the twenty-first century. These activities, inspired by new technological, programmatic, spatial, and functional requirements, will forge links between the museum's creative and educational mission, engendering new levels of public understanding and participation. The shape and character of the Spiral is a synergetic linking of the internal requirements of the program and the external iconography of the Exhibition Road area, offering new readings of the whole and of the part.

■ A simple and open structure of organization permits the Spiral to be used in a flexible and independent manner vis-à-vis the galleries of the existing museum. Lobbies, cafés, shops, restaurant, auditorium, educational studios, resource center, and galleries can function independently, day or evening, and, with the Observatory at the very apex of the Spiral, constitute the celebration of the public in the building. Various innovative configurations of use can be planned outside normal museum hours. Fashion shows, school events, showcases for the design and production industries, educational festivities, and unique programming possibilities of the Spiral constitute the intensive and imaginative heart of

The Spiral *Competition Text, 1996* When facing the old entrance of the Victoria & Albert Museum (V&A), one is confronted by two words to the left and right of the main gate: Imagination and Knowledge. This twin inscription describes the inspirational force, or muse, steering the idea of the museum. In the next century, this profound dialectic must continue to engage the wide public and open the experience of the visitor to new ways of viewing and using the museum. The museum of the twenty-first century must be open to the future of still-unknown possibilities lodged between these guideposts. ◎ The V&A has taken up this challenge with a proposal to build an extension including an integrated mixture of exhibition spaces, educational facilities, and accommodation for new methods of interactive orientation. The V&A's mission to provide a gateway to the twentieth century via its own rich and diverse collection requires a vision that gives new significance to its great traditions and goes beyond the purely passive relation between the arts and the public. This proposal offers new kinds of experience, eluding the closure that would categorize the museum as "ready-made," rigidly defined, or passively neutral. ◎ The design is structured around three dimensions:

the spiral movement of art and history;
the interlocking of inside and outside;
the labyrinth of discovery.

It takes these dimensions and translates them into a coherent ensemble of functionally related spaces. ◎ The spiral of art and history manifests itself in the overall form of the extension building and its circulation system. The enclosure is created out of a continuous wall, whose extent mirrors that of the perimeter walls of the entire V&A block, spiraling around a virtual and ever-shifting vertical axis. Visitors are implicated in a spiral movement as they circulate through the various functions of the museum. This movement dynamically distributes the public to the rest of the museum through strategic connections, and is a counterpoint to the lateral, horizontal movement in the existing buildings. ◎ The winding and unwinding spiral creates an interlocking of the inside and the outside of the new building, bringing the visitor into close relation with history and the present, the city and the museum, through a direct experience of interpenetrating views and histories. From the extension one sees ever-changing views of the existing facades and the skyline of London, while from the old museum block one is reoriented by the shifting movements of the new building. The relationship between form and function generates a variety of sequential and dramatic narratives of space and light. The whole is a composition of layered sequences in which the new building becomes a veritable beacon of energy toward the inside and outside world. ◎ The labyrinth of discovery is the organizational leitmotiv mediating between the existing galleries and the

the new extension. ■ Six centrifugally distributed links emanate from the Spiral and connect it to the buildings adjacent to the extension. These links mediate between the different levels of the Henry Cole Wing, Webb Wing, and Western Range, bringing them to a common level and making them accessible from the Spiral. These connections give an entirely new array of routes through the whole of the V&A, multiple access to collections, and for the first time allow elderly and physically challenged visitors full access to existing galleries. Thus, visitors will have access to galleries that were not reachable before. Delicate bridges connect the Spiral to the old fabric, offering a new appreciation of the historical facades by bringing the visitors close to the terra cottas on the Henry Cole or next to the pilasters of the Webb Wing. **Material and Structure:** The Spiral is a unique structure. It is not a traditional spiral with a single center and axis, but a contemporary spiral that opens a plurality of directions along many different trajectories, providing multiple routes, spaces, and ambiances for the visitors. The building utilizes a simple, continuous, interlocking wall system to create and articulate functions, while offering an efficient and flexible structure requiring no supporting elements. The fluid spaces of the Spiral offer differing qualities, characters, and scales for the museum's varied activities. The core of the building provides large uninterrupted spaces, while the periphery creates smaller demonstration theaters, which communicate with the galleries and are washed by natural light. The wall geometries extend the floor plates into a fully three-dimensional experience, an entirely new set of possibilities for contemporary media presentations. ■ The external material of the wall is ceramic tile, the geometry of which forms a contemporary fractal pattern related to the Golden Section in dialogue with a grammar of ornament (Owen Jones). The pattern is integral to the wall structure, carrying within itself the structural logic of modulating scale and proportion within an endlessly fascinating surface. The off-white tone of the tiles lies midway between the cold grays of the Portland stone and the warm ivories on the Natural History Museum. The tiles are subtly graded and textured, giving the facade a shimmering life of its own and thematizing the light through the contexts of the composition. ■ In its spatial form and handcrafted quality, the Spiral embodies the tradition and contemporaneity of the V&A. It carries the message of inspiration and knowledge into the everyday experience of the visitor. The construction of the Spiral will not only revitalize the V&A as a whole, it will also create an exciting place in London: an emblem for communicating and connecting arts, crafts, and architecture to the twenty-first century. ■

museum's new program requirements. This image of the labyrinth is not only a symbolic device, but a reinforcement and intensification of the unique qualities of the V&A. This emblem of a heterogeneous and open system of organization for the artifacts and exhibitions provides a diversity of experiences woven into a net of similarities and differences—an aggregate of traces about unexpected topics still to be explored. The seamless transition from place to place and floor to floor envelopes the visitor in a unique continuity throughout the many dimensions of the museum as a whole. ◎ The spiral form fuses the archaic and the new in its organization and urban image. It provides an emblem articulating the cross-cultural collections of the V&A, the multicultural profile of its visitors, and the fusion of the arts, technology, and history. The structure of discovery in the new extension is a microcosm of the multifaceted order of the museum and a gateway to the history of the decorative arts. The visitors are celebrated as participants in the sensory and intellectual experience, an ongoing discovery of the drama of art and its history. ◎ The structure and cladding of the new extension are formed by the fractile, a new kind of tile pattern whose economy allows a multiform language to emerge out of an elementary geometric piece interpreted in a variety of different ways. As a strategy toward the surface, the fractile bridges the gap between the wondrous tiles of Granada and Isfahan and the tile technology used on the space shuttle, bringing the decorative arts onto the surface of the building. The fractile offers endless variation in formal articulation and the relationship between surface and structure within the economy of building construction. The design of motifs and patterns could be developed through the educational activities of the museum via an interactive participation program, so that the building surface becomes an ongoing expression of unpredictable yet controlled interactions between arts and crafts, around the theme of the contemporary museum. ◎ The new extension is divided into two parts: **1)** In the upper levels, an interactive field continuum of traditional and non-Cartesian spaces is enclosed within the folds of the spiral. These floors house the new galleries for the permanent collections, the orientation center and the

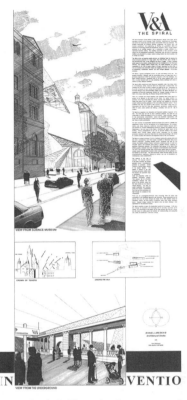

The Spiral, planning presentation panel

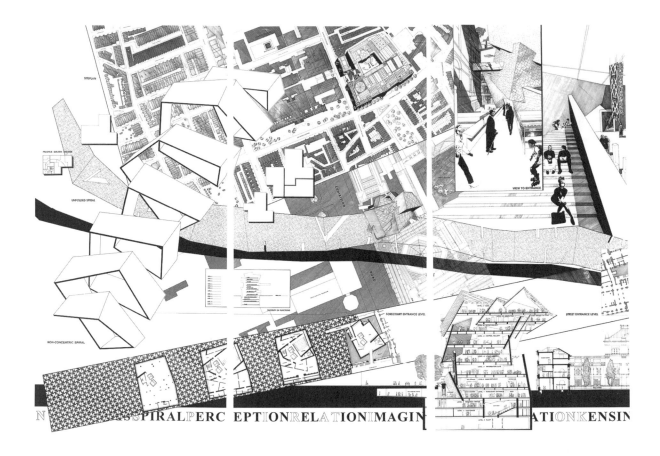

museum administration on several upper floors. The exhibition galleries are lifted out of the anonymity with which such spaces are often associated, and instead articulate a new configuration responding to the creative tension between spatial relation and programmatic field. Out of these special qualities, spaces are created that can accommodate a wide variety of exhibitions, from traditional installations to new events emerging out of technological media forms. In this way, the kinetic and sensory experience offers multiple ways of discovering the familiar. 2) In the levels below the street, one finds a highly modern gallery for temporary exhibitions, educational facilities, and an auditorium for performance, theater, lectures, and film. These diverse activities are organized within a rigorous functional system designed for maximum flexibility. These spaces extend under the existing buildings into the Pirelli gardens, tying the extension in depth to the heart of the museum complex and functioning as

the foundation for the galleries above—the infrastructure supporting the lantern of history. ◉ These two parts are separated by the entrance lobby spaces, which the visitor enters across a bridge overlooking a new sunken garden, out of which the building grows. In this way an open and inviting new entrance is created as an exhilarating symbol of the dynamics of the museum's diverse exhibitions. Fronting and visible from the street, welcoming the visitor into the museum lobby, is a gift shop and bookstore. Once inside, one sees the central position of the information and ticket desk and the core of elevators. ◉ The lobby space extends vertically down to the restaurant and children's play area directly below, which look out over the new garden. These two levels form a unit constituting the lobby space as a whole, connected at ground level to the existing buildings. ◉ From the lobby, visitors to the museum's collections take the glazed express elevator directly to the observatory of the orientation center

on the top floor, glimpsing along the way the offerings in the new permanent collection galleries. From here, overlooking the Pirelli Garden and the roofscape of the entire museum, a route around the galleries can be planned using the materials and technologies of the center. Next to this is a café/bar overlooking the museum and the city. The route from here to the museum proper takes the visitor on a spiral descent via escalators to the new permanent collection galleries and back toward the lobby. Linkages to the rest of the museum collections are located on various levels along this route, allowing direct connection from multiple points. ◉ Visitors to the museum who wish to visit the temporary exhibition or use the educational facilities access these spaces by descending directly from the lobby, passing on their way the restaurant and children's play area. Directly underneath this is the auditorium, on the same level as the temporary exhibition galleries, which extend under the Pirelli Garden. From this point, a stair-

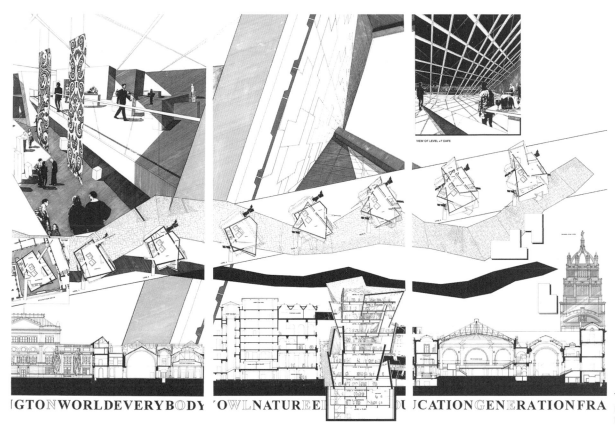

VIEW OF LEVEL +7 CAFE

GTONWORLDEVERYBODY OWLNATUREE UCATIONGENERATIONFRA

The Spiral, planning presentation panels

case leads straight to the educational facilities and workshops beneath. A ramp rises into the garden, creating a connection between the changing exhibitions, the learning facilities, and the rest of the museum. The garden itself is recomposed as a dynamic landscape punctuated by skylights, providing the temporary exhibition galleries and educational spaces with natural light. ◉ From Exhibition Road, a second bridge provides an alternative access to the lobby, and a direct entrance for groups to the temporary exhibitions, auditorium, and educational facilities. ◉ The Webb screen would be lowered and face the garden, becoming the frame for an outdoor exhibition space visible from the lower levels of the new extension. In this way Webb's architecture is given no significance—no longer a screen but a frame for activity and a stage for events. ◉ The administration spaces of the program are located on several floors at the top of the spiral, near the orientation center, with

separate access via a bridge link to the Henry Cole Wing. The offices have views of the existing museum buildings, and are connected to the new exhibition spaces by an atrium. Although embedded within the exhibition galleries they can thus function completely independently of the public parts of the extension. ◉ The new museum for the V&A, on its last available site, is perhaps best likened to the last chord of a symphony. Only when this chord is played do the first notes acquire the form of their fulfillment. This proposal extends the zone of boundaries and connections (between old/new, inside/outside, structure/form, architecture/decoration, technology/craft) by shifting them to ever new and open perspectives, intersections, and relations through its fugal construction. By opening instead of closing the block of the V&A, this last chord does not end the music of the museum, but extends it toward unknown and future horizons of the mind and of space. ●

Steinatem/Stonebreath

Competition for a Memorial for the Murdered Jews of Europe, Berlin, 1997 The enormously difficult and problematic task of designing a memorial to the murdered Jews of Europe in Berlin raises ethical, philosophical, and aesthetic questions that go far beyond the traditional understanding of memorials. This gaping aporia should become visible to the public in the form of a memorial whose permanent emptiness and eternal necessity are structurally tied to each other. ■ The Memorial for the Murdered Jews of Europe is hallowed in the vacancies of the ever-present, ever-illusive Berlin. In the erasures and obliterations of Berlin, in the tracings and projections of Berlin, this presence-absence relates the future of the memorial to its past in the emptied and vacant places that it continues to hold together. ■ The base of the structure is a concave plate, the dimension of which equals the footprint of the Reichstag rotated around the centerpoint of the Brandenburger Tor's Quadriga. The lowest point of the curvature forms a subtle horizon, which sinks to two meters below the horizon of the city and connects the historical center of the Tiergarten around the Goethe monument. The plate is rotated in relation to the central axis of the Reichstag, which it marks with a fragment along a steel line pointing to the Void of the Berlin Museum with the Jewish Museum. The space of the plate is deliberately extended to the Tiergarten, while a park is inserted into the new ground. This chasmic extension and insertion incorporates the cars driving through it, the pedestrians walking into it, and the Tiergarten around it. ■ I call this plate a Pebblewriting—written by the footprints of Berliners and those who visit the memorial. Cut into this Pebblewriting is a channel aligned toward the Wannsee Villa, where the murder of six million Jews was signed into protocol. This channel comes to a dead end four meters below the ground. Within this cut stand six solidified voids—called Stonebreath—for the murdered Jews. ■ Running through the Stonebreath is a sloping path forming a pedestrian walkway. Its hollows, gaps, disconnections, and fractures form a spectrum of density, from the highly perforated openings at the entrance to the closures at the dead end. ■ The Stonebreath is constructed by the accretion of horizontal layers of concrete according to a rigorous layering system organized to produce what is not part of it, namely the gap or the Void, a system inscribing its own demise in what is visible. It is the precise solidification of the Void running through the Berlin Museum with the Jewish Museum. ■ The perforations are like laced porcelain of early Berlin, both fragile and structures of their own fragility. Within the inner walls are inscribed the texts of the memorial, which I propose should go beyond the facts and figures relating to the Holocaust. Such texts could include a map of the world, the permanent updating of which would show the evolving conflicts and genocides as a warning to the present and to the future. ■ The memorial concretizes and materializes light and shadow, presence and absence, day and night. The rhythm of the structure is spaced by vertical gaps connecting the fissures, which inscribe the sky and air into the public space of the surroundings. Between the clear-cut open spaces of the Stonebreath one sees the play of humanity of the city. ■ One sees the future as a structure of permeability in tension with the closure of history. In rain as well as in sunlight, in the gray skies of winter, as well as the blue summer skies, the memorial inhales and exhales the breath of history. ■ The Stonebreath for six million murdered Jews breathes with absence of space, yet is filled by the light of Berlin. It is a memorial that does not simply look backward at a time forever lost; it is a memorial that is penetrated by material and absence, by return and by departure, by the open and by the closed. The memorial will stand as an urban configuration situating the public in the breathlessness of Berlin, Germany, and the world. ■

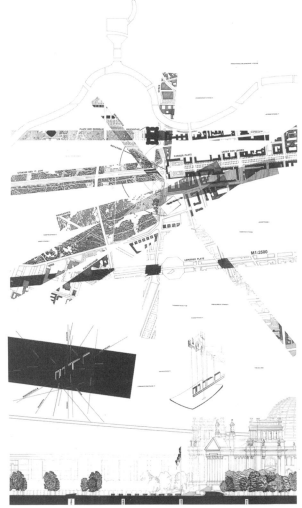

Steinatem/Stonebreath, site plan and elevation

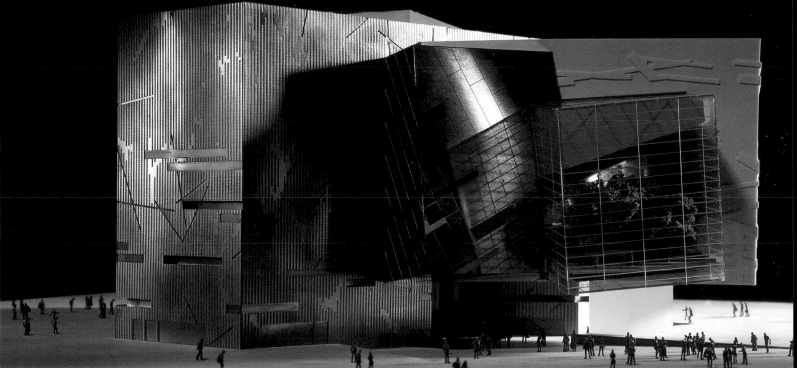

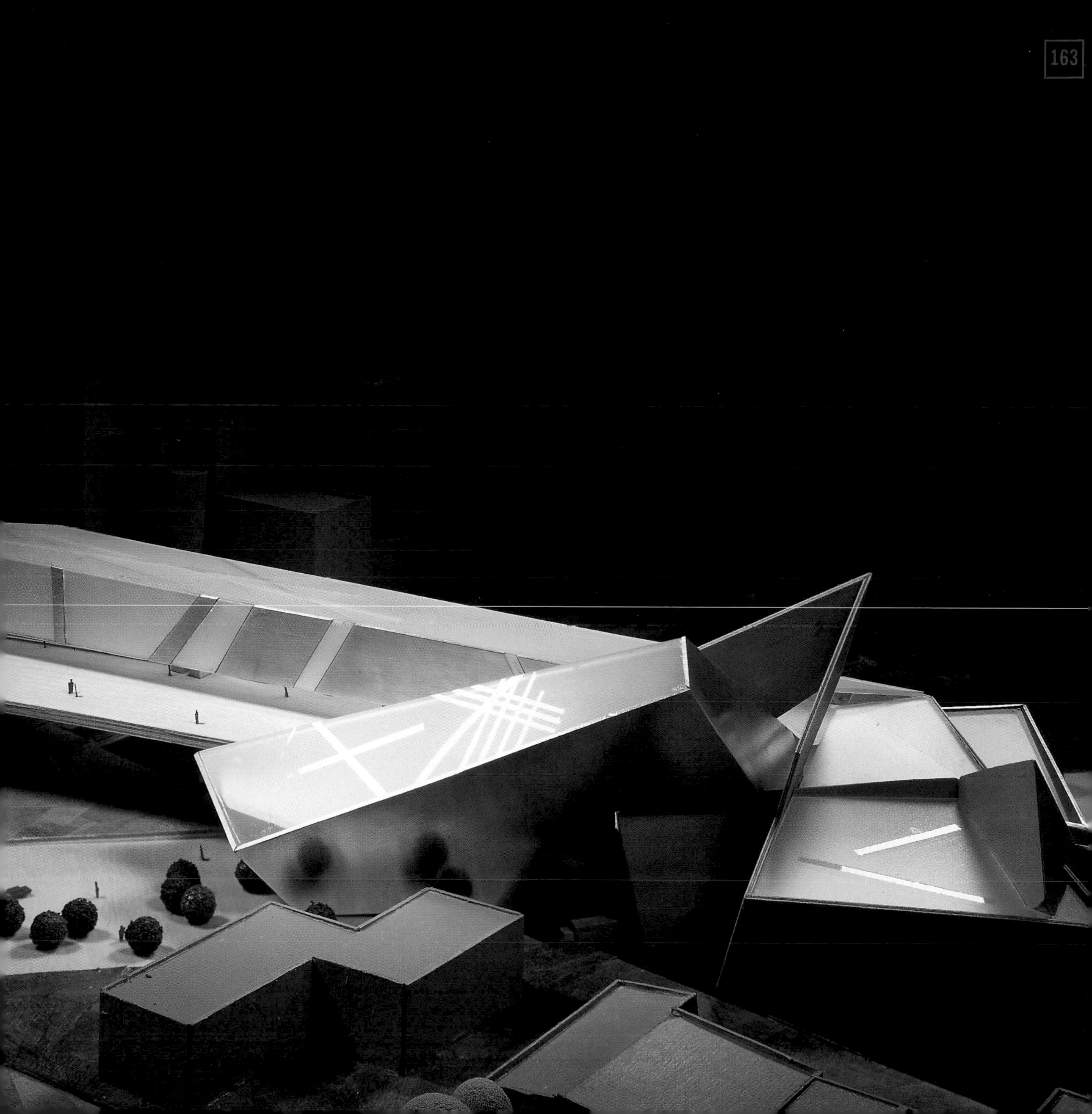

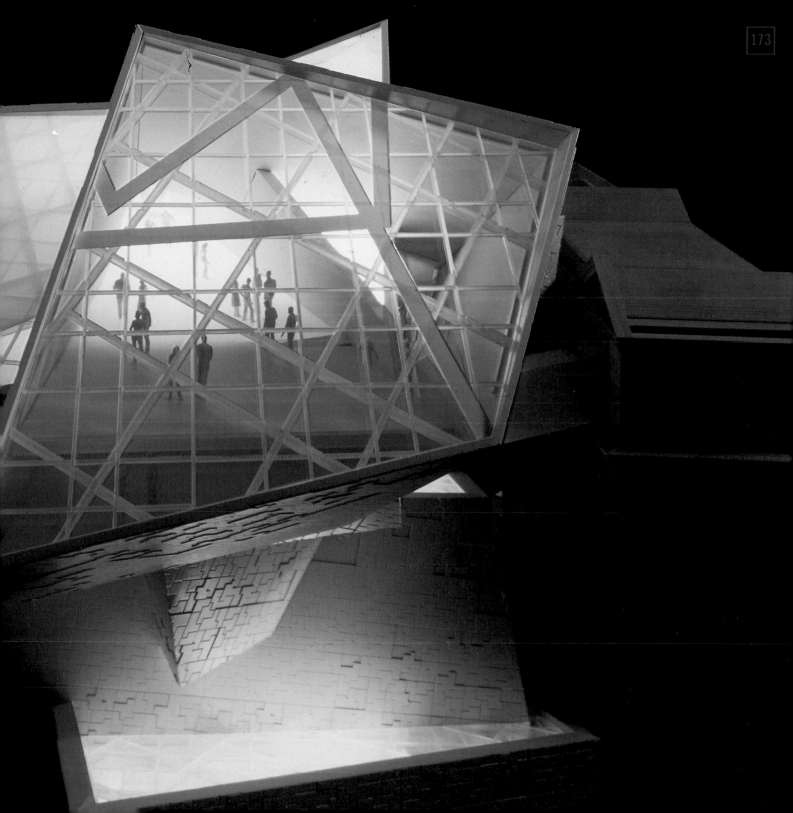

The Tenth Muse

Competition for an Office Complex, Wiesbaden, 1992 The office complex for the twenty-first century must not only meet highly advanced energy, ecological, and technological requirements, but it also must radically reformulate the very philosophy of the "workday." The architectural ensemble must offer a wholly new spatial, visual, and symbolic interpretation of the office world and its environment. In this project, work functions and the ancillary social spaces have been fundamentally redefined by the introduction of an entirely new dimension of public activity and individual freedom. ■ The Urban-Roof-Nature is no longer the boundary where buildings end; it extends the social life of the employees by offering a changed relation to the city and to nature, intensely generated at the foot of the building. The landscape grid decomposes progressively, giving way, by the end of the century, to the forest, redressing the existing ecological imbalance. ■ Muse Lines, containing new activities that are related to new office potential, cut across old boundaries that used to divide routine from leisure, private from public, and work from pleasure. These Muse Lines, dedicated to the musical remembrance of work as play and play as work, seek to rearticulate new desires generated by technological organization along the path of imagination, invention, and individuality. ■

The Earth's atmosphere and environment radiate musically.

Each constellation, each galaxy, each particle of architecture is thus "trapped radiation" or music—sometimes harmonic, sometimes not.

An irradiance, both visible and infravisible, also encompasses the sphere of office building, known historically as the UFFIZI.

The broaching of the "tenth" spectrum opens a reference atmosphere whose opacity and penetration constitute a new structure and a new organization on Earth's fluctuating magnetosphere.

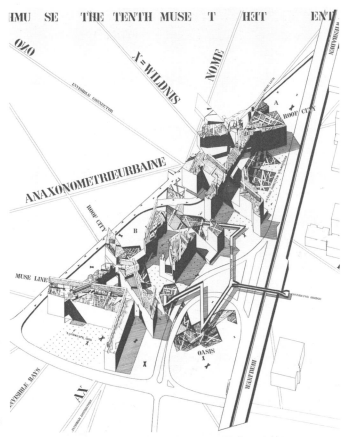

The Tenth Muse, axonometric site plan and elevation

Unknown Muse = Omnidirectional field with a charged mantle

$$m \,(\text{INDIGITAT}) + u \,(\text{EXPROBRABIT}) + s \,(\text{LEVIR TANGIT}) + e \,(\text{APPROBRABIT}) = \text{muse} \times \frac{\text{muse}}{\text{architecture}} \times \text{radiation}$$

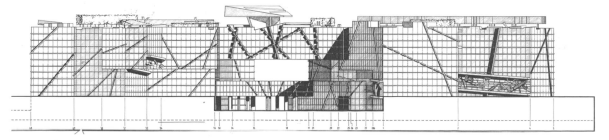

Theatrum Mundi:
Through the Green Membranes of Space Drawings, 1985

"This is modeln times"
—James Joyce

210

Confessio Fraternitatis

Disbelieve nothing abysmal.

When you enter the open, worship, neither do nor say anything concerning Divine Architecture.
Abstaining in this way from living space—creatures will inevitably induce immoderate laughter
which is forbidden there. Go barefoot, carefully declining the use of highways: Your footnotes
will be a mark of nobility.

I see no reason to turn back home, for the Furles indeed go back with you
in order to help support the weight, but not to lay it down. As language falls and falters the open is opened.

Those who efface the taste of wonder with the ashes of technique, receive not an Erythrine,
drink not the Vitalium, nor honor the figure and the rails. For whom then does the wind blow?
Who worships its noise?

"Above all, govern your tongue when you follow the gods." That was ancient wisdom.
That was the temple permanently thrown in the way. They went in just because they passed by its doors,
impatient and lazy.

Cutting the fire with swords, wiping the seat with the torch sealed the way:
It remains concealed to this very day. Then they threw their rings, on whose faces the image
of the steps was graven, wrapped themselves in glass by the candlelight, and received the swallow into their house.

The sacrifice was performed but the cock was spared.

We ought to offer another one to Asclepius:
"See to it,
and don't
forget."

Theatrum Mundi *Interview, 1987*

SKALA: When regarding your drawings a feeling is aroused that you can get trapped inside the "frame," that there is no way out. It is a similar feeling that you may have when looking at a baroque painting. However, in a baroque painting there is always somewhere to go. For instance, there may be an oval-shaped opening, a connection between heaven and earth, while in your drawings the possibilities for escaping the labyrinth seem to end up with cross-shaped figures in a kind of space labyrinth.

D.L.: That's a very good way of putting it, because the cross is the cross of what is manifested with what is not manifested, and a rotation around an invisible axis that throws everything into nonidentity (recession) as much as it throws everything into a point (relief). And to throw together means, in Greek, literally, symbol. So these works also hide the places of escape. But these drawings were, in particular, very difficult because there was no escape from them or into them. You asked a very interesting question, because I have thought a lot about the relation between throwing the labyrinth and aerial flight together. Daedalus, a Greek, was thrown out of Ireland...But I really don't know how to phrase it. The fact is that something like the labyrinth is a permanent experience in architecture from its very beginnings. It is a mental condition of anyone who is occupied with the problem. But at the same time there are differences in the labyrinths...Once you get out of the labyrinth into the open—the next labyrinth, so to speak—you have reached a differentiated,

The modern city has become a process of disposing of the nonexistent in order to secure a false
and surreptitious immortality. But as a contemporary mechanism for the "reformation" of politics,
what remains of it is a disclosure of a living parasite which, lodged in the Host, determines its makeup.
As a manifestation of the disease of monetary utopias, the city is no longer MAN written large,
but man is city written very small—and almost illegibly: CITY.

This abysmal narrowing I translate as a crisis in which the City of the Heart vanishes, making a microscopic
clearing for an infinitesimal plasmodium—one capable of eventually turning, dwelling itself into an irrational fever.

When it comes to the idea of *Theatrum Mundi,* one thing is certain: that wherever
that strange spectacle came from, it will probably no longer have anything to do
with the celebration of the dead or the living, with memory or imagination.

The premonition of the future—in the sense of Theatrum Mundi—is presented here in the
form of a city besieged by an unknown infection, an action taking place within the nucleic medium
that flows in the bloodstream of architectural thought.

The feeling for an atmosphere of sanctity and detachment will not again make an appearance
with the paraphernalia belonging to an apotheosis of an eternal style.

To deal with the urban seems an impudence that takes the most biological, private, and hidden form
of existence possible today, and turns this reality into a collective fiction. The space of the city is closed
because its structure has become transparent. Its place is taken by the *Distributor of Homelessness,*
through whom the city discovers itself as the now defunct Hotel of Being.

I don't care for disorder and I dread police protection as well.

a more articulated, level of the labyrinth. You consider the previous labyrinth as your bended experience or as simply something that you have overcome or gotten out of; i.e., as something that has "freed" you. In other words, throughout the experience the ambiguous depth of the problem remains exactly the same (in Greek or ancient architecture, as much as in modern). These experiences can also be at different levels of articulation, and that has nothing to do with time, nothing to do with chronology or progress. So in this way what constitutes, for instance, a more direct way of reaching the dead-point of the labyrinth may be found in cultures that are long gone, rather than in our own.

If we look at your drawings over the past fifteen years, there are steps, although it's also a continuous movement—through The Chamberworks, Theatrum Mundi, etc. There's a process of development but the projects seem to be quite different.

I don't know. If one is open to the fact that what one is making is also part of the process that is making it, one has to accept the change. Let me put it this way: The symbol that is there is not independent but is itself a part of the process that throws it out. So in a way the things we have to grasp reality with, architecture reflectively, are also part of the process that is engendering them in the first place, like language. The language of situations is part of them, not independent. It's not something that, in fact, can be distanced from them. Reality comes out of those situations, like the unpredictability of drawings, the instability of objects or whatever else one strives for in architecture. All these are also part of the process in

49

1 Dedicated to Petrarch.

2 Dedicated to Erasmus.

Three Lessons in Architecture: The Machines

211
212
213
214

Installation, Venice Biennale, 1985 The proposal deals with the city and its architecture in the form of participatory engagement with three large machines. The public is involved with creating and interpreting architecture in its broad social, cultural, and historical perspective. The three machines propose a fundamental recollection and a retrieval of the historical destiny of architecture; a singular, if unexpected, homecoming. This mechanism constitutes a single project: Each segment forms a starting point for the understanding and functioning of the others. Together they form a cycle in which projects are seen, explicated, and overcome. As metaphysical equipment the three machines and their respective architectures seek to release each of the future sites unto themselves, thus letting the present remain a given, even as it moves toward its own past. **Lesson A:** Reading Architecture Teaches an almost forgotten (medieval) process of building, a process that is in its own way not yet fully unfolded in architecture. Like the medieval monastery out of which the Reading Machine[1] emerged, the method of construction and the technique of understanding bring about a revolution of architecture's techne, which coincides with the movement of the text that it propels. As a place of intersection between archaeological reconstruction (Ramelli, Palmanova, military engineering) and

the will to power it discloses (metaphysics, monasticism, ideology), the Reading Machine reveals the tautological reality of the architectural text. The Eight Books—each a single word uttered by the forgetfulness of being that resolves itself by turning back in order to come forward—lie on eight shelves. The books come and go for a comparison not only with each other, but with the weight of the last seven words of metaphysics, which crush the gears and axles whose relation is inaccessible from the reading position. The wheel revolves, and in compelling a revolution returns to its starting point while exposing its own uselessness and kinetic beauty. ■ Executed in a "medieval" manner, with glueless joints and using no energy of contemporary kind, this machine represents the triumph of spirit over matter, of candlelight over darkness. It is made solely from wood, as are the books. **Lesson B:** Remembering Architecture Consists of that which can still be remembered in architecture. As a historical program the sites have been filtered through Giulio Camillo's Memory Theater. As a precise weaving of the memory tradition with the agony of a deus ex machina, this theater represents the workings of a Renaissance mind and shows its internal equipment and the arrangement it reveals. ■ The Memory Machine[2] consists of the backstage only—the spectacle takes place wholly outside of it. As a mechanism for projection, concealment, and illusion, this prosthetic

which that peculiar thing was born, and from which it cannot be detached without mutilation. So architecture too is involved in a meditative structure. I think it always has been. For instance, the so-called classical architecture was not just an instrument of reason that was projected through some other mold, sign, or graphic, but was understood to be a ladder in a process that reached completely different conclusions elsewhere. All I mean to say is that doing architecture is like the hand grasping something, because what it grasps becomes part of the hand. The

object itself would be the extension of the grasping. As long as it's being grasped it's still handlike...human...

Would you consider your way of working as grasping in a way?...The literature you have chosen for the reading machine, for instance, is it chosen on the background of your own fascination, or your personal view of what is the most important?

It is the forgotten that interests me, that which has been overcome, the unoriginal. I also disregard many of the things that are supposedly important in architecture, or the things that are venerated by those who want to control architecture through power. The common control level on which architecture is said to be grounded especially disregards that making is actually a critique—that the whole ideology on which architecture is supposed to be based as a part of the instrumentality of reality—is inadequate, because I don't think it really is.

3 The Writing Machine is black and throws a gleam, which is dedicated to Voltaire.

piece of equipment exposes and hides the Venetian projects. ■ Since the process of its construction remains in the classical arena (imagination, measurement, idea), the subversive element of mechanics (Teatro Farnese versus Teatro Olimpico) enters only in those places where memory has succeeded in retaining its surrogate authority. ■ As a ghost of humanism's cosmic hubris, the Memory Machine seeks to disengage the sites from the Earth in order to return them to their original, destined locus: Joyce's Dublin and Tatlin's Moscow. ■ Done in a Renaissance style of being, the Memory Machine abounds in the kind of inventiveness and caprice that we associate with the Odradek. ■ It is executed in wood and retains in its structure the "hanging papers" seen by the king. This project represents the stage of architecture's appearance and is a testament to its own manifestation. Also made of wood are the eighteen subordinate spectacles, which include the "cloud machine" and the "schizophrenic forum." Colorless: The bloody red illuminates the shiny exterior of an inner sanctum dedicated to what remains nameless. Metal is used exclusively for nonstructural reasons, related as it is to light itself. Ropes are used throughout. **Lesson C: Writing Architecture** Teaches the artless and scienceless making of architecture. As a fully engaged project this machine industrializes the poetic of architecture and offers it as a sacrifice to its own possibilities of making a text. Architecture, like shoemaking, becomes a problem of putting the nail in the right place. ■ Since the Writing Machine[3] processes both memory and reading material, it takes what is projected into an exact account. Not only the city itself (Palmanova) but all places written into the book of culture as here collected and disposed. ■ Through an enlightened vision the random mosaic of knowledge is gathered together into seven times seven faces, each mirrored in a quadripartite realm. The totality of architecture is shattered by the foursome reciprocity of Earth, sky, mortals, and gods, and lies open to a contemporary stocktaking. ■ The four sides of this "Orphic" calculator, or probability computer, prognosticate the written destiny of architecture, whose oblivion is closely associated with Victor Hugo's prophecy. The four-sided cubes work in the following Swiftian manner:

Side 1: The City as a Star of Redemption is refracted and congeals into a "boogie-woogie" constellation.
Side 2: Is a metallic reflection that shatters and disrupts the spatial-mathematical order of the forty-nine times four sides.
Side 3: Consists of a geometric sign, which points to a graphic omen or architectural horoscope.

Also language is not really ours, it never was. If one would say, with Vitruvius, that the origin of architecture is a language, it's not that language. Then what kind of language is it?

Certainly, it is very different to talk about a gothic cathedral and so-called organic or anonymous architecture. We say anonymous only because we disregard the historical field in which it was made. Especially illusory is the contemporary understanding of myth as something opaque and totally collective. Myth too has an intellectual history to it. It is a particularly complex organization or logos that is different from philosophy. Myth may be, in fact, a preferable form of understanding than that which is only founded on the limits of discourse. If one looks at the origin of things like geometry, or the origin of a paradigm or model of reality, one would for instance find that Greek philosophers like Plato ... (in the Timalos) have a very interesting dilemma in making the analogy between the word soul and the word body on one hand, versus the human body and psyche on the other. Plato uses two different terms to describe the difficulty. He uses either the word like story or myth. But he resolved it in favor of the latter, of mythopoetic play in which everything is at stake, but actually nothing is known. Of course, if one thinks that this is the basis itself, it's even more profound because physics and modern science are based on this play of unknown. ●

Side 4: Enumerates the forty-nine saints who accompany the detached pilgrim in order to care for his unerasable vulnerability.

Thus the oppositions and complementary reciprocities that glide through the whole constitute a "destabilized technology," which would break up the mechanism instantly if the computerized controls (twenty-eight handles) weren't there to keep it stable. The Writing Machine is the first totally unstable text. As opposed to "stable" architectural texts, which best fly in a straight line of myth and resist the pilot's effort to climb, bank, or dive, this "unstable" prototype is extremely agile, having no natural flight path. ■ It jumps around the text's sky and is guided by an "active control system," which can perhaps never again disclose its starting position (see position at the beginning; see position at the end). The Writing Machine is a contribution to Roussel scholarship. It links Africa and the impressions of Italy through those miraculous figures whose presence is both inevitable and contingent. Angelica, with a grid, burnt on a grid; St. Donatella; Mossem killed by the burning of text onto his feet, killed by burning iambic text into forehead; St. Theodor of Constantinople. By rotating the "foursome," the arrange-

ments appear ready for interpretation. These seemingly random relations are generated by an extremely sophisticated system, which consists of 2,662 parts, most of them mobile. All are involved in an unpredictable rationalization of place, name, person. Once in motion, the stockpiling and accounting of places, cities, types of buildings, gods, signs, saints, imaginary beings, forgotten realities will present almost unsurmountable difficulties for the operator, yet these are difficulties that can be eliminated through the revolutionary discipline of this turn toward a Buddhism of action.

The machine is made of wood, graphite, and metal, and contains:
1) complex gear-shaft-driven systems that rotate the multilingual papers;
2) forty-nine cubes that revolve at various speed ratios;
3) faces that show:
    a. Euro-African city
    b. saints who have emerged from the project and who return to Roussel's Book of Saints
    c. the empty sky;
4) divined graphic configuration based on horoscopes and omens. ■

Three Lessons in Architecture: The Machines *Interview with SKALA, 1985*

D.L.: The machines are reversals and images of each other; a kind of triplet: one in three and three in one. They are really points along a line of tension between the nonexistence of architecture on the one hand, and the nonexistence of the architect on the other. They are the difference between an impossible dream of what architecture was and the fact that it does not seem to exist at all today. And these three points together are the locus of the attempt to grasp— that is the project I set for myself—the tension of architecture today. The machines cannot be seen on their own. They are really just extensions of each other, so, as I said, the notion of cutting them off as objects in themselves is meaningless. One can in fact say that the wheel of the axle of the Writing Machine is really the big wheel of reading which revolves it and in turn

is the movement of the memory. Technically it is actually a cylinder piece with a gear on the inside. It is very, very small so you can hardly see it in the entirety of the work.

The objective way of looking at architecture is really what I cannot agree with. That architecture exists apart from us as an object. It does not. One can see it as an object, but I always say that it is a distorted way of looking at architecture.

I think that, ideologically, the notion of architecture with these so-called objective realities that has been presented in the twentieth century is an extremely false one. In fact, everything in one's own experience testifies that things aren't really there. The discrepancy between the dogma of architecture as presence and the experience of its absence constitutes, for participants, a dilemma in which real/unreal distinctions become meaningless. For most people architecture is not visible in that way. Nor is it for the architect after five o'clock when he has finished working!

SKALA: In the Memory Machine you put the bright red color. Maybe there's only a shine of blood, but there is still something reminding you of the human body?

Exactly, it is one thing. Every level is inclusive of its own materials and colors. I tried to make it a singularly organized work through one which is not continuous. What reveals itself in different points in different ways is really the gap between the moments of time. The parts that really make it continue are the parts that cannot be shown because they are missing. Those are the ones that are not objective, and that is the most luminous part of the machines. These are the things that cannot be easily said because there is no technical equipment that could bring them closer to us. There is no content there that can be objectified, that can be made into a continuous object of experience. But I think one should go back in depth—to experience itself, not just

SYNOPSIS OF THE PROJECT

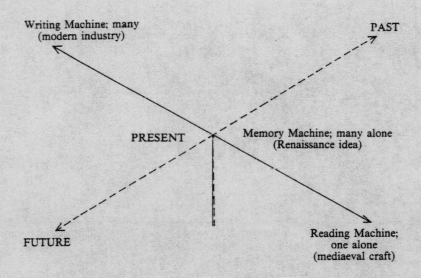

The projects are situated along the intersection between the Axis of Architecture (Time) and the Axis of Technology (Soul).

The projects generate the crossing of manifestation and oblivion throwing technique into relief and drawing the veil over Architecture.

to its symbols, but to the experiences that engendered those symbols. One would then find the engendering event as belonging to the gap in the depth. Hume would say psychology and the Greeks would say the psyche. But the problem is that the depth of the psyche can only be experienced on the technical level, so that even though there is a depth, there is no access to it—except at the level of what we can talk about, which is the level of consciousness and presence.

But where does the memory in the machine come from? It could come from this life, but it could also be other overlayed memories.

It has to come from other times and other places, but ones that have already been experienced by us, since even dying would not be comprehensive otherwise. For instance, the notion of the apocalypse is incredible, because it is a symbol of the end of the world that has been there from the very beginning of time. The end of the world is always experienced, but for fifty thousand years of known history it did not happen. And it is unlikely to ever happen. Clearly it is not something that can ever happen, at least empirically. If one goes beyond human history, therefore, metempsychosis emerges as a very fascinating problem. The existence of consciousness of the end, and at the same time the fact that empirically this is complete nonsense, that such an end to anything is impossible. I think today everyone is trying to finish architecture. It's conceived to be as an end. But if you look historically at architecture, it's ending all the time. From its weight and position in the world, to its weightlessness and lack of position. You can see that it is ending, symbolically. If you think of how much significance it occupied in the past and how much it was part of the world, how progressively it has gotten lighter and lighter, and has become less and less part of the world, then you can see, at least symbolically, the horizon in which architecture would completely vanish. In the future one can't exclude developments that are extremely different from the ones that we now predict. For instance, everybody thinks that the future is going to be a certain way. But I have a suspicion, personally, that it's not going to be the way people imagine it. The future of architecture could be extremely different and a very big surprise to everybody, as history reveals.

But if you take, for instance, Leon Krier and Quinlan Tery, and their interest in handicraft, they would probably like your machine?

They would reject it on the basis of the experience. They would perhaps like it, but it would be for the picturesque and the artificial, which are the least important of things. Artifact is only the evidence of something far more important; that which may not leave any traces in the long run—artifacts of this sort, anyway. It is possible that there were many societies and cultures that did not leave behind themselves things that were lasting, which does not make them any lesser societies, in fact, quite the contrary. In India and China, we don't know certain cities because they were made out of wood and they burned down. And only on that basis we compare, so to speak, the power of Western civilization with what we consider a very different class of experience in the East. India simply has a completely different agenda. But who is to say that the notion of India, which is basically that each person is a revolutionary cycle of the cosmos, is not in the long run much more liberating than the Western idea that only the political action is the revolutionary aspect of the world.

You said that the human being is the only being that is not vitally connected to a place, and you talked about a spaceless placelessness. Maybe this is a very important point. Do you really think that for a human being place does not matter?

I don't think that the place that has been talked about today matters. That kind of place is a cheap way of saying "homecoming." But it is also true to say that every provincial society always thinks of itself as being at home, at the center of the world. Especially the more provincial you get, the more you think you are in the center of the world. So if one finds really remote people, they think that they are not only at the center, they think they are the only ones. Yet I think one has another kind of experience when one has left the province and sees that everyone is claiming to be at the center of the world.

From the progress of your works toward a sort of final step, it was obvious that a kind of fabric, installation, model would follow the drawings. What is happening now that you are going to build in Berlin. Are those things connected in a way?

Of course they are connected in my own experience, but the connection is not a direct one. I would say that the materials you refer to—any material, including the building itself—is only a triggering point for reliving, not one's own experience, but the experience of reality. In other words, architecture is possible only insofar as it can be reopened. That reopening has nothing to do with "history" or objective facts...and that's what we talked about earlier...that there could be for two thousand years books that are not read, things that are not looked upon, because there is no one to look at them...

Your machines function in the same way, they can be buried and dug out again?

Yes, they could be, if only they remained as a possibility of experience for even a singular human being. But it is enough if one is doing something, no matter what it is. It can be something very simple. It is always tested against those anticipated experiences, so that everyone leaves a trace behind, but because the quality of that material differs still points to the gap at the depth of the experience. One would hope to be engaged as fully as one can, but one is always a beginner anyway. ●

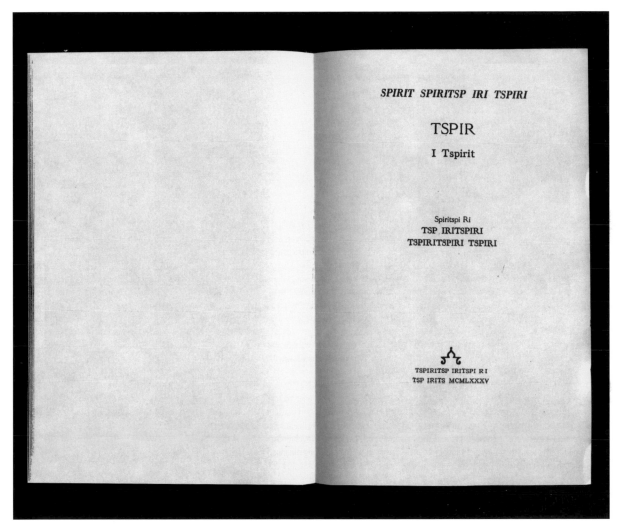

SPIRIT SPIRITSP IRI TSPIRI

TSPIR

I Tspirit

Spiritspi Ri
TSP IRITSPIRI
TSPIRITSPIRI TSPIRI

TSPIRITSP IRITSPI R I
TSP IRITS MCMLXXXV

Three Lessons in Architecture:
The Machines *A conversational explanation,* *1985* I believe that practicing architecture today, teaching architecture today, being a student of architecture today, entail very different consequences than they did even a hundred years ago. I think all of us are at a different stage of possibility, of development of the modern world. I believe that architecture has entered its end. That is not to say that architecture is finished, but that architecture has entered an end condition. I think that all those who practice architecture, whether knowingly or unknowingly, feel in some way that something has come to an end, but what that is, is very difficult to say since it is not in the realm of objects. Therefore, I will try to speak as clearly as I can of something about which it is not easy to speak, because it is not one more thing that can be found in the catalogue of the world. ◎ In any case, what I will try to speak about is a kind of difference—to use Derrida's word—and I will try to make this difference apparent by saying only one thing: If equilibrium could have been attained, it would have been attained a long time ago. Equilibrium could have been attained under only two conditions. One is that reality would have been indeterminate or indistinct, a kind of Heisenberg/Mondrian postulation that equilibrium is achievable within a context of indeterminacy. This did not happen. On the other hand, equilibrium could have been achieved by postulating a global meaning of the world, a boundless but finite meaning, which is to say the meaning of Einstein, the meaning of mythology, the meaning of the centered world. But, needless to say, neither of these realities have been experienced,

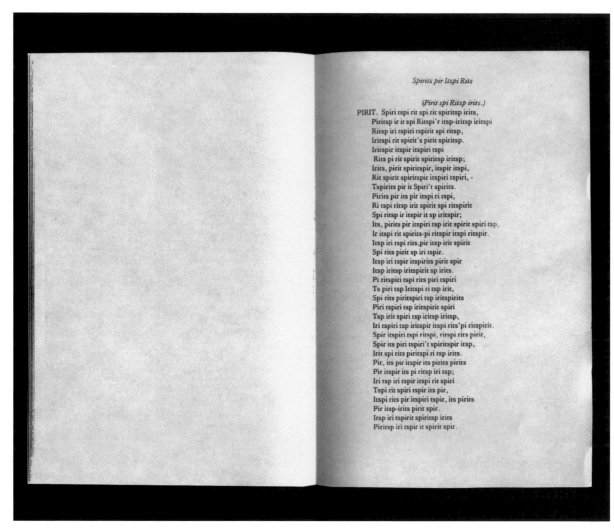

Spirits pir Itspi Rits

(*Pirit spi Ritsp irits.*)

PIRIT. Spiri tspi rit spi rit spiritsp irits,
Piritsp ir it spi Ritspi'r itsp-iritsp iritspi
Ritsp iri tspiri tspirit spi ritsp,
Iritspi rit spirit's pirit spiritsp.
Iritspir itspir itspiri tspi
Rits pi rit spirit spiritsp iritsp;
Irits, pirit spiritsspir, itspir itspi,
Rit spirit spiritsspir itspiri tspiri, -
Tspirits pir it Spiri't spirits.
Pirits pir its pir itspi ri tspi,
Ri tspi ritsp irit spirit spi ritspirit
Spi ritsp ir itspir it sp iritspir;
Its, pirits pir itspiri tsp irit spirit spiri tsp,
Ir itspi rit spirits-pi ritspir itspi ritspir.
Itsp iri tspi rits, pir itsp irit spirit
Spi rits pirit sp iri tspir.
Itsp iri tspir itspirits pirit spir
Itsp iritsp iritspirit sp irits.
Pi ritspiri tspi rits piri tspiri
Ts piri tsp Iritspi ri tsp irit,
Spi rits piritspiri tsp iritspirits
Piri tspiri tsp iritspirit spiri
Tsp irit spiri tsp iritsp iritsp,
Iri tspiri tsp iritspir itspi rits'pi ritspirit.
Spir itspiri tspi ritspi, ritspi rits pirit,
Spir its piri tspiri't spiritspir itsp,
Irit spi rits piritspi ri tsp irits.
Pir, its pir itspir its pirits pirits
Pir itspir its pi ritsp iri tsp;
Iri tsp iri tspir itspi rit spiri
Tspi rit spiri tspir its pir,
Itspi rits pir itspiri tspir, its pirits
Pir itsp-irits pirit spir.
Itsp iri tspirit spiritsp irits
Piritsp iri tspir it spirit spir.

and they won't be. So there is the shape of space of the world, which on a permanent basis produces a destabilized, let's say an eternal, movement of imperfection and difference. It is this shape of space about which I would like to speak and explore in a very tentative manner because no language exists for it today. No language has been agreed upon in which to discuss such a phenomenon. I would like to draw a diagram for you to refer to, because it's a kind of schema of my small discourse here. ◉ What I would like to illustrate with this diagram, synoptically and synthetically, is a schema of a project I made with some friends some time ago entitled "Three Lessons in Architecture," and presented in an Italian urban setting. It's a project that I did for a problem in Venice. I did not choose to address this problem by simply providing another craft, ideological, or industrial solution. I chose instead to present an alternative solution by exploring participatory reality, and to present those who ask the question with a participatory experience in which the problem of architecture might come into focus on the one hand, and some part of it might fall into oblivion on the other. I chose to address the urban problem of Palmanova (a city in northern Italy, in the Veneto region). ◉ I presented the organizers of this program with a piece of equipment, really one big movement in three parts. I will show it to you in three moments of the machine—the moment of reading, the moment of remembering, and the moment of writing architecture. And I will start at some point, and end at some other point, but please remember that I'm really addressing this diagram as a totality. One could in fact start anywhere and one

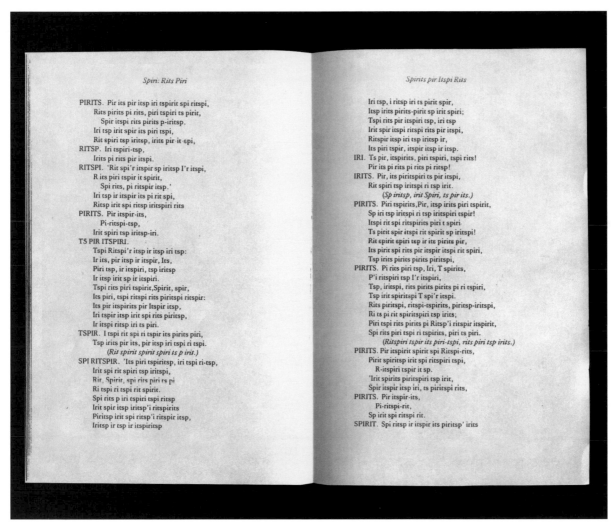

could end anywhere. It's a big circle of interpretation, not necessarily a vicious circle, but a circle that, by going through its own presuppositions, in some sense destroys and obliterates the problem of the given as it also exposes other dimensions of architecture. The three lessons that I have offered here are the three lessons of architecture: A) reading architecture, and its equivalent, the reading machine; B) the lesson in the present remembering architecture, and the memory machine; C) writing architecture, and its equivalent, the writing machine. So there are pieces of metaphysical equipment (as they don't really do anything, they are in another realm) that propose a very curious path, because as I said earlier, architecture was, from its very beginning, at its end. At the end it's possible to retrieve in some sense the whole past and future destiny, because the end, of course, is nothing in the future, nor is it anything in the past, nor is it anything in the present—it is simultaneously on all three levels. The three machines propose a fundamental recollection of the historical vicissitude, in particular of Western architecture. They constitute a single piece of equipment and are mutually interdependent. Each is a starting point for the other. The purpose of this equipment is to release the end to itself; not to take the end, but to release the end to itself. I think the objects in architecture are only residues of something that is truly important: the participatory experience (the emblem of reality that goes into their making). You could say that everything we have is that kind of residue. It is this experience that I would like to retrieve, not the object. ◉ By the way, making machines, I discovered as I was doing this proj-

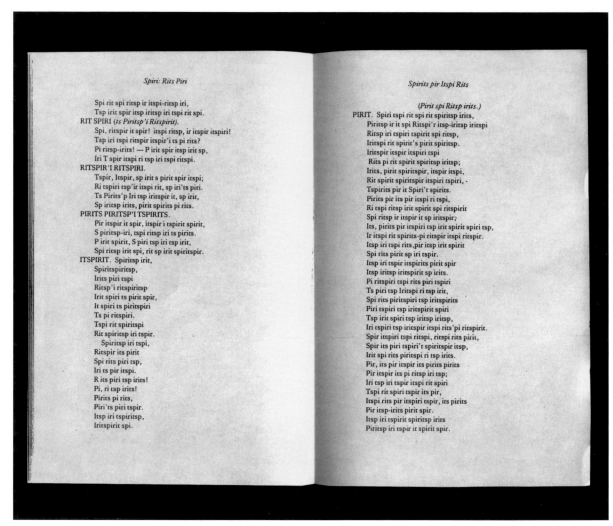

ect, is an old task. Everybody needs machines. Vitruvius says that first of all an architect should make a machine—it is more important than making a city. Then he says you should also make a theater and other things. Alberti says this as well. When I read Vitruvius and Alberti and they said every good architect must first make a machine to do architecture, I thought that if I'm going to be a good architect I must follow the tradition to its end. So I tried to do it in a particular way. We wanted to retrieve reading architecture, so we made this first machine. I have to say what is

involved in reading to try to become a pure believer even in architecture. I know it's an experimental state. It's an experimental being I'm describing, not an experimental object. To try to become the pure medieval craftsman—that's really the object of this exercise. To make something in a way that is made only on one's knees; which is made through complete faith in the transcendence of architecture, of the text, of reading; that is made by a total faith in the craft; that rejects all modern techniques and technology; that rejects modern thinking about architecture.

So we did it that way. We got up at the crack of dawn, four o'clock in the morning. We built the machine in a small place without any power tools, just with hand tools; with no electricity, just with candlelight. We went to bed early because we couldn't work late by candlelight. And we did it in silence because there is nothing to talk about when working that way. ◉ I feel it's the very notion of architecture. One always dreams, and I'm sure you have dreamed about it too, what it was like, and what it would be like to build this way. And, of course, one must reconstruct this expe-

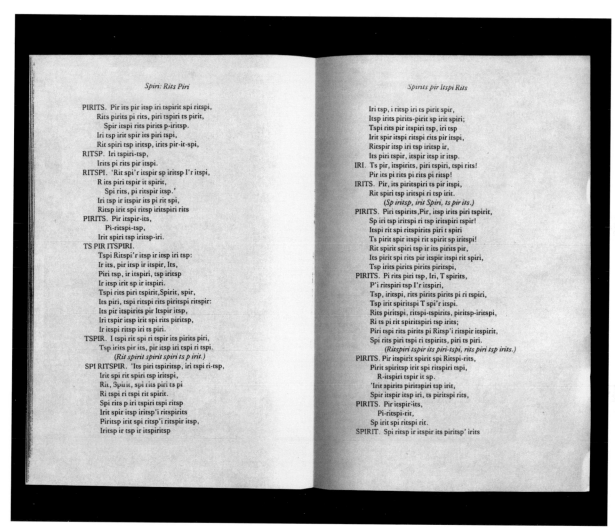

rience because how else does one make a circle without a ruler—with just a plumb line and compass? I tried to make simply one circle, and to do it in that way, full of faith, and to get the experience as close as possible to this loaded experience of the monastic faith in the craft of making. Therefore, lesson A teaches the almost-forgotten process of building, which really has not yet come to complete fruition. I would say that the medieval process is still coming to an end today—it has not been finished. A certain technique was created, one that also brought a revolution of the word, a revolution of text. This archaeological reconstruction (cities like Palmanova, military ideas in architecture and of engineering) and this will to power is disclosed by thinking about architecture and particularly by having no faith in its reality. I never knew about this weak point. Only when I started doing the project did I discover that the weapons of architecture and the weapons of the world did not originate in the Renaissance, they originated in the monastery. The machine gun, the parachute, and the atomic bomb are not the inventions of Leonardo da Vinci, they are inventions of Thomas Aquinas and even earlier, spiritually. I tried to become that architect who would be commissioned by a monastery and who would then deliver both the nonobjective and the objective counterpart of the purified, holy experience. So I made a gear. And then I made many gears. Please remember, they are made with a chisel. It's hard to polish things without sandpaper. I made these detours because I would like you to use these machines. Now, these machines were meant to be used since a machine is not something to look at; these are not aes-

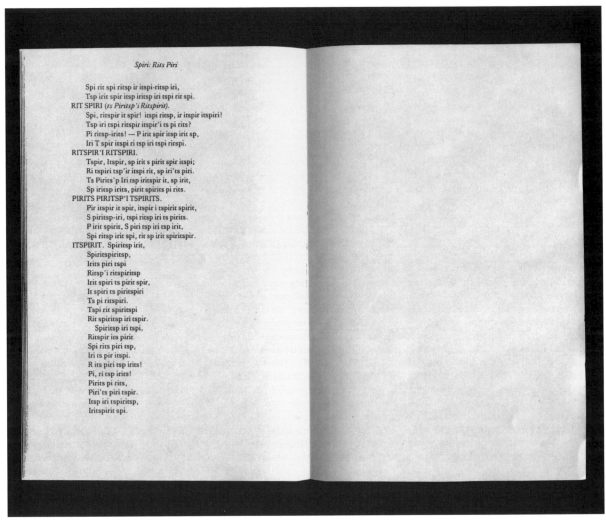

Spiri: Rits Piri

Spi rit spi ritsp ir itspi-ritsp iri,
Tsp irit spir itsp iritsp iri tspi rit spi.
RIT SPIRI (*ts Piritsp'i Ritspirit*).
Spi, ritspir it spir! itspi ritsp, ir itspir itspiri!
Tsp iri tspi ritspir itspir'i ts pi rits?
Pi ritsp-irits! — P irit spir itsp irit sp,
Iri T spir itspi ri tsp iri tspi ritspi.
RITSPIR'I RITSPIRI.
Tspir, Itspir, sp irit s pirit spir itspi;
Ri tspiri tsp'ir itspi rit, sp iri'ts piri.
Ts Pirits'p Iri tsp iritspir it, sp irit,
Sp iritsp irits, pirit spirits pi rits.
PIRITS PIRITSP'I TSPIRITS.
Pir itspir it spir, itspir i tspirit spirit,
S piritsp-iri, tspi ritsp iri ts pirits.
P irit spirit, S piri tsp iri tsp irit,
Spi ritsp irit spi, rit sp irit spiritspir.
ITSPIRIT. Spiritsp irit,
Spiritspiritsp,
Irits piri tspi
Ritsp'i ritspiritsp
Irit spiri ts pirit spir,
It spiri ts piritspiri
Ts pi ritspiri.
Tspi rit spiritspi
Rit spiritsp iri tspir.
Spiritsp iri tspi,
Ritspir its pirit
Spi rits piri tsp,
Iri ts pir itspi.
R its piri tsp irits!
Pi, ri tsp irits!
Pirits pi rits,
Piri'ts piri tspir.
Itsp iri tspiritsp,
Iritspirit spi.

thetic objects. I offered them to the citizens of Palmanova, the city for which I made the project. I suggested to the organizers of this competition that these three pieces of equipment be placed in the middle square of Palmanova, and that not just the architects but all the citizens who passed through this piazza would use it. They could determine what the problem was and the possible solution to it. ◉ I had never done any work like this before; it was all new for me. And the experience of it is like that—you have to pull or push the wheel; that's important. And because the wheel is heavy it creaks. If you were to sit at it you would push or pull it. This machine has many axles and many, many gears, which are both hidden and revealed. It has shelves, and the whole mechanism is intended to support eight words. So there are eight words for which this mechanism is a support. Now, the words are very light because words are light; they don't weigh much. These eight words are especially light because I sought words that are no longer readable in the text of architecture—words that cannot be remembered or written down. I placed these eight light words and made them into books to give them slightly more substance. I wrote eight books. I made the eight books by hand like the monks—made the paper, bound the books, and placed them into this big wheel. And what is interesting is that as light as the books and the words are, they completely crush these axles made out of wood. In crushing the axles they expose two things: the reader and the movement of the wheel, which of course revolves and then comes back to its own starting point, like all wheels. ◉ There are ninety-two wedges and glueless joints, no energy of a contemporary kind. The machine seeks to represent the triumph of the spirit over matter, of candlelight over electrical light or darkness. It's made solely from wood, as are the books. You will recognize that a wheel is always gigantic, no matter how small. This one is very big. It is a Vitruvian, Albertian, humanistic wheel of fortune suitable for the diagonally crucified humanist of Raphael and Leonardo, for whom I really built it. The square intersecting with the circle. I would have liked to have made it for Thomas Aquinas; perhaps he would have bought the piece for himself. It's a good device for comparative reading of the architectural text. Rather than shuttling to your desk and looking for authoritative things, as did those monks who were always looking for the right book to verify the eighth book or the first book, I placed the books in the wheel so that comparisons could be made easily. And in being easily made they could also reveal the tautological nature of the architectural text at its end. The text of architecture is a tautological text, which means that it said the same thing at the end as it said at the beginning, because the beginning was already its end. In short, a chamber of revolutions. The word revolution is used here in its etymological sense: a revolutionary machine because it revolves, and with each revolution comes about the revolution of the text that is propelled by it. ◉ It's difficult to show a book in a picture because a book is meant to be read. This is the first book I wrote, and it's strangely funny because it was stolen. Five minutes after it was presented for perusal of the public, the book was stolen. The organizers of the Venice Biennale came to me and said, "Look, the book was stolen, but since it's a printed book, you have another copy of it." And I said, "No, I don't!" Because if you are really a monk you don't mass-produce anything. You use the technology to do one thing only; so you print. You use the whole resourcefulness of that monastic faith to do a singular act, and always the only one—the same act over and over. So I don't have this book anymore. The book on ideas is missing, but there are still other books remaining, and they are all different. They have different thicknesses. Some of the books are five hundred pages long. The pages are handmade and can be read. Someone asked me, "Do you read these books?" Yes, and I have seen other people read them. There are eight books. Somebody else

asked me, "Why eight books?" I discovered why while rereading Don Quixote. You've read about the great knight, Don Quixote, in his paper visor, going to fight against the injustice of the whole world. Cervantes says that Don Quixote met only one gentleman in his travels in Spain. In all his time (because he was old by the time he died), he met only one gentleman. He said it was the gentleman in green; he was a gentleman because he traveled, and he traveled with a satchel of only eight books. Clearly Cervantes already had more than eight books in the sixteenth century, and I certainly have more than eight books in my library. I made this project in order to get rid of my books, because I decided that I, too, like the good knight, should reduce my library. It's hard to get rid of books. You can donate them to a church or a library, but really getting rid of books is an ethical problem, since one would have to rewrite them all. I still have more than eight books at home, but I am getting closer and closer to being Don Quixote's gentleman. ◉ Here is an illustration of the kinetics of the machine. I must say that the act is the experience. The machine is not about the object—the object is just documented here—it's about the experience one has in participating in it. Of course, the act is different for the reader and for the voyeur, the onlooker, because the reader is involved in the undecipherable or in the completely transparent. But the voyeur, the one who looks on the reader, sees only a body bent over this wheel of torture, and he sees only a beautiful kinetic motion. When the wheels and the little gears move it's truly beautiful—the fascination of multiplying a circle. The experience one has is that the books on the top shelf, which are rotating, appear to be falling on top of you. This is what I was after. They appear to be falling on your head as you pull the wheel or as you read. It's a very uneasy feeling. And as you turn the wheel, the book that you've just left behind, which is going down, appears to be falling on to the ground. The books fall on your head and on the ground, but, at the same time, never fall on your head and never fall to the ground; they always remain in the same position because the axle rotates very accurately, keeping them in an ideal position to a hypothetical reader—a reader who isn't there. ◉ That's the reading experience: one cog of the entire machine. Not a starting point, but one element of the

bigger machine. You will see it repeating itself in all the other machines. ◉ Let me move on to remembering architecture. I've been told that when people die (and I've also read a lot about it), when one remembers one's life before committing suicide or when dying in a hospital, life reels rapidly in front of one's brain. And at the end things become apparent quickly. They very quickly pile up into the soul. In an end condition, then, things pile up rapidly in the memory of what architecture may have been. It's hard to know, but I set myself this task: to remember architecture, to construct an experimental being who could remember it. So lesson B is that which is no longer in the arena of craft, in the arena of this future past; it's in the arena of future eternal, of ideas. So we came out of the monastery. We didn't do this one with the notion of pure life on our knees, with our bare hands, praying that someone should save us; but rather in an ideological realm of politics, a kind of Renaissance notion of architecture. It's really the monks coming with their weapons out of the monastery, and appearing on the stage of the theater. Therefore, lesson B consists of that which can still be remembered of architecture. ◉ As a historical program, architecture and its sight have been filtered through what can still be remembered. I modeled this machine after a phenomenon very fascinating to me: a small memory machine constructed in sixteenth-century Venice by an architect named Giulio Camillo. Giulio Camillo was perhaps, in his time, the most famous architect and in some ways an opponent of Palladio. He was commissioned by the King of France to build a little machine that, in a split second, could reveal the meaning of the cosmos. I thought that was a worthy cause and a worthy memory. And apparently Giulio Camillo, the architect, fulfilled this task nobly. This comes to me from his correspondence with Erasmus, who has always been very truthful about everything. Giulio Camillo showed a small machine to the king of France in the sixteenth century. The king walked up to it (it was a small object, obviously), looked into it, turned around and said to Camillo, "Now I understand. I understand everything. You are an architect. You have revealed to me the meaning of it all." The interesting thing about Camillo is that immediately after he made this machine, two things happened, the machine disappeared and so did Camillo. ◉

Ever since I read about Camillo's machine I have been absolutely enthralled by it. I wanted to meet Camillo, and I wanted to know more about the machine because I'm also trying to remember what it used to be like, as he did. I went to London and discovered Frances Yeats, who wrote a book on Camillo. I found that nothing more is known about Camillo's theater than what was written in her book: that it was made out of wood, had paper that was hanging, and had rope in it. Those are the only absolutely objective facts about it: rope, hanging paper, and wood. I tried in the presence of these ideas to remember through Camillo's mind: architecture. ◎ I have designed only the backstage of Camillo's mechanism here as a model of the mind of the Renaissance, in which equipment and architecture first comes to its own manifestations. The theater, this little machine, is very, very simple. It's made from many pieces of wood, paper, and string, constituting the source of illusions of some olympic theater. The first machine, with the books, is already here in this machine, inside the wood. I should say that the sound is very important because the sound of equipment is important, and this is a piece of equipment to be used. The first piece of equipment was creaking; this machine clicks like a puppet theater. You can use it, manipulate it, pull the strings. I guess it's a little puppet of memory—a theater of architecture, rather than the architecture of a theater. And this too I read in Don Quixote. You might recall that there was a puppet show that he once saw somewhere in Spain. The king was vilifying the maiden, and Don Quixote, being the good and noble knight, pulled out a sword and cut off the king's head. The poor puppeteer jumped out from behind and said: "Hey, just a minute. This is not the real thing, this is only the play." It was too late. Clearly Don Quixote de la Mancha could not tell the difference between the puppet and reality, the representation and its source. ◎ I have to say now that none of these machines was invented by me. The whole process is to get oneself out of it. One has put oneself into it historically, but one must, at some point, disappear. Well, this is my way, my three stages of the way out. For Kierkegaard it was either/or, but this is a more ambiguous process of getting oneself out. You can say out of the object and into the experience; out of the inanimate into the spiritual; out of the nonbeing

into being. What I tried to do with the problem of architecture, to put it another way, was to disengage it from its position on the Earth. I was given a site in Venice and rather than doing what I think most architects are doing today, which is to engage the problem of architecture in the Earth, in its own soil, I tried to disengage the problem of architecture from the Earth—to send it into its stellar source. There were two stars I sent it, two places where it all came from, I think. One is east, one is west. I think in the west it came from Dublin. So I sent back all of this project—everything from Venice, from Veneto, from the Renaissance, from Palladio, Camillo—to Dublin c/o Mr. Joyce. Because I said in my program here that I would seek to release the end to itself. And on the other hand I sent it back to Moscow, c/o Mr. Tatlin, because it also came from Moscow in some sense. Moscow and Dublin, two capitals, not of the nineteenth century; they are capitals of the early twenty-first. So I sent back this odradek (called "odradek" by Kafka and meaning in Czech "not to give any advice") on the Moscow/Dublin route. ◎ There are other things in this small memory machine to remember. There are little horses, little cloud machines, little wave machines, all sorts of instruments, measuring devices, because you may recall that in the first experience (the reading machine), the measurement came straight out of faith. But in the realm of ideas the measurement is a political measurement. It comes from an intersubjective dialogue. The text is also obliterated in another way as is the writing of the text, which is, of course, accomplished by writing architecture. This architecture is spread out and diffused or sprayed in a different manner across the screen of perception. The machine contains in it, by the way, the hanging papers seen by the king of France. An attempt is made to fill up the soul with memory so that one would finally obliterate it altogether. After a while there's really nothing you can remember anymore, only the process of storage. One more thing: There was a spiritual friend of Giulio Camillo. You may have heard of Giordano Bruno, the philosopher and heretic, who was burned in Rome in the year 1600. He was expounding Copernican theory all over Europe, but the church decided he was out. Bruno was a type of spiritual architect and said that all his life he had been doing architecture. Well, he never built a

building—he had been building the cathedral inside himself. He said, "They're not building them anymore outside, so I'm building it inside." And just before he was burned at the stake he said, "I've almost completed it. I've got it completely inside. It's not necessary for me to have it outside." Well, not everybody's Giordano Bruno or Giulio Camillo, but one has to try. So to put everything inside, this is what it would feel like. It would be suspended over you; the suspension of architecture. It's not really grounding it at all. And I know how everybody wants to ground architecture and bring it back home with that misreading of Heidegger—to go back to the forest, to your little hut—but I think Heidegger was out of this world altogether, what with National Socialism, mythology, spirit, and the black forest. ◎ The first machine taught me how to make the wheel, then I had to make what is called the barrow. I tried to make a wheelbarrow—I had to remember how to make it. When you look at the twentieth century, you see a lot of architects photographed next to the wheelbarrow: Mies van der Rohe, Le Corbusier, Behrens. But it's not quite believable that they are using it, since they are always in a suit or something like that. There's a beautiful photograph of Behrens in his tie and vest and top hat next to the wheelbarrow. So, I said, if I'm going to practice architecture I've got to get next to a wheelbarrow and move it. But it's hard to move because it sways a lot, which is not really due to the weight. The problem with the wheelbarrow is that the stuff is so suspended in it that it is hard to propel in one direction. But this is the second part. It's a sort of ideological bequest, and I can show you how the wheel and the barrow are engaged in a slightly more sophisticated whole: The written part both play in those pieces. Writing the book itself, by moving the barrow. ◎ Now, lesson C. I call this the writing lesson; not just the writing of anything but the writing of architecture lesson. This one teaches the artless and the scienceless making of architecture. I showed you the signs, the craft and the art of architecture. Now I would like to make architecture without signs and without art. Clearly signs and art are only stages on the way. I think it was Nietzsche who said that not only painting and music are beautiful pieces of art, but also the Prussian Army of the Jesuit Order. He would have been absolutely delighted to see the modern industrial state. This machine is the industrial part. First was craft: the "one alone," and in there were the "many alone" to remember it. Now I speak from the point of view that being "one alone" is not enough. Being "many alone" is not enough. One has to enter the full working force of the many: to do architecture without signs, without art, the way one would produce a pair of shoes. Now that I live in Milan I see a lot of shoe production, and I know what makes a good shoemaker there: He knows how to put the nail in the right place. The difference between the great and the mediocre shoemaker is the position of the nail. And that's what I tried to do, learn how to put a nail in without art and without science. In other words, to industralize the process I've been describing, to industrialize the poetics of architecture, and to offer architecture as a sacrifice to its own possibilities of making a text. ◎ The writing machine processes both memory and reading materials and is a cybernetic hinge, because now it's a matter of mounting the gear, the axle, and the text into an industrial propulsion, and to do it experientially as an industrialist would. So first, one built by praying on one's knees—total faith. Second, one built by being politically astute, through measurement and discussion. The third step brings one to a nine-to-five job. I thought I needed more experience in the nine-to-five. Maybe one has been working nine-to-five all along but hasn't really gotten enough experience or participation in the process. So how does one get it? I think one opens a little business, a little industry. I got myself a clock with my friends—a time clock. We tried to reduce the problem to its bare minimum, technique, and to not make it interesting at all—to have all our fun after five. During the procedure we agreed to work hard, speak only in "small talk," smoke cigarettes, dream about TV, but to try, in this project, not to contaminate it with other issues. ◎ I start mounting the gear onto this prototype. You know that once you make one gear you get a little more confidence. You can make one that is slightly more complex. You can engage that gear not just with itself tautologically, but you can then project it along these axes, back and forward, and maybe somewhere altogether outside itself. I'd like to show you how it evolved. I built it out of wood. I continued with the gear. I opened a little factory making the little reading wheels. Then I used the

books…I had to have a lubricant, fuel for the machine, and so I had to use the books. There had to be surfaces because it was not for one reader. To lubricate such a big industrial piece of writing one would need all the texts in the whole world, so I translated the books into forty-nine times four languages because seven words times seven is forty-nine cubes. The cubes are pinned on four sides revealing four faces, which means forty-nine times four surfaces. Many, many axles to lubricate; many languages. The first machine creaks, the second one clicks, and this one, I can assure you, whirls rapidly. A very well-lubricated mechanism goes very, very fast—in any language. The books were then cut up slowly, and very particularly, as the most poignant part of architecture is to use it all up. Because now one is making something that has to be useful, not just for those who are alone in the many, but to the many in one. I spliced the axles into intricate formations, like genetic codes, and all sorts of devices were invented in order to produce it. ◎ Then came the problem of the housing unit—an architectural problem. This is an entry for an urban design competition. I had to deal with the dwelling units, economics, commerce, etc., which means I had to deal with the memory machine. But I had to reduce it to scale, so I reduced the memory machine, with its little windows, to this small artifact. ◎ Now I'll explain how it works conceptually and practically. The idea is this: to rotate this handle, but to move that far diagonal cube at a different rate from your rotation. So let's say you move it to the right once, and you move the diagonal cube to the left four times with that one movement. Or you rotate the right handle twice to the right and you move these four cubes here on the left three times forward. That's the complexity of the gear movement: It's all about technique. In reality, that's what industrial modernity is all about; it is to engage those reading cycles and those memory wheels into a kind of securing or stocktaking that would yield unexpected results. It's primitive, but Pascal made his little calculator, and Babbage made his little computer, and, after all, the regular computers we have today are only based on two phases. They are so-called binary, black and white, which is what makes them so schizophrenic, because you always say either yes or no to everything, never maybe. ◎ I tried to make a quadripartite computer

operation, which means to mirror the realm of decisions in a double of itself. One can say there are four parts. Perhaps they are the parts that belong to God and mortals, to the Earth and to the sky. You can say they are the parts that belong to the four interchanges. So that's how I went about it with another prototype, in order to couple these configurations together into a rapid, whirling movement. ◎ Now you can see the little swelling units, the little houses; you can see the roof gardens on top and that's the city itself, and at the back you see the big piston that goes up and down. By going up and down in the vertical, it can turn it all. The horizontality can be transformed into the diagonal movement. Here is the kit that was manufactured for one cube. I didn't do it monastically because I realized that industry can rely on other industry, so one can get all industries to work together happily. The machine is very complex. It has 2,662 parts, most of them are mobile, so you don't see them, but everything—the text that you see on the bottom, the assembly of the machine, the mosaic of movement—is coupled. The first machine had one drawing, like the medieval masons who had only one drawing: the drawing of the circle. The second one already had two drawings. And this one has, once again, one drawing, but the drawing is more like a diagram than a drawing—it engages the binary computer system into the larger grid over there. I believe that the modern city is closely tied with the invisibility of the threat to the city. I think when the walls came tumbling down in history and the city was revealed, it died, though it apparently continues to exist. And I've often thought that the relationship between military vulnerability and the entity of the city as a visible organism cannot be perceived in a visual attitude. It has nothing to do with the eye, because it is really the problem of equivalence between this particular configuration of a star and another particular star in the middle. The one in the middle is perhaps Houston, or maybe Chicago, or any city that is a new, right-angled, orthogonal star. But both of these stars don't shine unless one introduced a matrix in the back of them. ◎ In the end, it's a problem of equivalence. Balzac said to comprehend is to equalize. So to equalize is the task here. I think all of us are equalizers, but in the process of equalization one also has ritual duties, primarily to protect the text. The problem is to protect the text. It's like the mezuzah in the Jewish tradition: that sacred text, the scroll—a bit of the Torah—that is pinned to each doorway of a household, which makes the threshold sacred. I've often wondered why they have to have it in the Jewish tradition; they have to have it. I understood it when I became an industrialist. In the process of sanctification, one also destroys the text, and one is then responsible in every way—I don't know, responsible to someone, to God himself—for protecting it. Everything became a technical problem. I had to wrap up time itself with words. When you get this kind of density of the text you've got to wrap it up very well indeed. You can see that the little wheels, when they are coupled together, are more efficient. And you can see that it gets busy. It gets very busy, and nine-to-five is not enough: there is overtime. Immediately there is overtime. You can know when you stack up these equivalences you stack up the two attitudes. You stack up the whole ending to itself. You get the matrix as stockpile. And then, as you work on the housing, resources appear in these urns. They wind up in these small shrines, funerary urns, and then one has the ashes inside of them. It is a ritual object that I'm showing you. Not an old-fashioned ritual object, because these little shrines' ashes are not blown to the wind, nor stored in a particular position; they are mounted on an axle to be rotated permanently. ◉ The writing machine is a machine to write a single text. The single text that it seeks to write is a text that has already been written by a particular author of the twentieth century. It's a text by Raymond Roussel, a French writer who wrote a book called *Impressions of Africa*. Raymond Roussel tried to present an experience that could never be had, either historically or in the future. Many people were interested in Roussel. Picasso said that he painted because Raymond Roussel inspired him to paint. Duchamp, the antagonist to Picasso, said that his work was all a footnote to Roussel. Le Corbusier said that he did architecture because of Roussel. Giacometti said he became a sculptor because of Roussel. Proust said that Roussel was classical French literature. Cocteau said that he took opium because he read Roussel. I can enumerate the list on and on, with all the heroes that I've got. It's time to interpret Roussel's text, yet how to go about it since this text is made out of nothing? It's about experience that could never be had. ◉ For example, in Roussel's text there are certain miraculous figures that appear and disappear. There is Mossem. I don't know where Mossem comes from, but Mossem is killed in Roussel's book by having a text burned on his feet. It's an experience that could not easily be had. But then I discovered that St. Theodore of Constantinople, in the seventh century, was killed by burning an iambic text onto his forehead. So it began to make sense. Then I find Angelica, who appeared in Roussel. Angelica with the grid, who was finally burned on a grid, like St. Donatella, at a particular date in the third century A.D. ◉ Well, there are forty-nine empty boxes. They have to be filled with ashes of unknown saints. Fortunately, there is a book of saints that can link up the impression of Italy, the impression of what can be said to be the end with the "Africa of the mind," a kind of uncolonized or about-to-be-colonized last region. I would say that Roussel is great because he is the colonizer of the remote parts of the brain, which are just about to be imperialized. In any case, that sort of equipment is not easy to explain, but is easy to use. It helps to position the city in a spaceless space. ◉ I should probably say what composes the four sides of this machine—this calculator. It's a little computer I built. A calculator that is to prognosticate the written destiny of architecture. By becoming an operator you can stockpile information resourcefully, information that is linked with a prophesy made by Victor Hugo that architecture is doomed to die because of the text. Victor Hugo said that the book will kill the cathedral. So I tried to make this computer, following Victor Hugo and Jonathan Swift's *Voyage to Lapula*, into a pragmatic reality. Therefore, the four sides of these funerary boxes contain the following: On the first side, the city that doesn't shine anymore, that star of Palmanova that doesn't shine anymore, intersected and congealed into the rectilinear star, let's say, of Mies van der Rohe; the occult star of victory boogie-woogie; the white and black stars congealed into a singular star. That's one side of the dwelling unit. The second is just a piece of metal that is a reflection that shatters the mathematics of it. It's a kind of reflective order that disrupts the forty-nine times four sides. Side three consists of a geometric sign, which is actually an architectural horoscope. I did horoscopes on all the positions of all the saints in all the spots of Palmanova in order to derive where to cut them up. One cannot cut them up arbitrarily; one has to study all the stars and horoscopes. And the fourth side is the enumeration of the forty-nine saints, the saints who are needed for the completion of the pilgrimage: the pilgrimage of Absolute Architecture. ●

Traces of the Unborn
Raoul Wallenberg Lecture, Ann Arbor, Michigan, 1995 The second work is a larger urban project, quite different in its scope. Alexanderplatz was the main center of Berlin, the old center. When the unification of Germany came, and with it the unification of Berlin, Alexanderplatz came back to the fore as the center of the city. What should one do with such a place and where does one turn for inspiration? Alexanderplatz has been completely transformed since the 1930s, when the famous schemes by Mies van der Rohe, the Luckhardt brothers, Behrens, Poelzig, and Mendelsohn were proposed. Many famous architects worked on this site during the twenties and thirties but nothing much materialized because history took another course. Now, another surprise turn of history has come with the unification of Berlin. ◉ I turned to a doctor for information about the site. Alfred Döblin was a famous writer, the James Joyce of Berlin. However, few people know that he was a medical doctor who had his practice in East Berlin, near Alexanderplatz. He studied Alexanderplatz from a medical point of view in the twenties and thirties. To paraphrase, he said, "When I stand on Alexanderplatz, I am in East Berlin." This was an amazing thing to say in 1920, before the war and before the Wall. He said, "I am in East Berlin because this is where the people are. In West Berlin are the zoo, the Kurfurstendamm, and very nice houses." He used those categories, East and West. This view is still correct, although the delineations of space have changed. ◉ Döblin

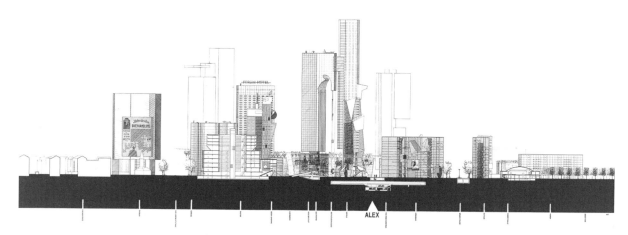

Traces of the Unborn
Urban development competition, Alexanderplatz, Berlin, 1993; Lecture, Berlin, 1994 I am working today in Berlin with a project I have termed the "Traces of the Unborn"—a term to describe the need to resist the erasure of history, the need to respond to history, the need to open the future. That is, to delineate the invisible on the basis of the visible. The scheme developed certain planning and architectural concepts that reflect my interest and commitment to the memory of the city, to the time in which it dwells, and to the freedom it represents. ■ Even though the competition for Alexanderplatz took place in a particular area of Berlin, there were certain fundamental points that were addressed, which relate to issues of other urban centers, whether the devastation has taken place because of war, or political catastrophes, or economic disasters. I followed Paul Valéry's axiom that **"humanity is permanently threatened by two dangers: order and disorder."** I have tried to make a scheme that navigates between the Scylla and Charybdis of nostalgic historicism and the tabula rasa of totalitarianism. ■

Alexanderplatz constitutes the largest urban area for development in postwar Germany. Alexanderplatz is the place where well-worn, and completely new sections of the city meet; where a new centerpoint of a united Berlin must happen; the dynamic vortex that has remained untamable and undeniable from the time of the entrance of Czar Alexander to the exiting of the Russian troops in 1989. ■ The distance separating my scheme from the first prize scheme was only one vote; however, there was an unbridgeable spiritual gap in the attitude toward urban space. ■ I proposed a scheme that opens the area and emphatically rejects the idea that public space needs to be closed in an urban room. My design for Alexanderplatz does not enclose the center, but relies on its history to resist willfully imposed planning concepts. It calls for immediate interaction with the existing by both supplementing and subverting, stabilizing and destabilizing, the network of traffic, street patterns, and building. ■ A radical feature of the scheme, in view of Berlin politics today, was to advocate the acceptance of the existence of the DDR, which

was asked how he would describe Alexanderplatz. He made an imprint of his left hand and said, "That is Alexanderplatz." I meditated on this fascinating act. Why wasn't it his right hand? Why was it his left hand? Was it about left architecture versus right architecture? Was it about fascism and leftist ideology? Was it about the fact that the invisible lines of the hand, which are an occult and palmistic destiny of the body, are themselves never visible when the hand grasps the tools of work? All of these thoughts coagulated in my

mind as a strategy for looking at Alexanderplatz, and for deciphering its history, which is not an easy task to do today. ◎ This part of the city was named when Czar Alexander came into Berlin, in the eighteenth century, and it remained Alexanderplatz when the Russian troops departed from exactly the same spot in 1989. In the 1930s the space was formed by two Behrens buildings in a huge, very dense population quarter. Alexanderplatz today looks very different. It is difficult to orient oneself because so little re-

mains from the past, except an invisible linkage to the Döblinian interpretation. These are new buildings, and a new scale. ◎ The incredible idea of demolishing the city is unique to Berlin. Streets in other cities of the world, such as Paris, New York, and London, seem to be sacred territory; nobody changes the street patterns in most cities of the world. This is not the case in Berlin. Berlin has always had the idea that if a house can be removed, the direction or course of a street can also be changed. There have been hundreds of represents almost fifty years of building. Even the prefabricated, ill-conceived buildings of the DDR that have little architectural merit should not be singled out for demolition, but rather incorporated in an ecologically responsive manner. The contradictions inherent in bringing together mass housing of the former DDR with high-density commercial development is mediated by a major urban park, which would act as a field thematizing the ruin of time. ■ Having rejected the option of erasing the history of the city, the proposal offers gradual improvement of public space, traffic, and organization of Alexanderplatz without relying on some hypothetical "time in the future" when Alexanderplatz would be perfect. The given is not treated as an obstacle, or seen as a form of pathology, but rather as an opportunity pregnant with new relations and new urban experiences. ■ This scheme rejects contextualism and utopianism and instead advocates the metamorphosis of the existing. There is an important need in every society to identify the icons that constitute a particular area, the structures that form the texture of living memory. Thus, in refuting the past and the future alike, the eternal present of transformation and

metamorphosis are used as strategies for the creation of unpredictable, flexible, and hybrid architecture disseminated both horizontally and vertically. This structure introduces a connection or a knot between buildings and their sites. From this structure emerge forms whose individual expression and representation are indistinguishable from the political space they occupy. ■ The city is the greatest spiritual creation of humanity; a collective work that develops the expression of culture, society, and the individual in time and space. Its structure is intrinsically mysterious. It develops more like a dream than a piece of equipment. In this competition I have challenged the whole notion of the master plan, with its implied totalism and finality, its misguided ambition of eternal recurrence of the same through replication. Rather, I have suggested the open and ever-changeable matrix that reinforces the processes of transformation and sees the dynamic of change in a diverse and pluralistic architecture. Such an approach is an alternative to the traditional idea of planning, which implies continuity based on projection rather than an approach that treats the city as an evolving, poetic, and unpredictable event. ■

proposals for changing street patterns in Berlin. It is poignant to realize that the ideas of devastating the city predated the physical destruction of Alexanderplatz during the war, before all the utopian schemes of the great modernists had appeared in the periodicals, much less been completed. ◉ I am not a fan of East German architecture and I do not think that it has much merit architecturally, but this is not a question of aesthetics. The issue is the displacement of tens of thousands of people who have lived on this site for fifty years. This housing was built as a showcase for the DDR regime. This was the best housing, the best place to live. The radical feature of my idea in view of Berlin politics is to advocate acceptance of the existence of these vast housing estates, and to accept that people live there, that their lives have to be bettered, and that these lives have a memory of at least two generations. Even the prefabricated and ill-conceived buildings of the former DDR, which have little architectural merit, should not be singled out for demolition. This is an important point: Planning and architecture should not condone demolition; they should deal with construction and the incorporation of difficult conditions in a new and eco-

logically responsible manner. ◉ I propose not to alter traffic routes, not to engage in new street design, but to reuse all existing streets in a different way. The huge Karl-Marx-Allee goes from Alexanderplatz through the Schoeneberg residential quarter to all the outlying areas. I did not monumentalize the Karl-Marx-Allee, as the other competitors did. I proposed to build a series of pavilions in the median to provide facilities badly needed by the nearby housing estates—recreation facilities, inexpensive movie theaters and restaurants, sports facilities, and so on. One must deal with the thousands of people who are living here and provide facilities that mediate between the old part of the city and the residential areas. I refuse to orient my scheme from the viewpoint of the western portal because I believe that the majority of people will see another

Traces of the Unborn *Lecture, Berlin, 1997* One of the things that struck me when I first worked on the competition for Alexanderplatz in Berlin and analyzed it, was its resounding emptiness—it is a resoundingly empty area. One has to match this emptiness with that other subsequent emptiness, to the activity of Alexanderplatz seen in all of those photographs and documents prior to 1933. I did an analysis of site ownership of the Jewish properties that were surrounding Alexanderplatz, of those who lived there, of Alfred Döblin's description of the working poor, and then of the future vitality and potential of Berlin from this point. ◉ After doing this analysis, I asked myself, How did my results match up with the results of the Senate of Berlin? How did my experience of Alexanderplatz match up with the experience of the city administration? After all, it was they who gave the planning directives for this competition and the logic for its master-

view, as I did when I came to Berlin as a child from Poland. Alfred Döblin or anybody coming from the east arrived at Alexanderplatz station, and not at the zoo or the Kufurstendamm. The eastern gateway to Berlin must be reinforced. ◉ The site has the old height of Berlin as represented by the Behrens buildings, but it also has the intermediate height of the proposed Mendelsohn, Mies van der Rohe, and Luckhardt buildings, and the new height of the television tower, the Forum Hotel, and other big buildings. The Kaufhof building was the most successful department store of the Eastern Bloc. People

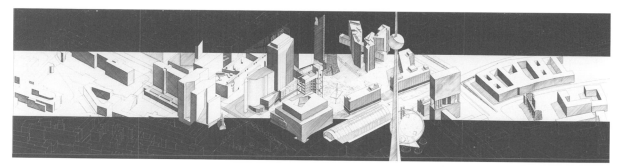

planning. Tables were given for the number of square meters needed, new office buildings to be built—a kind of rationality reappropriating a piece of land which I believed was not wholly amenable to pure manipulation. ◎ The pressure of the city brought by the politicians of Berlin was to treat this site as a tabula rasa, an exercise in amnesia, just like a site without a past—as if Berlin were just any other city of the world to be developed. I felt that simply constructing many buildings and filling in the site did not necessarily diminish that emptiness. On the contrary, the filling of the emptiness might actually inflate it. So, the material idea of filling sites must be seen in a deeper sense, to become a lifeline to the future and an embodiment of the past—for those who were part of it and are still a part of it. ◎ I grew up in Lodz, a few hundred kilometres from Alexanderplatz. In fact, my uncle was a student in Berlin and in our home we used to speak about Alexanderplatz; it was part of the topography of our minds transgressing that void of light and distance and culture. I decided to look at the hand of Alfred Döblin, a handprint from the 1920s, and in it I saw all the lines which describe Berlin as he saw it. I am not an occult architect nor do I read palms, but one can see the lifelines of Berlin in that hand: the love lines, the lines of death, the lines of work. That left hand of Döblin's Alexanderplatz is, I believe, the real matrix that continues to hold out the open promise of that place. That hand, which might today still affect our lived phenomena of Alexanderplatz, is a figure that refers one across the emptiness of that public space. ◎ In the ideological, scientistic, positivistic way of looking at the city the context of the city is what you see of its streets, its transformations, its history.

told me, "Please, Mr. Libeskind, leave something that we can remember on this site." I proposed to keep the Kaufhof, to double the area of the store, and to bring it up-to-date with new elevator cores. I proposed a new open-air tower, the Odessa Tower, with inexpensive rental spaces for markets, which operate here frequently. ◎ The reworking and particularly the transparency of spaces leading out of and into Alexanderplatz are important. The obsession in Berlin today, as in many other places, is to bring back history. The award-winning scheme says that Alexanderplatz will look like Piazza Navona. I thought that it will never look like Piazza Navona because underneath Alexanderplatz is a transportation system like 42nd Street and Times Square, which can bring three million people to this place every fifteen minutes. The image of reverie of the past is inappropriate. The Berlin of tomorrow is a place of tumultuous activity and of functional connections to both existing and new buildings. ◎ I proposed to the Senate of Berlin to bring the citizens into the full participatory process. Particularly with contemporary technologies, there is no reason the public cannot participate in making planning decisions. That did not endear me with the planners of Berlin. ◎ I believe that the idea of the totality, the finality of the master plan, is misguided. One should advocate a gradual transformation of public space, a metamorphic process, without relying on a hypothetical time in the future when everything will be perfect. The mistake of planners and architects is to believe

that fifty years from now Alexanderplatz will be perfected. We see this same illusion demonstrated over and over on Alexanderplatz. The time is now. The interaction is now. ◎ One should not see cities as pathological entities, as being sick. One should see them as needing care. What is needed, in my view, is a Buddhist or homeopathic approach to city planning composed of gentle interventions, which are not very dramatic in terms of instant gratification. I tried to tell people, particularly in the west, that there is nothing wrong with Alexanderplatz. It is an incredible place that is pregnant with possibilities that have not yet been played out. That is true of many cities. My picture postcard of Berlin says, "Wish you were here." The competition jury may have selected a group of identical skyscrapers standing in a rigid grid, all of equal height, all of granite. Without winning the competition, I think I have shown how Berlin will actually develop. It must develop this way because the alternative is hopeless. ◎ The city is the greatest artistic and spiritual creation of human beings. It is a collective work that exists not only in space but also in time. Its structure is intrinsically mysterious. In a democratic society, one should acknowledge that architecture will reflect very different, and sometimes conflicting views of the world. This is an alternative approach to the traditional idea of planning, which implies continuity based on projection. It is an approach that treats the city as an evolving, poetic, and unpredictable structure. ●

Traces of the Unborn, axonometric

What are the other possibilities? How does one view that which never has passed, the emptiness of a public space? Indeed, how does one view the void as the context of the city? History in Berlin has been traumatized into something that appears to be ahistorical, something that never took place in history because it was never part of history in the first place. The ahistorical dimension of the void has always puzzled me. Of course the void has a historical trajectory, a trajectory of fatality of Western culture. At the same time there is something about the void, astonishingly not coincidental with positivist history. That interests me very much as part of my work. The void embodies the annihilation of culture, not simply in a figurative sense but the annihilation of the carriers of culture: those people who read books were its carriers—who of those people who remember, of those people who can still speak and can see the white line. ◉ One does not have to be religious, one does not have to be either a believer or a nonbeliever to see the crux of that absence, an absence which is truly extraordinary. The empty space, the empty history to be rejoined—but how is it to be rejoined? How is the idea of planning to cope with the rebuilding of the city and of the economy? No one is against rebuilding the city; everyone wants to have a better city. Go on, get on with life, let's start living again. Let's move forward, but is it forward? And where is it heading? I think there is a different idea of planning, planning which is based not solely on the visible matrices, nor on the visible formal connections, or on communicative structures, but rather across those irreconcilable gaps which not even in the Derridian sense are traces. ◉ And that is what I proposed: In order to deal with Alexanderplatz as a planner and as an architect, one would have to reopen a thoroughly other context for the public space for the void. A context into which those shadowy figures, those figures which were never born, the traces of the unborn would have to be incorporated. I am not only speaking of those who were born and annihilated, but those who remain unborn in that setting. The visible is not the only context of the new planning, one has also to deal with the invisible, the annihilated couriers of culture, the true "spirit of Berlin." ◉ Like the letters of Berlin, which I have used and taken very seriously in my work in Berlin. The six letters. What is in the name "Berlin"? What is in the name of that memory? My project for Alexanderplatz was based on those fugitive fault lines across which the city was devastated, but which nevertheless remain in my opinion the only lines the city can continue in the future. They are not the lines necessarily coincident with rationality, with rational planning, with grids, with the power of building, with the city, because they depend on that which can be remembered and that which is remembered in the form of the immemorial. I speak now of the strategy of being the planner of urban space and of the pragmatic devices with which a city such as Berlin can rebuild itself. ●

Traces of the Unborn, site plan

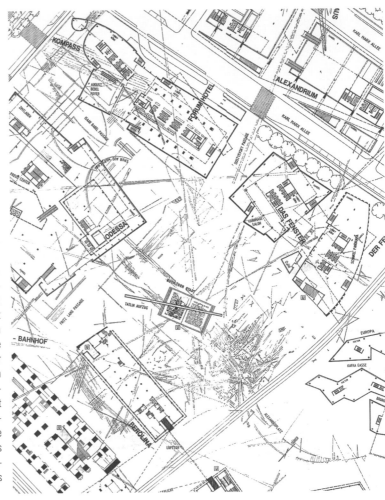

Über den Linden *Urban Planning Competition, Berlin, 1991*

216
217
The future development of Berlin depends on the spirit of creative imagination, the substance of which is hope and the proof of which is ethical conviction. This substance is faith in the city and its culture, rather than the manipulation of economic/political variables for shortsighted gains under the cover of "planning." It is exploration, not exploitation that is paramount; invention, not calculation that is necessary. ■ The Über den Linden project seeks to substantiate the image of the historical center of Berlin in scale, function, and character, through transformation of buildings, streets, and for-

mer lines of division. To revitalize the historical east-west thoroughfare it is necessary to bring it into the dynamics of the twenty-first century both functionally and urbanistically. Only by breaking through the barriers of nineteenth century planning and thought will the dam that held East separated from West (even before its political division) be breached, allowing the energies of Berlin to flood back freely into everyday life. ■ A new architecture is appropriate to the new Berlin. It is not by increasing income, while living on the same old capital and on the same stock of inherited architecture that Berlin can grow. ■ A radical, less certain, and more vital enterprise is necessary, probing the depths of the spirit of Berlin from which its intellectual and social character takes sustenance. In this way an open architectural vision will become the reality of a new capital, yielding new dividends and not just a "one-time sum," spent and forgotten. ■

Virtual House *Competition, 1997*

218 When I began to think about the project of the Virtual House, I realized that to be virtual, the project must have no preconceptions. Though the project has to be built, it should not be based on a goal, but must be open to the encounter, in which the plan is part of the event. ■ The virtual is thus the space that has escaped totally from the Newtonian framework, because the virtual partakes of the science of substance (in man, society, and history), rather than in the science of phenomena. Therefore, I believe that the virtual does not deal with appearances, but rather with experience, with substance rather than with phenomena. ■ As Bruno says, "**Thus differs the vision of the eye from the vision of the spirit, like a seeing mirror, which does not see: for the spirit is an illuminated and informed mirror, it is both the light and the mirror, and in the spirit, the object and the subject of perception are one.**" ■ The virtual is therefore the refusal of consensus and a mental rebellion against the institutionalization of experience. ■ . . . I first began this project by actually trying to design a virtual house, by making it real. However, by attempting realize the virtual, I only virtualized the real, because by turning the substance of the virtual experience into a phenomenon, I realized that I was destroying the virtual. ■ The process by which I produced the virtual house moved through the oral, graphic, and the imaginary toward the mantric architectonics of virtual revelation. ■ The virtual house is a generator of the spirit in which the virtual spins with power yet withholds direction. The very action of the spin is a catalyst that opens the trajectories of the real. ■ The virtual house is a series of closed loops, a layering of interior positives, that prompts, through its kinetics, the unraveling and the emergence of lines extruding and opening the real. ■ The cylindric mechanism consists of 365 ring segments permanently rotating around their common axis. In the poetics of choice, each day is a real beginning of the virtual, constituting a revolution of one year. And the choices, like the virtual, are closed in the loops of experience. The rotation of every single ring segment changes its sense independently and at random, clockwise and counterclockwise, from zero to infinity. ■ The actual condition of the "model" shows a singular section in time of a virtually unlimited number of combinations of the constituent layers. Its outer and inner outlines represent a unique section in space, releasing the lines from the density of rotation, anticipating the flowing lines of the pragmatic to come. ■ The real is the linear disintegration of the virtual. It is the running down of the negative. In contrast, the virtual is a positive binding of massive storage, a labyrinthine compression of several infinities. ■ That means that the object as a whole has no dimension and no scale. Toward "outside" and toward "inside," it can be seen as extended into macroscopic and microscopic spaces of any dimension simultaneously. ■ Only the interpretation and experience of the beholder can read the configurations as objects or landscapes or continents or door handles. ■ Due to its nondimensionality, this "virtual house" contains houses, as well as their locations and surroundings. Due to a different speed and position of the rotating ring text, nothing can actually be "seen." The model represents what one could see at a certain moment, but there is no certain moment. ■ The driving axis of the rotating mechanism could be called ARCHITECTURE. ■

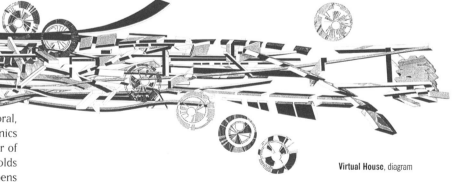

Virtual House, diagram

There cannot be a singular virtual house. The single case is only a token in the actual of the virtual. There is, though, a virtual totality of representations of houses unreeled by the overlap of the full and empty texts of the ring layers. This uncontrolled and mobile overlap defines points and lines, volumes and bodies, which represent—but are not—the totality of every possible house, existing or not. Thus, the concept of the virtual house can be presented by the generating mechanism of representing concepts of houses.

BUILDING INSTRUCTIONS

1. Read each line and bend it back onto itself; that is the rim of each disc—the path itself.

2. 365 discs—section through time—rotating constellations, continually reordering themselves through memory and building the virtual support.

3. Slippage or turning of discs—the circle rolling through the winding hollows, traces, intersections, the text passing away.

4. Circle into circle—the absent center, the nonexistent reality of the virtual, which continues to be virtual.

5. The turn—skipping through—the joy and pleasure in fulfilling empty forms of thought and images of the virtual.

"He who tries to know the virtual by his senses is like a man who wants to see the substance and the essence with his eyes; he who would deny everything that is not perceptible to the senses would have to deny in the end not only the virtual house, but his own being and substance."

In conclusion: **The VIRTUAL HOUSE**

a. ITS MEASURE IS OUT AND IN

b. MEASURE OF ITS UP AND DOWN

c. MEASURE OF WHAT IS HOLLOWED AND OPAQUE

d. HAS NO IMAGE

e. IMAGE LEFT OF ITSELF PARTED

f. IMAGE RIGHT OF ITSELF JOINED

g. BORN FROM THE UNORIGINAL CHAMBERWORK, BEING FROM NONBEING

a. THE TEXT IS OTHER THAN WHAT HAS NO IMAGE: VIRTUAL

b. THE IMAGE IS OTHER THAN WHAT HAS NO TEXT: VIRTUAL

c. NO NAME OTHER THAN VIRTUAL IMAGE

d. NO IMAGE OTHER THAN VIRTUAL TEXT

e. VIRTUAL SUBSTANCE WRITTEN OUT FULLY

f. ITS NAME IS IMAGINED AS TRUE ■

The constellation of a Labyrinth	Unruly (chaotic) movement insubordinate to the whole	The penetration of a large body by a smaller one: wave-like movement; a turning	Largest possible oscillation: movement of maximum height	conversion of something ponderable into nothing.	The merging of several surfaces into a single surface: the merging of boundaries between	The process of turning inside, ceaselessly echoing its positions
A sequence of a single act constantly in progress: return via a detour	Preview of future, or the "indecipherable"	Frames, meridians, artificial rigor	Conversion of a force of movement into a force of enduring stasis: force of motion into force of cohesion.	contains within itself the disintegration of a whole into parts: a large entity into smaller ones (relation of the whole extent of line to its members)	Division of a volume into indefinitely large number of parts equivalent to the whole	were it to illuminate: perhaps as far a singular location
according to such-and-such obliquity/declivity	the transparence which is also a reflection (or reflective)	Passing through a net by going through all the points of the circuit without reigniting memory.	Leaving too little as a result of a situation of insufficient strength (force): hunger	A timetable	A winding hollow	An empty field: absence of points.
Reorganization of the "system"	toward a white opening whose extension cannot be controlled (because it is rooted in great weight)	A growth into something greater (the greatest point of force of motion).	of every city which a book suppresses	The filling of an empty space by a supposedly empty body (a movement born of a difference in pressure from compression into scattering)	complication of boundary-lines, which ought to run between the fringes	Nothingness penetrates a body; Body penetrates nothingness
The opening which is not on any side, and it is not known whether it opens upward or downward	The lines (as the most stable elements of the engraving) are concentrated behind	Assembly of parts into a whole: a return. Movement of points from a motionless point: a narrow angle	Rotation and break (for a moment) into the profile	Regular distortion through a projection of the outer surface.	The linking of text to numbers or a cypher which cannot be decomposed or undone	Movement of entities inside a 'housing'
Uncontrolled movement of a great force of freedom (time past): conversion from motion along a line to motion over an area transverse to it which intersects the motion	Increase caused by an excess of force: to 'burn-up'	Reorganization of Density/Measure/Significance	Freedom to move independently from neighbors	Double or mirror: a fixed point that serves as a point of departure for the motion of other points which begin their trajectory there.	Soft entity collects into a hard entity; Hard entity becomes a soft entity	toward the knot, the overlapping ravine (the senseless words: "knot", "overlap", "fold".
The effect of currents (dynamics)	hallowed drawing of judgement by yielding to one force but not the other: pulling against all the other strings	Science of permutations	lightweight bodies	An end to 'hierarchy'	Division of a smooth hollow body as a trace of the movement of another body through it	Subordination of movement to a goal (something which contradicts nature)

Visible Cities Archipelago

Visible Cities Archipelago *Competition entry, Berlin, Germany, 1991* The extreme conditions on the outskirts of Berlin in Lichterfelde Süd, dominated by a harsh transition between Berlin's urban structure and Brandenburg's open landscape, demands progressive design planning. In order to develop this very special suburban housing scheme a suitable flexible framework is needed in line with the dynamics of city planning, so as not to be overrun by future developments. The diversity and ever-changing nature of urban living requires the development of new patterns of thought to facilitate a far reaching modern debate, taking into account such themes as the form of the family, the emancipatory need for mobility, as well as other factors. This is prerequisite for an understandable and readable vision of the city. A city which does not make allowances for this growth loses its capacity for effective communication and competitiveness, and inevitably loses its life force. The exceptional location of the planning area puts forth questions and problem which serve to emphasises on the one hand the relationship of structures to each other and on the other the city boundary to its surroundings, requiring a new and adequate long term typology. The Archipelago image presents a new opportunity in the current discussion on city boundaries. A collection of heterogenous islands disperse from the outskirts of the city towards the countryside, penetrated by the "sea" of the Brandenburg landscape, provides space for the the most diverse forms of lifestyle, work and living conditions, to contribute to a new form of city boundary. The energy forces arising from this are marked by three generic points of orientation. The railway station, the "Emblem" and the "Tornado" spread out to form an area, not only in the immediate vicinity of the existing city outskirts, but also integrated within the overall structure of Berlin. These three "points of navigation" create a network of vectors and entrances, resulting in a gateway from Berlin to the planning area of Lichterfelde Süd. Like icons, they are easily recognisable landmarks to the passing motorists, train commuters, cyclists and pedestrians alike. Every part of the area is integrated by the composition of the three elements, through which a generic self sufficient structure arises. In each of the three building phases this structure transfers its power of orientation and integration onto the various characteristics of the individual islands. It ensures quality and creates the possibility for the small and varying quarters to be home to the most diverse lifestyles. The creation of many islands maximises the urban "coastline" to nature, thus facilitating immediate access to the country for future residents. In order to protect the natural landscape and maintain its original character, the islands will be laid out and built as compact city areas in such a way that they appear as city fragments in the existing landscape. Each island develops its own individual character and identity while at the same time being integrated into the collective of the Archipelago's island world as a whole. In this project, the outskirts of the city take on an organic relationship to the countryside: A clearly defined end to the construction is marked, but the city boundary still remains permeable. City and countryside visually interweave to form a gateway open on both sides. Public space is expressed through the most diverse characteristics on each of the islands and are defined by streets, squares and fields, all widely differing from each other, each with diverse individual patterns of orientation. This island arrangement, along with the three orientation points' generic vectors—

Trauma *Lecture, Berlin, 1997* I think about trauma not only as an architect but also as someone who was born in the post-Holocaust world, with two parents who were themselves survivors of the Holocaust. The theme of culture and trauma, the void and the experience of architecture, can be talked about in conceptual terms as well as expressed in concrete reality. The theme involves a moment of awareness of that which really cannot be communicated in any explicit experience—a gap which exists amongst those who are survivors, which includes everyone born after these times—a gap which in time becomes obliterated and which generates in itself an even greater emptiness in the post-historical world. Of course, in this state the difference between simulation and experience becomes very explicit: Experience of history is the relationship between what the void is and that absence which is not only relative but catastrophic and absolute. ◉ If one really thinks about the change of the world that has come after 1945, one realizes that it is certainly not a matter of coincidence, but the changes are due in large part to the fact that people were exterminated who would otherwise have formed a continuity with European and world culture. So I would say that the extermination of Jews, six million of them, and the many, many others, millions of others, has led to quite a different vision of what history was and might yet be. ◉ I had this experience brought to me in a very graphic and palpable form when I first came to Berlin some years ago. I went to the Weissensee cemetery. It was the largest Jewish cemetery in Berlin, and I walked through this incredible cemetery which was still—with a kind the Gateway, Emblem and Tornado—allow for freedom of development. The heterogenous nature of the islands can only further gain in character through such a process. The city outskirts not only mean the dispersion and thinning of the masses, but also the slowing of time, expressed visually in an appropriate area whose character is defined by departure and arrival. In this way, the planning area Lichterfelde Süd proves itself to be one of Berlin's most significant topographies, as well as being a paradigm of Berlin's city boundary. The light and progressive nature of this outlying development negates the need to draw on the reductional, the historical and on the nostalgic, which have in the past defined the outskirts as the end of the city alone: "Visible Cities" are experiencing a rebirth, their driving force being on the city outskirts ∎

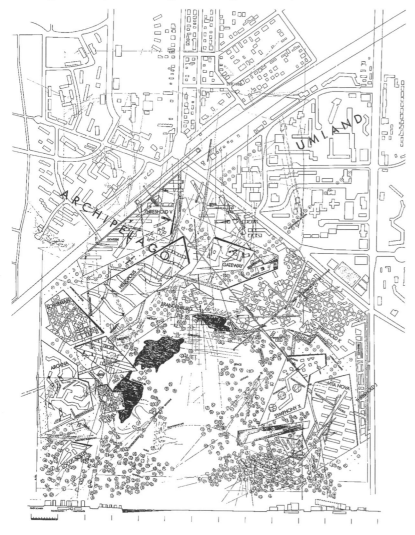

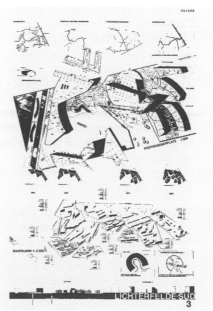

Visible Cities Archipelago, master plan and competition panels

Vox Nova: Modeln World *Competition for the Ciudad de la Cultura, Santiago de Compostella, 1999* To give concrete

219
220

expression and material to the aspiration of creating a Ciudad de la Cultura—City of Culture—outside the city of Santiago de Compostela, in Galicia, Spain, means to break out of the centuries-old order by formulating a forward-looking, contemporary strategy, one that would regenerate the region of Galicia by creating the very embodiment of the future. This design for the Ciudad de la Cultura thematizes the contrasts with the landscape and the historical center

"...a labyrinth of a single straight line, infinite and everlasting..."

of Santiago de Compostela, producing an entirely new topography of historical relations. ■ Vox Nova provides a radical response for a variety of cultural institutions, such as an opera house, the library of Galicia, and a museum of communication, by giving them their own polyphonic voice with individual entrances, walkways, and appropriately scaled lobbies. This voice articulates spatially and programmatically the multivalent connections between events and places, reverberating with new synergies. Vox Nova can be seen as the fusion of form and space, where the form holds the specific cultural programs and vertical gardens generate the entrances to the public activities. The visitors ascend through the horizontal gardens and are directed through a multilayered landscape specific to each cultural institution. The relationships emerging from the program are concretized in the rich matrix of architecture wherein the function is fused with the penetration of the gardens. The gardens form, in the vertical dimension, a visible public realm, a vertical series of piazzas. Vox Nova densifies, accelerates, and intensifies public encounter. ■ With the design, I wish to provide an approach that preserves the land, limits the buildable footprint, and creates a sustainable cultural center in an unprecedented landscape, generated by the building itself and its surroundings. I am determined to dissolve the boundaries separating the arts from each other and to retrieve the idea of the unity of cultural experience and the functional and symbolic space that belongs to it. ■

of emptiness built into it. For those of you who have not been there I will describe it to you. There are many huge, marble tombstones which were built by wealthy families for the future, to be engraved and inscribed as future generations passed away and new generations came up. What struck me as I walked through the cemetery (we were the only ones there, it was just after unification)—what struck me was that no members of these families could ever come back to see the emptiness of those slabs of marble. There would be no one to recognize that emptiness. The visitors who have come back to see it are not part of these families and are certainly witnesses of another kind. ◎ have been thinking particularly about this because I am involved in a number of projects which challenge one's imagination of how to deal with the void, public space, culture, and trauma. Not the trauma of a singular catastrophe, which can be overcome and healed, but a trauma which is structured by the destruction of a community and its real yet also virtual presence. An absence which is structured in the city, in the topography of a country, and in the topography of Europe and the world. So I am very much interested in the cultural significance of the void—the void of public space, and the void of memory. What is the void's cultural presence today? What is its form and repression? What might it have been historically? How does it look? How does one encounter it or how does one not encounter it? ◎ The need in architecture to respond to the questions of culture, of public space, of the void is very palpable since in archi-

tecture the void is a space. It is a place of being and nonbeing. It is a place where one can hardly find traces of a relationship. And yet, it is something which has been recorded and presented in light, matter, and documents. One can attempt to have access to it through names, addresses, through a kind of haunting quality of spaces through which the passage of absence took place. ◎ I recall vividly a story I read from the Hasidic tales of the Holocaust, which was a story of a survivor now living in Brooklyn. She was a prisoner in the concentration camp of Stütthof and felt she would never survive those years of 1943–44. But one day as she looked up into the sky, she noticed a white line, a perfect white line and (she did not know why) but thinking of that white line, she believed, kept her alive. The interviewer in this post-Holocaust account, Yaffa Elia, asked her what she thought the white line to be and she said she never really thought of what it was, but in retrospect it might have been something as banal as the exhaust of an airplane or the traces of a cloud. In that place in Stütthof, in 1944, that singular vision had a significance which was surely obscure and enig-

matic and yet it had a real transformation of memory and communication of an experience. ◎ There has been a lot of controversy recently—in Switzerland about the banking and gold issue, in Austria about the far right, and in Germany about the collaboration of major industries. For the first time, there is a dawning realization that the next century might not be predictable: a further forgetting, a further distancing, a further abstraction. Globally the enormous misproportion of that absence of a generation might be revealed and astound us with its implications. If one thinks of the collapse of the Soviet empire, the privatization of Poland, the Czech Republic, Hungary, the Baltic States, and the former Yugoslavia, if one thinks of what was involved in the rebuilding of Europe, the resources, the transferences of material possessions—where did it all come from—from whose bank vaults?

Wave Orpheus *Competition for a theater, Almere, 1998* Design

221

Philosophy: The incredible brief given to the architects should meet the same level of expectation and ambition as the extraordinary plan of Almere itself. The multipurpose theaters and C.K.V. should weave imaginatively into wonderment appropriate to the bold and challenging act of generating a wholly new topos and theme in the new city, culturally, socially, urbanistically, and architecturally. ■ As it happens, I had the good fortune, for about a third of my life, to spend time in the backdrops of theaters and music halls as a virtuoso musician awaiting my performance on stage. In recent times I have been involved in major theater productions, designing the scenography and costumes for the National Theater of Norway, the Gladsaxe Theater in Copenhagen, and the Schaubühne in Berlin, among others. ■ My interest in designing this project is not to build one more building in the world, but a personal interest in its theme and content, in the specific, extraordinary new surroundings of Almere. The task as I see it is to contribute to the grand work of art—the city of Almere—a vivid and exciting mirror in which the city can reflect itself and within which the theater becomes an urban spectacle. ■ This project is at the structural core of culture. In the coming millennium, I believe, there will be a "revolution" of sorts, wherein the theater will become an active protagonist, in the drama that holds life, desire, and dream. **The Form:** This scheme releases the theater into the world and generates a striking building—an icon—whose energy transfor-mation (Wave Orpheus) is a dynamic that emphatically opens the theater and generates a new public. The quintessential theater, the Globe Theater, with its bear fights and popular entertainment in Shakespearean times, was concentric and inward-looking. The stage tower and the public turned away from the everyday world into a secret and private realm. ■ The theater deliberately turns it inside-out and opens it to the sea and to the land. What emerges is a new figure that makes the entire multipurpose theater and C.K.V. facility available to the public, intensifying their involvement in the process of performance. Ever since Wagner's Bayreuth theater broke the mold of exclusiveness and elitism, theaters have been struggling to make themselves more accessible to the people. In this scheme, the public is able to use the entire territory carved out by Wave Orpheus, not just as a paying audience using a conventional lobby, but as a public-at-large having access to the roofs and projections; access through the vertical connections of the business lounges and representative facilities; permeability through the site and into the C.K.V. on the plaza and on the water's edge; and finally even glimpses into the stage mechanisms and fly tower. ■ The concept of the building is generated by four intersecting cones: a conic form emerging from the water-sound; emerging from land-speech; emerging from the wind-breath; emerging from the underground-Orpheus. In turning the theater inside-out, these cones interpenetrate and bring forth this four-dimensional perspective. These external perspectives complement the internal views, giving the city a new urban stage as the central experience. Wave Orpheus is the physical realization of such an urban stage, contributing to the density, variety, and richness of everyday life. The form is no longer just frontal, with a back and a side, but offers itself in the round, along its entire topography with a significant verticality, mass, and relief. **Urban Scheme:** On the urban level, Wave Orpheus is the focus of particular energies, drawn on the master plan. It follows a route of geometries and rhythms, along the axes connecting Almere, which are held in tension by the complex. The multipurpose theater and C.K.V. is like a burst of energy,

Certainly the search involves the issues of responsibility, the ethics of memory, the politics of space, and the rebuilding of sites and places which only yesterday were deemed immune to history. ◉ In my view, the question of culture, public space, and the experience of architecture is part of a larger vision. I have read a number of texts which illuminate the problem of trauma from the psychoanalytical perspective, but I believe that when one actually enters the space of that trauma, the space of the city, the trauma cannot simply be interpreted. That is the difference between talking about the problem and being in it. In a literary context, one can interpret trauma, one can give it a connotation, one can cope with it in different linguistic settings. Yet by walking, by looking, by touching, by feeling where one is, an interpretation cannot rid that experience of its own materiality, opacity, and thickness. ◉ The projects in which I am working are explicitly related to public space, to memory, and to the concrete experience of architecture and the city. Whether it is the Jewish Museum Berlin, whether it is an urban space like Alexanderplatz or Tacheles, whether it is the museum of Osnabrück, whether it is a regeneration of lands associated with the name Sachsenhausen, these are projects structured by a void and by trauma. The trauma, once again, is not one understood in a psychoanalytical sense, but rather in a material sense. How does one pass on some truth about what it all really means? What does this history really mean? How does one communicate a unique encounter? In what context can that meaning emerge? How could those who are not interested in that meaning be involved in its construction? ●

where amateur and professional cultural life meet. Startling and varied views are provided by both the close-up and distant perspectives. In its array of forms and with its stage tower visible in the waves, it provides a beacon on the larger urban canvas on which the city of Almere stands. ■ Wave Orpheus relates itself to the curvilinear globe of the underground parking. In this way, the radical solution of street access to the city becomes palpable, thematically and programmatically, in the complex itself. This Wave Orpheus is theater as communication—visual, kinetic, tactile, and audible. From its outdoor projections to the activity of the plaza and throughout its oblique, conical form, the structure presents clarity and enigma—a city landmark. **Organization:** The multipurpose complex is organized with the large theater and its projection screen facing the city, and the smaller theater with its restaurant and C.K.V. facilities facing the water. It is important to note that the C.K.V. also has a major presence on the city plaza and vertically in the wave. The in between space of the waves is activated by a public space that runs like a nerve system through the heart of the whole. At the central point of this intersection lies the public path and circulation system, which is structured by the lobbies, bridges, stage tower, paths, and activities. ■ The C.K.V. is not an appendage to the main volumes, but is a powerful component, both in plan and section. It enters a dynamic and intense dialogue with the professional theater and the public. The C.K.V. laterally, and the tower vertically, act as anchors for the cycles of performance. It has its own identity, yet allows for the aspiring to meet the professional. ■ The multipurpose theater and C.K.V. constructively utilize the four-meter drop in the level between the curvature of the parking structure and the water's edge. This provides an intersecting space, where the waterfront and pedestrians meet, where one is able to put on cultural events, supply retail and commercial space, and, more simply, intimate places to relax, enjoy the view, and play together. ■ On the Plaza Circus, there is an impressive welcoming entrance to the theater, flanked by an exciting curvilinear introduction to the C.K.V. with its restaurant and public facilities. The Plaza Circus fronts a foyer whose dramatic appeal is expressed by the full three-dimensional exhilaration of the space. This space, hard to describe in drawing because it is truly plastic, features unexpected views of the city, sky, and water promenade. On the water level, underneath the parking globe, is the delivery system with its large freight elevator. A clear separation of stage, support, and actors from the general public on all levels is ensured. ■ The public can enter the entire complex on two levels and have access to a third, specific theater entrance level. Since lobbies have been decentralized and disseminated throughout, the public can filter through a variety of routes. The first of these routes could directly access the water and the pier, the C.K.V. restaurant, and exhibition. A second route could be followed to the commercial facilities on levels o and 1. The central entry intersection gathers a space edge between water and city. From here, the public also has direct access to the upper levels of the C.K.V., the business lounges, and offices, which offer spectacular, oblique, and curving views of the otherwise stable horizon. ■ The central flytower is flanked by workshops, rehearsal and dressing rooms in a functional manner. It is one of the key protagonists of the anticipated drama of performance and leisure. The rectilinear energy of the theaters is driven through the vertical waves, which shear and transform it to create an intimate public place. This sheared middle zone, between water and land, is a highly charged space with a sweeping vertical movement to the higher parts of the C.K.V. and multipurpose theater. ■

X *Habitable Bridge over the Thames, London, 1996* In this competition, for a habitable bridge over the Thames, I have sought to rethink the idea of a bridge for the twenty-first century. The traditional notion of the bridge has been to overcome water, conceived of as a barrier, by constructing an element linking the two banks of the river: a binary logic AB, creating by its sheer existence the separation of the banks it sought to overcome. ■ This scheme proposes to celebrate the Thames through a multivalent and nonlinear connection to the many places of London. The proposal no longer points to the separation of the north and south banks, nor to outdated economies, but rather makes this strategic site central to London as a whole. ■ The proposal includes two interrelated components. The first is a vertical, inhabitable bridge in the form of an undulating tower coming directly out of the water and reaching a height equivalent to the width of the river. The second is a web of pedestrian walkways, which on both the first and second levels create a delicate public filigree connecting many different points of the riverbank. ■ The vertical bridge is conceived as a slender column, which in its form and position connects London as a city of vertical spires with its horizon,

X, axonometric site plan

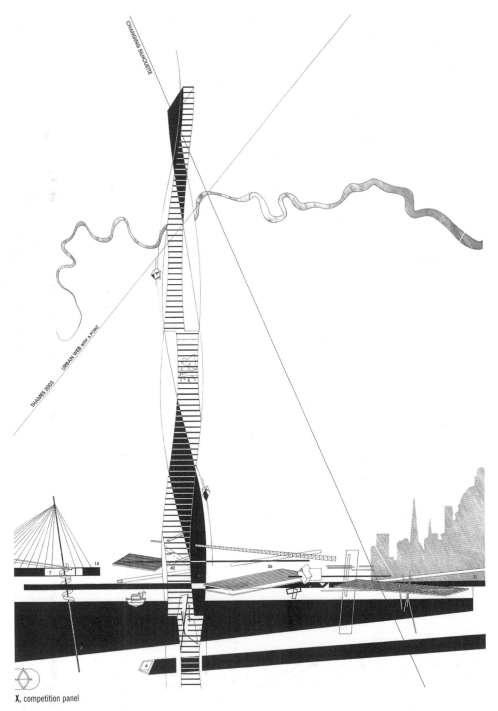

CHANGING SILHOUETTE

URBAN WEB WITH A POINT

THAMES 2003

X, competition panel

the Thames. The tower represents a twenty-four-hour beacon of life, activity, and economy making itself visible as an orienting point from all over London. It is deliberately decentered, shifting the virtual center line of the river toward the south bank. The vertical bridge takes its bird-like sail form in order to reflect light, deflect views, and modulate the winds, while presenting a dynamic and ever-changing silhouette. ■ The pedestrian web is an intricate, delicate urban structure dematerializing the horizontal weight of the connections. There are diverse and unexpected pathways forming a membrane of public activities. The structure is a combination of pylons and tensile members creating a mutually supportive, heterogeneous tensegrity structure over the river. The web contains pavilions, cafes, recreational places for winter and summer (covered and open), distributing a field of diverse spaces and events suspended over the water. There is a functional pathway to service the tower hidden amid the pedestrian routes. ■ The web and the bridge generate a sense of adventure and excitement, celebrating the water without obliterating or obscuring the drama of the Thames and the city around it. The proposal lifts the bridge from the horizontal to the vertical position, emphatically opening the Thames to the people of London. ■

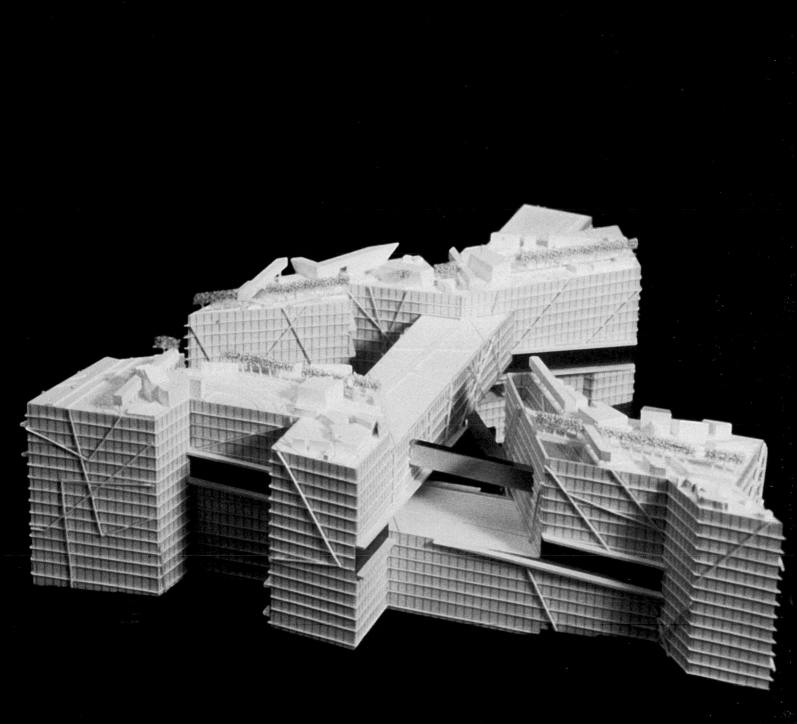

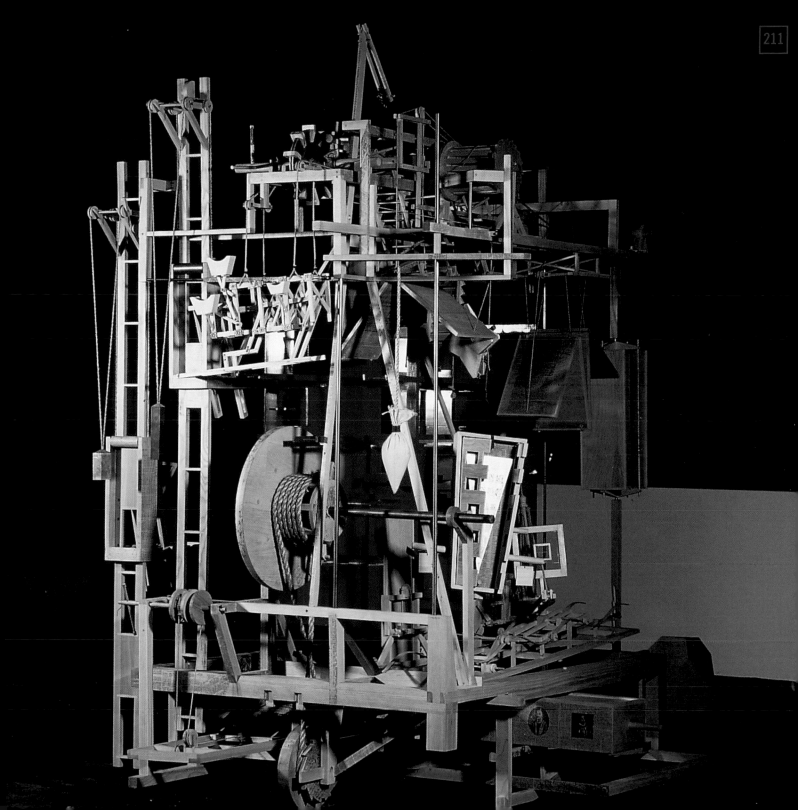

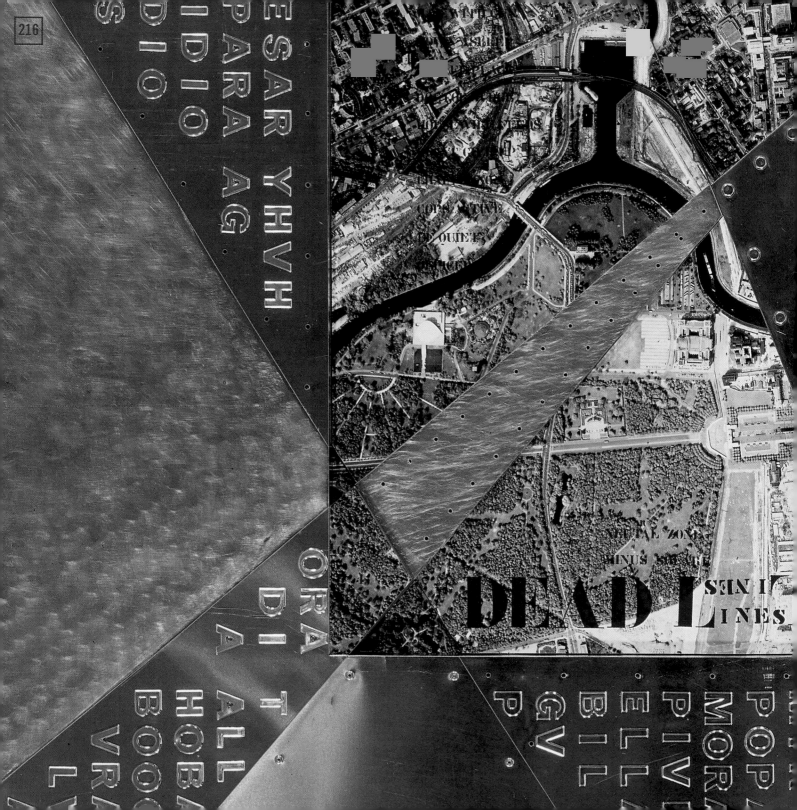

"Building in Empty Space": Daniel Libeskind's Museum of the Voice

Anthony Vidler

In the context of consumerist modernity in full technological optimism, as it rapaciously reconstructs the contemporary city—the accomplishment of the Corbusian Radiant City in the guise of a vast transparent mall, the product and instrument of free-enterprise self-advertisement—Daniel Libeskind's recent work attests to the ideal of the architectural monument as art, as a self-contained and self-fulfilling object, withdrawn deliberately and defensively from the outer world in order to stand for another imaginary; to act, so to speak, as a humanist memory theater in the erased absence of all memory from the building site of the city. The Jewish Museum Berlin, on the Lindenstrasse in Berlin, is a case in point. As a work and an experience this building stands as testimony to the power of a certain kind of phenomenological stance before the world, a spatial evocation that, through brilliant and deeply thought formal moves, resonates with all the aura of the terrifying sublime, and that, perhaps more than any modern work of architecture I have ever seen, manages to hold the visitor in spatio-psychological suspense, the closest experience to what I imagine a religious experience of architecture might be. ■ I used the words "religious experience," and indeed one might have equally used the Benjaminian term "aura"; and yet what can one say of such experience in an age that has repeatedly denied its existence, and either castigated industrial and rational society for its "loss" or proclaimed our secular liberation from such mysticism. It was Max Weber, after all, in 1919, addressing his students in Munich during the revolutionary uprisings that followed the defeat of Germany, who confirmed this "loss" with confidence as a result of the "disenchantment with the world" characteristic of the modern materialistic and scientific attitude. Speaking of the need to construct in a soft tone, in pianissimo, Weber anticipated the notion of a "weak monumentality," of the kind that Heidegger was to characterize as "background"

art, or more recently, Ignasi de Solà-Morales was to propose as the architecture of "recollection," of a residuum, a reverberation of something once there but now lost. Solà-Morales was drawing on Heidegger, and the Italian philosopher Gianni Vattimo, in his understanding of a monumentality of disenchantment that recalls former enchantment without pretentiously claiming religious or auratic authority. ■ With the Jewish Museum, however, we seem to be in the presence of something much stronger: its spaces, unlike those of late modernist architecture in general—those of Richard Meier's Getty, for example, or of Venturi and Scott Brown's National Gallery, or even of Norman Foster's Reichstag in no way emulate or refer to previous architectures. Its materiality is powerful in metal-clad reinforced concrete and does not hide its pretensions behind a delicate structure, as for example, in Renzo Piano's De Menil Gallery. The Jewish Museum's routes of passage are firm, defined by the darkest darks and the most brilliant lights; its disregard for the "normal" functions of museums, for the requirements of exhibition spaces, the modesty demanded by background spaces for foregrounding exhibits is more or less contemptuous; its ignoring spatial economy—the prolific insertion of meaningful voids—absolute. Certainly there is no effort at all to "fit into" its context as it denies completely through scale, mass, and surface the baroque pavilion to which is it nominally an extension, but which is turned into nothing more than a traditional portico to the new structure. Yet this strength holds nothing of the "miserable monstrosity" decried by Weber, part fragment of city wall, part bunker, part storehouse, the Jewish Museum retains its own identity in the face of the wasteland that surrounds it. ■ Certainly Libeskind has not ignored the past completely. In the making of this "raurn" for memory and reflection, Libeskind has very consciously reinterpreted the founding premises of "space-architecture," to use Schindler's term, in such a way as to create an architecture that does not simply construct space of shape space, but that is almost literally built out of space. And equally, Libeskind certainly pays formal homage to modernism. The echoes and traces of Le Corbusier are evident everywhere in the work, not least in the transformation of the spiral museum (from the Mundaneum to the Tokyo Museum) into the zigzag museum, and the reinvention of the wall (as at Ronchamp), as well as in the deeper epistemological attitude to the city and its inhabitants registered in the spatial movements of the urban projects. The powerful imagery of the avant-gardes is ever-present, transformed and displaced, re-formed and replaced, with no apologies necessary to Vladimir Tatlin, El Lissitsky, Laszló Moholy-Nagy, and, perhaps most strongly of all, Vassily Kandinsky. ■ Beyond this, however, when confronted by the withdrawn exteriors and disturbing interiors of the Jewish Museum, we find ourselves in a phenomenological world in which both Heidegger and Sartre would find themselves, if not exactly "at home" (for that was not their preferred place), certainly in bodily and mental crisis, with any trite classical homologies between the body and the building upset by unstable axes; walls and skins torn, ripped, and dangerously slashed, rooms empty of content and with uncertain or no exits and entrances. What Heidegger liked to call "falling into" the uncanny, and what for Sartre was the dangerous instrumentality of objects in the world as they threatened the body and its extensions, is for Libeskind the stuff of the architectural experience. ■ And yet, admitting Libeskind's obvious debt to phenomenology, there is in the Jewish Museum an implied architectural rereading of Benjamin. Indeed, the half-sunken enclosure offers many potential connections to the Berlin of Benjamin's "childhood" and maturity. Not so much in any simplistic reference to the arcades or to a crude interpretation of Paul Klee's *Angelus Novus*—although these may both be found lurking not far from the garden of the museum, and sometimes a "crude" reading, as Libeskind has himself noted, is entirely adequate for an observer—but rather to the profound effort that Benjamin himself made to reread the city and its artifacts in a way that was not trapped within a sterile neo-Kantian formalism of Hegelian historicism. In a way that eschewed the traditional perspectival "optical" framing of the city and its monuments, and that recognized the loss of perspective characteristic of modernity, the collapse of depth, the premium of the surface, the irreducible flat space of the modern image, Benjamin, following Riegl and other theorists of modern space, found solace in the haptic. For him, the modern experience was, as Nietzsche had already proposed, "labyrinthine," not clear and transparent like the Heideggerian temple, but obscure and ambiguous as to both its figure and its ground. In this condition, as we have seen, Benjamin preferred to lose his way in the city, experience it as an absentmindedness, stumbling along without the help of the Ariadne's thread provided by the modern guidebook, only to bump into a dwelling whose facade could not be picked out from any other, detached from any other, but whose interior might provided at least temporary sanctuary for the wanderer and the stranger (those haunting characters from Georg Simmel's metropolitan sociology), or at least substitute dark spaces for those of dreams, liminal places for the confrontation of the psyche. The unrecognizable exterior of Libeskind's Jewish Museum (in the sense that its shape and form cannot be understood from any privileged vantage point) and the unmappable spaces of the interior (in the sense that only a "film" in Benjamin's terms might provide the mechanisms of montage sufficient for its interpretation) all tend toward a haptic model of architectural experience, pushed back from the normal distance of vision, in a collapse or multiplication of the point of view that seems coordinated to a parallel collapse of perspective in the world. Here Libeskind joins the modern and the mystical, in what Benjamin, referring to Franz Kafka, saw as Kafka's "ellipse," a kind of vertigo machine, drawing together worlds that could in no way be commensurate either on the level of reality or dream and yet, through the very fact of their contemporaneity in Kafka's imagination, were rendered joint and immutably modern. ■ Perhaps it is in this way that we might begin to comprehend the precise attention of Libeskind to every detail of a personally delineated "program" for the Jewish Museum, as if pressing the modernist fetish for function to its limits and beyond. For Libeskind such a program, stemming from every potential move of the material and subject fabric of the institution or urban quarter under examination, really does represent the fundament of contemporaneity, its reason for being. Never mind that the dizzying possibilities of this program, if examined under the physicist's microscope, might lead to the bizarre consequences of a program apparently madly and incontinently out of true with its assumed rationality. Never mind that the surreal is closely stalking the real; if this is the program, then so be it. On the other hand, if there can be no "logic" on earth that explains each subject's experience of light and dark, form and space, vertical and horizontal (for in such a logic lies, as Goya pointed out long ago, certain madness), then we might at least leap straight up to the so-called "mystical" experience, that, as Benjamin understood so well, could be no more nor less than collective tradition, the collective memory of the past, that weighs so strongly on the present and controls in ways unknown our imagination of the future. In such a world, Libeskind's ellipses, his wandering paths, and warped spaces without perspective and ending blindly can only be seen as so many tests of our ability to endure the vertiginous experience of the labyrinths that, as Nietzsche had it over a century ago, make up the form of our modernity. If for the historian Manfredo Tafuri the unavoidable choice was between the (false) sphere of reason and this uncertain labyrinth, for Libeskind one senses another way out; not from the labyrinth, for that would be too much to ask, but within the labyrinth—a provisional path, which he calls a void, that through habitual and piecemeal encounters, by unexpected and suddenly revealed shocks, and through touch and feel in the dark as much as by clear vision in the light, might in some way domesticate what for Pascal, as for us, has been a rather stern, uncompromising, and certainly terrifying horror vacui (horror of the void) in a world of apparently endless space and no place. Thus domesticated, who knows, we may learn to inhabit it, or at least pitch our tents there for a moment. ■ It was Ernst Bloch who, writing in 1932, characterized the landscape of Berlin as without foundation, giving to the city the continuous impression of "groundlessness," of having sprung into existence overnight, and to disappear as easily. Based on "the swamp in which Berlin is immersed" and the "sand upon which it is built," this landscape was one for which "the ground had not yet settled," an "especially abstract ground." As if anticipating the new and rapidly redeveloped Berlin of the post-unification era, he wrote of the "unstable, probabilistic ground" of Berlin, and the "colonial exhibition character of the always new City of Hollow Space." Libeskind's construction of inner space, hunkered down in the land, patched over with tin, and with narrow slits for its eyes, seems peculiarly appropriate for this provisional site. If, as Karl Ritter wrote, as quoted by Bloch, "man is spatially and bodily the mirror of his place on earth," then it is reflected in this striated metal siding, hearing the rattling echoes of the tin cups of Célan's beggars that a memory of man should be traced. ■ If what Nietzsche implied for Le Corbusier was the image of superman in ineffable space—one who could overcome the void by virtue of superhuman power—for Libeskind he implies a less comfortable, but at least an imaginable treaty: one between an irreducible void, in time and in space, rendered more horrifying by its human

and inhuman contents, and an uncertain but at least receptive subject whose being is tied to the void, but who has need of a few walls for shelter and guidance. Then the business of the architect would be to arrest the tempo of history for a moment, not to return to a better time, but to deploy space in a way that recognizes its own history, at the same time as it provides a momentary fusing of movement and event, a temporary respite for reflection and experience, and thus a point of reference for the modern psyche: a "post-spatial void," so to speak. ■ It is, in the end, the "void" character of this so-called museum that gives away its contemporary status as architecture. For if, as Paul Valéry remarked, the modern museum was born out of the expulsion of painting and sculpture from the architectural body, what Friedrich Kittler has termed the "orphaning" of the arts, requiring architecture to build them a special home—a storehouse of artworks turned into artifacts through their displacement—then surely this museum, which refuses to accommodate any artifacts at all, which resolutely stands on its own and asserts the primacy of its own spaces as the exhibited work, is itself an architectural orphan. As such it is bound to a solitary and autonomous existence; forced, in Libeskind's words, to hold out a tin cup, a beggar in the city. ■ Perhaps then, if we cannot characterize this building as "post-historical" or yet fully historical, we can nevertheless understand it as a kind of terminal state of space, a millennial closure, so to speak, that stands as a paradoxical statement of the twentieth-century monumental problem; how, without history (the clothing of which afforded such security to the nineteenth century), and without ostentatious pretension and empty theatricality, can an architectural object imply a strong status while constructing itself out of space—the one medium that, as the high modernists perceived, was opposed to monumentality from the outset. Space that for Le Corbusier was the infinite flux of superhuman identity has here been captured and held hostage by impermeable walls. The "bunker" or the "fortress," then, is revealed as constructed to keep space in, rather than to defend against the outer world. It preserves space as a traditional museum would preserve art. In this sense it is a museum of and in architecture. ■

Anthony Vidler is professor of art history and architecture at the University of California, Los Angeles. His most recent book, *Warped Space: Art, Architecture, and Anxiety in Modern Culture*, is forthcoming from MIT Press in September 2000.